The Fall of the Berlin Wall

THE FALL
OF THE
BERLIN WALL

The Revolutionary Legacy of 1989

Edited by Jeffrey A. Engel

OXFORD
UNIVERSITY PRESS

SCOWCROFT INSTITUTE
OF INTERNATIONAL AFFAIRS

THE BUSH SCHOOL OF GOVERNMENT AND PUBLIC SERVICE
TEXAS A&M UNIVERSITY

OXFORD
UNIVERSITY PRESS

Oxford University Press, Inc., publishes works that further
Oxford University's objective of excellence
in research, scholarship, and education.

Oxford   New York
Auckland   Cape Town   Dar es Salaam   Hong Kong   Karachi
Kuala Lumpur   Madrid   Melbourne   Mexico City   Nairobi
New Delhi   Shanghai   Taipei   Toronto

With offices in
Argentina   Austria   Brazil   Chile   Czech Republic   France   Greece
Guatemala   Hungary   Italy   Japan   Poland   Portugal   Singapore
South Korea   Switzerland   Thailand   Turkey   Ukraine   Vietnam

Copyright © 2009 by Oxford University Press, Inc.

Published by Oxford University Press, Inc.
198 Madison Avenue, New York, New York 10016
www.oup.com

First issued as an Oxford University Press paperback, 2011.

Oxford is a registered trademark of Oxford University Press.

Library of Congress Cataloging-in-Publication Data
The fall of the Berlin Wall : the revolutionary legacy of 1989 / edited by Jeffrey A. Engel.
    p.   cm.
Includes bibliographical references and index.
ISBN 978-0-19-538910-4 (hardcover); 978-0-19-983244-6 (paperback)
1. World politics—1989–   2. Post-communism.   3. Europe—Politics and
government—1989–   4. United States—Politics and government—1989–
5. Soviet Union—Politics and government—1985–1991.
6. Russia (Federation)—Politics and government—1991-9   7. China—Politics and
government—1976–2002.   8. Berlin Wall, Berlin, Germany, 1961–1989.
I. Engel, Jeffrey A.
D860.F35 2009 909.82'8—dc22   2009013105

"The River," by Bruce Springfield. Copyright © 1980 Bruce Springfield (ASCAP).
Reprinted by permission. International copyright secured. All rights reserved.

9 8 7 6 5 4 3 2 1

Printed in the United States of America
on acid-free paper

Now those memories come back to haunt me

they haunt me like a curse

Is a dream a lie if it don't come true

Or is it something worse

—Bruce Springsteen, *The River*

ACKNOWLEDGMENTS

No book is ever truly a solo endeavor. This is particularly true of an edited volume, and especially a project, such as this, which owes its existence to so many sources of support.

This book evolved from a January 2009 conference, *The Cold War Is History*, hosted by Texas A&M University's Scowcroft Institute for International Affairs, the research and programming arm of the Bush School of Government and Public Service's International Affairs Program. Primary support came from the Institute's Ansary Foreign Policy Conference Fund, ably administered by the Bush Presidential Library Foundation. To Hushang Ansary, and to Ambassador Roman Popadiuk and his staff, hearty thanks, indeed. Additional financial support arrived from Texas A&M University's European Union Center and its Melbern G. Glasscock Center for Humanities Research. Much appreciation goes to their coordinators, Guy Whitten, James Rosenheim, and Donnalee Dox, as well as to Jason Parker, who carried the ball in the College of Liberal Arts for this Bush School program.

Faculty and staff at the Bush School did their typical herculean effort to make the January 2009 conference not only a public success, but also an extremely productive workshop for the volume contributors and their commentators. Griffin Rozell coordinated the entire affair, ably assisted by Mary Hein, Beth Roberts, Sue Robertson, Matt Henderson, Ron Szabo, Mark Kacer, Carrie Lytle, Janeen Wood, and Aurelia Figueroa. Deans Richard Chilcoat and Benton Cocanougher provided both leadership and logistical support when needed most. Ambassador Larry Napper's cool advice was invaluable throughout.

Each of the contributors to this volume benefited greatly from the formal comments solicited for the workshop and conference. Particular thanks to these experts for their thoughtful work: Frank Gavin, Gale Stokes, Larry Napper, and Randy Kluver. Additional contributions came from participants in the workshop itself, including Roger Reese, Peter Hugill, Charles Hermann, Jasen Castillo, Christopher Layne, Jim Olson, Richard Chilcoat, and Mike Absher. Andrew Preston offered his usual good advice and editorial help from afar. While each essay in this volume has a primary author, all who attended the workshop will agree that its synergy ensures that no idea in the book can claim single parentage. The work showcased in this book is only possible, at the end of the day, because of the indefatigable efforts of Warren Finch, Robert Holzweiss, and their team of archivists at the Bush Presidential Library, who made available— often for the first time—many of the documents employed in this study. Deep gratitude to Armin Cantini as well, who generously allowed reproduction of personal photographs taken in Beijing in 1989.

Susan Ferber, as always, provided the advice, guidance, and enthusiasm necessary to move the project from idea to book. Thanks owed to her know no bounds. So too with Katherine Carté Engel, who opened her home, and cleared her packed calendar, to ensure all got done. Victory might know a thousand fathers. But one mother alone can do the rest.

CONTENTS

CONTRIBUTORS

JEFFREY A. ENGEL teaches history and public policy at Texas A&M University's Bush School of Government and Public Service, where he is also the Evelyn and Ed F. Kruse '49 Faculty Fellow. He is the author of *Cold War at 30,000 Feet: The Anglo-American Fight for Aviation Supremacy,* which received the American Historical Association's 2008 Paul Birdsall Prize in European Military and Strategic History. A member of the editorial board of *Diplomatic History,* and a member of the Society of Historians of American Foreign Relations' Executive Council, he is also the editor of *Local Consequences of the Global Cold War* and *The China Diary of George H. W. Bush: The Making of a Global President,* the private diary of former President Bush during his tenure as de facto U.S. ambassador to Beijing in the 1970s.

CHEN JIAN holds the Michael J. Zak Chair of History for U.S.-China relations at Cornell University. He is an expert in modern Chinese history, Chinese foreign policy and security studies, and Sino-American relations. His major publications include *Mao's China and the Cold War, China's Road to the Korean War,* and *The Road to Global War: A Chinese Study of the Origins of the Second World War.* In 2005 he shared an Emmy Award for Outstanding Achievement in News and Documentary Work for his role in the documentary film *Declassified: Nixon in China.*

MELVYN P. LEFFLER is the Edward Stettinius Professor of American History at the University of Virginia (UVA). He is also a faculty fellow at the Governing

America in a Global Age Program at UVA's Miller Center of Public Affairs. Leffler has served as the president of the Society of Historians of American Foreign Relations and has been the recipient of senior fellowships from the Norwegian Nobel Peace Institute, the Woodrow Wilson International Center, the United States Institute of Peace, the Kluge Center of the Library of Congress, and the Lehrman Institute. Some of his major works include the Bancroft Award–winning history of the Truman administration's national security policy, *A Preponderance of Power,* and *For the Soul of Mankind: The United States, the Soviet Union, and the Cold War,* which was awarded the American Historical Association's George Louis Beer Prize.

SVETLANA SAVRANSKAYA is the director of Russia Programs at the National Security Archive at George Washington University and teaches courses on Russia, Central Asia, and U.S.-Russian relations at American University in Washington, D.C. She also organizes various conferences and programs in Russia and the former Soviet states, including a summer school for young faculty in Gelendzhik. She is the author of several articles, book chapters, and electronic publications on Soviet and Russian foreign policy and the end of the Cold War, including "Unintended Consequences: Soviet Interests, Expectations and Reactions to the Helsinki Final Act," in *Helsinki 1975 and the Transformation of Europe,* edited by Oliver Bange and Gottfried Niedhard; "In the Name of Europe: Soviet Withdrawal from Eastern Europe," in *Europe and the End of the Cold War: A Reappraisal,* edited by Frederic Bozo; and an editor of *Masterpieces of History: Soviet Peaceful Withdrawal from Eastern Europe, 1989.*

JAMES J. SHEEHAN is the Dickason Professor in the Humanities and Professor of Modern European History, Emeritus, at Stanford University. He is a former president of the American Historical Association and an expert in the history of modern Germany. Some of his major publications include *The Career of Lujo Brentano: A Study of Liberalism and Social Reform in Imperial Germany, German Liberalism in the Nineteenth Century; German History, 1770–1886;* and most recently, *Where Have All the Soldiers Gone? The Transformation of Modern Europe.*

WILLIAM TAUBMAN is the Bertrand Snell Professor of Political Science at Amherst College. He is an expert in Soviet and Russian politics and foreign policy and a 2006 recipient of a Guggenheim Foundation Fellowship. He has authored and edited several works, including *Stalin's American Policy: From Entente to Detente to Cold War; Globalism and Its Critics: The American Foreign Policy Debate of the 1960s;* and the Pulitzer Prize–winning biography *Khrushchev: The Man and His Era.*

The Fall of the Berlin Wall

Chapter 1

1989: AN INTRODUCTION TO AN INTERNATIONAL HISTORY

Jeffrey A. Engel

The world changed in 1989.

At the start of the year, the globe's strategic map looked much like it had since the end of World War II. Communist leaders in China and the Soviet Union held power. Their American counterparts, skeptical of the sincerity of recent calls for change throughout the Communist world, prepared for a reinvigorated Cold War of unknown duration and ferocity. Europe prepared for another year divided along fault lines imposed by conquering armies nearly a half-century before.[1]

A year later, communism would be dead in Eastern Europe and dying in the Soviet Union itself. China would be once more in the grip of hard-liners wary of reform, and once more on the precipice of isolation. Washington would be looking to capitalize on its Cold War victory. Europe would soon be rejoined. The future—our twenty-first-century present—would be at hand. And no one had seen it coming.

This book recalls the heady days of 1989 and explains how leaders in the world's four principal strategic centers—Europe, the Soviet bloc, China, and the United States—viewed the reforms and protests that swirled around them and considered the revolutions and suppressions they witnessed, fostered, and even fell victim to. It explores how policymakers in each thought the end of the long-running Cold War, which had marked their entire adult lives, would affect their nations and the world. Ultimately, it reveals how global leaders yearned to find some safe passage through rocky shoals of change that none of them fully anticipated or, in some cases, even desired. For leaders such as Mikhail Gorbachev of the Soviet Union, Deng Xiaoping of China, George Bush of the United States, Helmut Kohl of Germany, and Margaret Thatcher of Britain, the global battle of communism versus capitalism framed their entire worldview. Each recalled the struggles of World War II. Yet each had risen to power in the years that followed, believing their own society held the key not only to Cold War victory, but to the future itself. By the end of 1989, they would each come to realize what Thatcher had announced a year before: the world of their youths was gone. "We're not in a Cold War now," she told a skeptical American audience in December 1988. Because the Soviet Union had, in her opinion, ceased its quest for global domination, the Cold War was "all over but the shouting."[2]

Those shouts eventually reverberated throughout the world, and continue to echo decades later, though not everyone readily accepted Thatcher's opinion. "There are those who want to declare the Cold War ended," Secretary of Defense Dick Cheney cautioned at the start of 1989, arguing "we must guard against gambling our nation's security on what may be a temporary aberration in the behavior of our foremost adversary." Change seemed unquestionably in the air throughout the Communist world. For American Cold Warriors, long trained to view any Soviet action with caution and fear, skepticism proved the watchword of the day. Even the most optimistic did not anticipate that the Soviet Union itself would cease to exist in but a few short years. As recalled by longtime Washington powerbroker Robert Gates—who in 1989 was deputy national security adviser—"I know of *no one* in or outside of government who predicted early in 1989 that before the next presidential election Eastern Europe would be free, Germany united in NATO, and the Soviet Union an artifact of history." Indeed, many in Washington shared Gates's far more pessimistic concern that the Cold War threatened to turn hot once more. They worried that Gorbachev's widely heralded reforms were designed not to transcend Soviet communism, but to preserve its strength. Many in Moscow, including Gorbachev himself, hoped for the same, yearning to alter and thus preserve their beloved Soviet state, not to see it powerless, poor, and ultimately dismissed. Gorbachev's was a race against time, pitting reforms he knew were required— but whose details continued to elude him—against the structural flaws of his nation's system, ideology, and very history.[3]

Chinese leaders, who had initiated reforms of their own during the 1980s, feared above all else their nation's tendency to excess in the face of wholesale change. They consequently believed their government had to maintain order and enforce stability at any cost if their country were to survive its own great transformation. Following decades of enforced deprivation, justified by the quest for ideological purity, Deng Xiaoping and his ruling cadre hoped to catalyze their archaic economy, spurring growth by allowing personal wealth only recently considered anathema to their doctrinaire society. They sought to change China, but without simultaneously losing the communal zeal and nationalism that had largely defined their country since its 1949 revolution. More immediately, they sought some means of managing the social and political transformation sure to result from their economic reforms, believing only strict government control could ensure that the mayhem and violence of China's recent past did not reappear. In 1989, they proved right to worry. And they proved as well the violent lengths they would go to impose stability and thus retain power.[4]

While communism faced an existential crisis in 1989, and Americans pondered a world without the enemy that had largely defined their own society for decades, many in Europe's capitals looked out over the transforming international landscape with greater contentment, though with no less trepidation. Leaders throughout this continent, particularly in its Western half, largely interpreted 1989 as confirmation of their vision for a unified continent, designed less for absolute power than for peaceful coexistence in a world dominated by far more powerful global players. This is not to say that European strategists viewed the events of 1989 with a single attitude. Kohl, for example, thought the long-sought unification of his country might finally be at hand. Thatcher and French leaders feared a unified Germany, recalling all too well the demons of invigorated German nationalism. "National character basically doesn't change," the British prime minister believed, adding that she "knew perfectly well what Germans are like." French leader François Mitterrand coolly—and incorrectly, it turned out—calculated that the force of history would prevent the kind of reunified Germany that haunted his past. "I don't have to do anything to stop it," he boasted. "The Soviets will do it for me. They will never allow this greater Germany just opposite them."[5]

Even the uncertainties of a future dominated by a resurgent Germany did not deter European leaders from interpreting 1989 as vindication of their post-1945 hopes. When protestors throughout the Soviet bloc chanted for freedom and change, they were in effect asking to join the peaceful, stable, and growing European society they saw just beyond the iron curtain. They wanted to be European, because that identity had developed real meaning since the traumas of World War II. "This was more than just a matter of rhetoric," historian Tony Judt has concluded. "Sometimes the thought was inflected as 'the market economy,' sometimes as 'civil society'; but in either case 'Europe' stood—squarely and simply—for normalcy and the modern way of life." Western leaders fully understood Europe's appeal. They had worked since 1945 to construct the kind of peaceful and prosperous society others would find appealing. They were simply unsure how much they wanted to share in their bounty with former Communists behind the iron curtain. Neither was it clear if the European ideal formed in the incubator of broader Cold War tensions could survive beyond its confines.[6]

Strategists schemed and politicians pondered in response to the events of 1989; yet, simultaneously, throughout the world people far removed from the halls of power revealed that they cared little for the opinions of leaders in the world's great Cold War capitals. Indeed, one should note from the outset a central paradox inherent in this book: it is a study of great power politics, of elite leaders, and of international affairs. The history of 1989 is most often told from a different perspective, as a tale of popular unrest. The story of Eastern Europe's democratic revolt is most often that of ordinary citizens, banding together to reject the forces that violently ruled their lives. As historian William Hitchcock has concluded: "The events of 1989 must be seen as the final breakthrough, after four decades of struggle, of a citizen's movement with a history that pre-dated Gorbachev and in fact reached back into the 1940s. Gorbachev did not give Eastern Europeans their freedom in 1989. They took it."[7]

People took power indeed. Poland held free elections in June 1989, the result of years of internal struggle epitomized by the decades-long rise of the Solidarity movement. For the first time a country within the Soviet empire voted Communists out of office. In that same fateful spring and summer, Hungarian crowds numbering more than three hundred thousand marched to rebury and to honor Imre Nagy and the fallen heroes of 1956, whose failed rejection of Soviet rule left an independent streak finally exercised by the free elections of May 1989. Millions more throughout the country watched the proceedings broadcast live on television. No longer could discontent be isolated or contained. Before the year was out, Hungarians explicitly rejected socialism, renaming their state the Hungarian "Republic," rather than the more Stalinistic "Hungarian People's Republic." No longer willing to serve as prison guards for Eastern Europe, Hungarian officials opened their border with Austria that spring as well, opening a spigot through which thousands of disaffected and frustrated East Germans made their way to the West. By year's end a newly elected government in Budapest informed Soviet officials that their troops were no longer needed—or, for that matter, tolerated—on Hungarian soil.[8]

Germans too marched for freedom. Throughout the German Democratic Republic, often considered the most doctrinaire of all the Soviet client states, thousands of ordinary citizens demanded change in the fall of 1989. Thousands more voted with their feet or, as often, with their tiny and underpowered Trabant automobiles, whose lack of speed and options symbolized the very society that created them. They left their homeland in search of a better life in the West, leaving behind not only their lives—and those Lilliputian cars on the streets of Prague or Budapest—but a dying regime ill-prepared for change and unwilling to relent. "We took power in order to keep it forever," East German leader Erich Honecker boasted and simultaneously warned. In January 1989 he brazenly promised that the Berlin Wall, which physically divided a city and symbolically split the entire continent, "will be standing in fifty or a hundred years!"[9]

Those whom Honecker claimed to rule, inspired by events in their fellow socialist states and by Gorbachev's sweeping rhetoric, disagreed. They turned out by the thousands for candlelight vigils and raucous marches throughout the autumn of 1989. The once-feared East German leader proved no longer capable of controlling through force and terror. Upon hearing Hungary's foreign minister promise in early September that they might cross into Austria "without any further ado," twenty-two thousand East Germans fled in just three days. By October, however, crowds of equal number began chanting something new and arguably more ominous for the teetering regime: "We will stay HERE." They would not abandon their homes and homeland, but would instead force change from within. A week later their chants reminded the nervous police and government officials charged with maintaining order that "we are the people." Believing opposition to his rule was "futile," Honecker authorized his troops to fire on the crowds. They refused. Within a week, he was purged from power. When told by a nervous and confused government spokesman late in the evening of November 9 that visits to the West would be approved without delay—in other words, that they might leave at will—East Berliners joined with their Western neighbors at the despised wall that for decades had divided them. It's concrete, barbed wire, and feared killing zones had stood for twenty-eight years, two months, and twenty-seven days. In a single night, crowds took axes and hammers to its base and danced on its once formidable peaks.[10]

The change born in Poland and Hungary, catalyzed by the fall of the Wall, rippled with seismic force through the rest of Eastern Europe. In Bulgaria the hard-line Communist leadership headed by Todor Zhivkov—who had led his party since 1954—suddenly resigned the day after the wall collapsed, ceding power before the wave of reform could overwhelm their government. In Czechoslovakia popular unrest led to a largely peaceful collapse of Communist rule in the weeks that followed. Throughout the region reformers swept away with shocking speed the governments that had ruled them for decades. Only in Romania, where, in Judt's apt phrase, "Communism had degenerated from national Leninism to a sort of neo-Stalinist satrapy," did widespread violence erupt. Nicolae Ceaușescu, who had ruled with an iron fist for more than twenty years, baldly promised there would be no similar reform so long as he remained in charge. During the summer he had joined with Honecker in pleading with Gorbachev to authorize a military crackdown against the "breakaway" Polish and Hungarian regimes. Despite wielding an army unmatched on the continent, including some 390,000 troops on East German soil alone, the Kremlin refused to intervene, forsaking the iron fist it had assiduously maintained since Stalin's day. Although the Wall came down on November 9, the real end of Soviet domination in Eastern Europe occurred far less dramatically in a secret meeting months before, when Gorbachev told his socialist counterparts that the Kremlin would never again crush Eastern European reformers with force. He had promised much the same publicly in the preceding months. But it was only when he told the hardest of Eastern Europe's Communist hard-liners that they were truly on their own did the message seem real.[11]

Ceaușescu would not give up so easily. On December 15, soldiers and police acting on his orders fired on demonstrators in the western city of Timisoara. Crowds throughout the country swelled in response, leading Ceaușescu to call for a massive public demonstration of support to be held in front of the Communist Party's headquarters in Bucharest. For the first time, however, the assembled masses did not rally behind him, but instead shouted him down. He fled in fear. By Christmas, he and his equally feared wife would be dead, condemned by a hastily summoned citizen's tribunal for crimes committed against their own people and shot hours later. Save for their fate, the story of 1989 in Europe might well be told as a story of leaders simply getting out of the way of those they presumed to lead. The story of dissidents in China might be equally well known today, were it not systematically dismissed by the Chinese government, which is hardly eager to celebrate the lengths it took to retain power.

This broad story of people power has been told. Less understood are the mind-sets and maneuvers of statesmen charged with leading the world's most powerful states as they confronted this unexpected groundswell of popular pleas for change. Some, like Kohl, welcomed the opportunity to achieve the ultimate goal of their lifetime: a unified German state. Some, like Gorbachev and Deng, sought change they could control. Others, like Thatcher and Bush, feared what change might bring. "A profound cycle of turmoil and great change is sweeping the world from Poland to the Pacific," Bush declared when visiting Eastern

Europe in 1989. "It is sometimes inspiring, as here in Warsaw." Yet sometimes, Bush lamented, "it's agonizing, as in China today." Only weeks before, thousands had died when Chinese leaders refused to cede to their own people the very power their fellow Communists in Europe ultimately granted. This book, focused on the world's grand strategists, reveals at once how little control policymakers held over the events of 1989 and yet at the time how their decisions, made in the face of such unexpected change, structured the world we inhabit today.[12]

The year 1989 was a global phenomenon in every sense. Crowds and reformers around the world spoke directly to each other, not just in response to the dictums of their national leaders. Gorbachev was like a modern Pandora, unleashing forces he could not control. Domestic reforms he initiated in response to a weakening economy inspired similar calls for change in Eastern Europe and China. Sometimes he embraced the change he inspired. Crowds handpicked by East German officials for their loyalty signaled the regime's demise, for example, in October 1989 when their patriotic chants celebrating the fortieth anniversary of their state transformed, almost in unison, into pleas for the visiting Soviet leader to "save us, Gorby!" Standing beside him on the reviewing platform, Polish leader Mieczyslaw Rakowski leaned over to wryly note, "It looks as if they want you to liberate them again." Gorbachev welcomed their enthusiasm, reminding East German officials they would receive no Soviet support in suppressing the crowds. Just as often, however, the results of his reforms shocked even Gorbachev himself, such as when reformers in the Baltics took to heart his public support for national self-determination, wrongly believing he included parts of the Soviet Union itself as candidates for independent sovereignty. Soviet police fired on the crowds in response, a widely publicized shedding of blood Gorbachev could neither understand nor condone. "Naturally," he conceded in 1990, "I feel troubled by the fact that I did not succeed in keeping the entire process of perestroika within the framework of my intentions."[13]

In an earlier age diplomatic events had largely developed through formal notes passed from one clerk to another. At the least, in centuries past the slow pace of news granted policymakers time to consider their responses to distant events. The late twentieth-century experience was different, faster, more reactive. Just as their European counterparts played to the television cameras, Chinese students consciously crafted symbols—a female statue of liberty, most famously—designed to inspire international sympathy. Protestors in a multitude of countries carried placards labeled not in their native tongues but instead in English, the better to be understood by audiences continents away. Throngs of demonstrators interacted as never before and, with the aid of global media outlets, moved events with shocking speed. To take one famous example, Secretary of State James Baker only learned of the Tiananmen crackdown after his son watched the carnage on television. In a slower age, the chief diplomat of the world's most powerful country would have had the luxury to be out playing the golf match he had planned for that morning. Instead, he and his government were forced to respond, and quickly, because cameras ten thousand miles away beamed images no global witness would soon forget and thus no superpower could possibly ignore.[14]

At such a pace, governments could only react to events, rather than control them, leading repeatedly to the conclusion that seemingly similar events occurring almost simultaneously across continents and regions were somehow intertwined. Chinese officials viewed protests in Eastern Europe during the first months of 1989, for instance, and vowed not to lose control of their populace the way their fellow Communists had. Beijing's violent domestic crackdown made American leaders wary of promoting subsequent change in Eastern Europe too vigorously, lest they inadvertently instigate similar violence behind the iron curtain. That violence in China simultaneously revealed to Communist leaders and to opponents alike throughout Europe the lengths their own governments would *not* go and thus exposed the ultimate frailty of their regimes. Being largely unwilling to retain power solely through force, such states forsook the monopoly of violence that had for generations undergirded their self-proclaimed right to rule. Transformations in one region, in other words, affected decision making and events in others. Changes in one state or region inspired new calls for change and transformation. These in turn reverberated throughout the entire global system.

Echoes from 1989 remain audible years later, because the ruling elites of each society—be they Chinese, post-Soviet, European, or American—collectively concluded that 1989 offered useful lessons for the future. Each seems to have learned a different lesson, however, as the chapters in this book reveal. That these lessons vary is perhaps not surprising. The Cold War's winners and losers were hardly evenly distributed throughout the globe. For some, 1989 offered a blueprint for future success. Believing in the universality of their democratic values, West European and American leaders pushed hard for speedy democratization and development of market economies behind the former iron curtain. In time they endorsed eastward expansion of the North Atlantic Treaty Organization (NATO) as a military bulwark for political and economic integration. For thwarted Chinese reformers—or for ruling elites stripped of power, such as those in the former Soviet Union—1989 revealed what not to do if authority and prosperity were to be retained. That same NATO expansion that promised so much to the West appeared threatening in Moscow, especially when it became clear that Russia was not included in most Western conceptions of Europe. So, too, does a wide chasm continue to separate China's economic and cultural integration with the wider world from its government's continued rejection of commensurate political liberalization. Current fears over a new or renewed Cold War, therefore, find their origins in how the superpower conflict ended.[15]

Those different strategic lessons of 1989 portend a future of conflict, which ironically runs counter to the initial conclusion most widely gleaned from that momentous year. Optimistic strategic observers at the end of the Cold War perceived an end of history. They quite famously envisioned a future not so much of absolute peace than of a relatively more peaceful struggle for power between democracies alone. Given the curious fact that no two democratic states had ever gone to war with each other, a whole rationale for American foreign policy developed following 1989's wave of popularly inspired democratization. Active democratization from abroad as a means of promoting long-term peace emerged as the driving force behind Washington's hegemonic aspirations following the Cold War. Russian leaders, conversely, came to believe in the economic power of the market, while simultaneously learning to mistrust Western proclamations of democratic and supposedly market-inspired values. Wealth, and an ever-widening gulf between haves and have-nots, appeared in Russia beginning in the 1990s. That decade and the first years of the twenty-first century also brought less political freedom than Boris Yeltsin or other democratic reformers of the Soviet Union's final days might have envisioned. We now know that history would not end so quietly, or so quickly, as many thoughtful observers hoped or prayed at the Cold War's end.[16]

Each of this book's authors delves deeply into the fate of a single region in 1989, bringing to bear distinct records and literatures in this melding of international history. Collectively their histories underscore four points. Two have already been mentioned in this introduction, specifically (1) the intertwined global nature of events throughout this epic year and (2) the way policy makers drew fundamentally different lessons from those events. A third conclusion may seem implicit, but demands explicit discussion: Personalities matter in history, even when considering events widely understood to have been the result of mass action rather than individual agency. The story of 1989 is largely the story of crowds. But masses of people only formed because of, and often, in spite of, reformers such as Gorbachev and Deng. Russia and China choose different paths in 1989 largely because of the individual personalities and proclivities of these two men. Even in a story of crowds, leaders matter. To write history merely from the ground up, or exclusively from the top down, is insufficient if we are to understand the dynamic interaction between leaders and those they led. The world that developed after 1989 was only possible because statesmen helped form it—even when they were merely responding to events far beyond their power to control.

This book's fourth and final conclusion is equally important: Save for in China, where events from this period have largely been purposefully obscured and systematically erased from the national memory, the story of 1989 is largely celebrated. Even those who look back on the Communist era with nostalgia marvel at the generally peaceful manner by which the East European regimes ceded power. These were, in Czech leader Václav Havel's famous phrase, "velvet" revolutions, largely devoid of the violence and mayhem that more frequently accompanies wholesale change. But 1989 need not have turned out quite so well. Tiananmen could have been repeated in Europe. Force might have been deployed. Ethnic tensions and long-festering hatreds might have more widely consumed democratic impulses, as happened to great tragedy and suffering in Yugoslavia only a few short years after the Wall came down. Yet, for the most part, in Europe at least, events did not swirl out of control. Society did not crumble. Anarchy did not reign once the cauldron of change erupted from decades of built-up pressure. War did not erupt. It was a close thing, however. Looking closely at the events of 1989, we are reminded that with but a small push in another direction, the world we now inhabit might well have been different indeed.

As the odd man out in this history—as the state in which violence determined the course of events—China is the ideal place to begin this introduction to the events of 1989. Dismayed by the growing power of reform movements through-out the Soviet-dominated half of the Communist world, Chinese Communist Party officials met in March to discuss "the unrest in Eastern Europe," conclud-ing that "every effort should be made to prevent changes in Eastern Europe from influencing China's internal development." What was undermining Com-munist rule abroad, they worried, might infect their own country.[17]

They had good reason to fear. Inspired by events in Europe—but to an even greater extent prompted by the transformation of Chinese society in the decade-plus since the death of Mao Zedong, who had ruled since 1949—Chinese masses demanded change to a degree unseen in a generation. Students began to march in favor of reform in mid-April 1989. Their teachers quickly followed their lead, as did workers and citizens from all walks of Chinese life. By the end of May, tens of thou-sands were encamped in Beijing and throughout China's cities and villages. Some called for change. Others engaged in hunger strikes. All demanded to be heard.

As luck would have it, Mikhail Gorbachev arrived in Beijing at that very moment. He was there for the first Sino-Soviet summit in over thirty years. In his wake arrived hundreds of camera-toting reporters, many of whom eagerly turned from the staid protocol of a state visit to the unusual spectacle of mass protests swelling before them. News of the events in Tiananmen Square was therefore beamed immediately throughout the world. Chinese officials could not hide their internal disruptions; public scrutiny left them little choice but to react—or else to admit their lack of power to their own people and an increasingly vigilant global audience.

Deng was as responsible for these events as anyone. He had returned from the political wilderness and survived China's treacherous political squabbles more than once in order to head a fundamental economic transformation of the regime, beginning in the late 1970s. Within two years of Mao's death in 1976, Deng had purged the most passionate of Mao's supporters, who had for more than a decade during the Cultural Revolution of the previous decade committed atrocities in the name of purifying their regime's true Marxist-Leninist nature. Pushing aside more doctrinaire calls for communist orthodoxy, which had proven unable to foster the kind of economic growth seen in capitalist nations, Deng continued Mao's plans to reintegrate China further into the global political system, while simultaneously instigating reforms once considered heretical. Deng had long been Mao's point man on economic reforms, a position of great power and great personal danger. Three times he was sent into domestic exile. Each time he survived and returned. His family would not prove as fortunate, however. His son lost the ability to walk when thrown from a rooftop by zealots, termed "Red Guards," inspired by Mao's pleas for political purity. Deng knew firsthand, therefore, the price of change and the real cost of defeat.

Following Mao's death, he moved quickly to institutionalize the economic reforms he believed necessary for China to fulfill its true potential. Ridiculing the oft-heard rallying cry of the Cultural Revolution that it was "better to be poor under socialism than rich under capitalism," Deng countered that "to be rich is glorious." Hoping to unleash pent-up economic demand, he allowed peasant cultivation of private agricultural lands, ownership of private property, and widespread foreign investment. He famously argued that effectiveness mattered more than political orthodoxy—collective farming made ideological sense, for example, but had resulted in starvation for millions—by offering that "whether a cat is black or white makes no difference. As long as it catches mice, it is a good cat."[18]

In other words, what mattered to Deng and his supporters was whatever made the Chinese economy boom. Under his leadership, formal diplomatic relations were reestablished with the United States in 1979, and even the long-simmering border dispute with the Soviet Union relaxed by the mid-1980s. Arguing that the Cultural Revolution of 1966–76—which had seen schools closed, universities ransacked, and authority figures from all walks of life ridiculed—had produced little more than "a generation of mental cripples," Deng reinvigorated China's educational system. English, once banished as a sign of Western influence, was studied once more. Chinese students ventured abroad in increasingly greater numbers. Their perceptions of life's options in a new Chinese state multiplied.[19]

Private wealth and individual opportunity grew under Deng's leadership, but for many Chinese it was not nearly enough. Real power, including the opportunity for social advancement, still rested with the state, and more specifically with the Communist Party. Eager to manage the pace of change and a firm believer in the communist cause to which he had devoted his life, Deng vested power, including the new centers of economic power that his reforms produced, in the hands of party loyalists. This helped him retain central control over his changing society, but also led almost inevitably to widespread corruption—or, just as importantly, the widespread perception of corruption—as private connections and wealth proved as important to success as ability.

Given a taste of opportunity and inspired by Gorbachev's example of the change possible within a socialist state, once-divergent facets of Chinese society converged in the spring of 1989 to demand more. For professors openly ridiculed during the Cultural Revolution, the educational emphasis of the 1980s inspired a new claim to social status. Students called for economic and scholastic opportunities in line with ability more than with family status. Workers demanded even greater market freedoms. As Chen Jian argues in the pages of this book, Deng's retreat from the orthodoxy of Mao's legacy inadvertently opened his regime to questions about its own legitimacy. If the strict doctrine of the previous era had been wrong—if the black cat were in fact on par with the white, despite what past zealots had repeatedly preached—then who was to say that Deng's regime itself was free from reproach?

Such widely known critiques of 1989 had initially percolated through Chinese society in the final weeks of 1986, when students throughout the country protested against perceived government fraud and dishonesty. Deng successfully discredited these protesters, further solidifying power by forcing the resignation of Party General Secretary Hu Yaobang, a leading voice for political change within the government and a favorite of the student movement. It was

Hu's death in April 1989 that sparked the unrest which ended in so much violence that June. As news of his passing spread, students in Beijing assembled to mourn, demanding further reforms in his honor. "Those who should have lived, have died," some chanted in a clear rebuke of Deng and his cadre, which remained atop the government, "while those who should have died, have lived." From Beijing the protests only spread. A crowd estimated at 10,000 marched in Chengdu on May 18. Only four days later it was conservatively estimated at more than 100,000. American consular officials reported crowds in Shenyang of twice that number, while American ambassador James Lilley warned Washington that "the seeming coordination with protests elsewhere, the similarities of political concerns, and the genuine enthusiasm of students and others demonstrate how deep and widespread public sentiment against corruption and for democracy is throughout China. Its spread to Guiyang should be a telling sign to central government leaders in Beijing."[20]

Within that central government, party leaders met repeatedly to coordinate a response, noting with alarm that what seemed to motivate the protestors was not only a desire to change China, but also a yearning to participate in the momentum of change sweeping the globe. As Zhao Ziyang, General Secretary of the Chinese Communist Party, warned his colleagues: "Times have changed, and so have people's ideological views. Democracy is a worldwide trend, and there is an international countercurrent against communism and socialism that flies under the banner of democracy and human rights. If the party doesn't hold up the banner of democracy in our country, then someone else will, and we will lose out." Generally sympathetic to the protesters, Zhao reminded his fellow party leaders that "the student slogans that uphold the Constitution, promote democracy, and oppose corruption all echo positions of the Party and the government."[21]

While protesters were drawn from throughout Chinese society and were hardly unified either in their goals or organization, some common points about them can be made. Specifically, democracy in a Western sense was less their aim than was further liberalization and a purification of the political and economic spheres. Words like *freedom, liberty,* and *democracy* are amorphous by their very nature. American policymakers found them malleable both during the Cold War and after 1989. Chinese protesters embraced such terms in the hope of inspiring domestic reforms, while linking their struggle to similar reform movements in other parts of the Communist world, in order to solicit support abroad. "We Salute the Ambassador of Democracy," one student sign read as a welcome to the visiting Gorbachev. Another asked, "In the Soviet Union They

Have Gorbachev, But What Do We Have in China?" Issuing a "New May Fourth Manifesto," some students purposefully tied their cause to the much-celebrated 1919 protest against a Chinese government considered too corrupt and ineffectual to combat foreign incursions and influence.[22]

Their message was clear: These students walked in the footsteps of previous popular movements that had been instrumental in the fall of previous Chinese governments, which (like the current government) had proven unable to withstand the temptations of power. "Today, in front of the symbol of the Chinese nation, Tiananmen," one such well-publicized manifesto read, "we can proudly proclaim to all the people in our nation that we are worthy of the pioneers of seventy years ago." An unsigned poster prominently displayed in the square—"big character" posters long served as respectable message-boards for Chinese reform movements—offered a similar critique (and a dire warning): "Today, the Communist Party, especially its members who are government cadres, has already become a new privileged class of Chinese society....Of course, actual power is in the hands of Deng Xiaoping and his relatives, disciples, sycophants, and card buddies....Great turmoil across the whole of China is imminent. The Communist Party's day of reckoning is about to arrive."[23]

Turmoil meant something quite specific to Deng and those around him. They knew from bitter personal experience the potential of unruly crowds to inflict pain and damage. All to well, they knew what happened to leaders who left unchallenged zealous calls for societal purification. A strict accounting of the damage wrought by the Great Proletarian Cultural Revolution remains difficult to this day. Millions of lives had been disrupted when Mao's effort to reassert his power inspired his most zealous supporters, students especially, to promote ideological purity at any cost. Anyone associated with the Soviets or the West, with the outside world more broadly, was suspect. Anyone too well educated, or set apart from the masses in any way, risked trial and justice at the hands of the mob. Urban elites were sent to live in poverty on collective farms. Authority figures from all walks of life had been stripped of their social standing, beaten, abused, cast off. Tens of thousands had died. Far more suffered humiliation and saw their lives completely ruined.

Deng and his cadre well knew such traumas firsthand. When he saw protesters in the very central square of his capital calling for change and promising that "turmoil was imminent," Deng immediately thought of the pain and suffering that riled-up students bent on reform had only recently caused. He knew it was time to act. The government's official mouthpiece, the *Renmin ribao* (People's Daily), had in late April castigated the protesters not only as unpatriotic, but also dangerously engaged in stirring up the chaos of the past. The editorial in fact derived from Deng's own words to the party leadership. "Under the banner of democracy," it read, the protesters "were trying to destroy the democratic legal system. Their goal was to poison people's minds, to create turmoil throughout the country, to destroy political stability and unity. This was a planned conspiracy, a riot, whose real nature was to fundamentally negate the leadership of the Chinese Communist Party and to negate the socialist system." Deng later told military officers that "the word 'turmoil' [*duanhuan*] exactly describes the problem" with the protestors. They were stirring forces that they could not hope to control and that could not therefore be tolerated. As Premier Li Peng argued in response to the appeals for sympathy and genuine reform made by Zhao Ziyang: "Our first order of business should be stability. Once that is achieved, we can talk about reforming the political system." While Chinese officials debated, the crowds only grew in size and enthusiasm. On May 15, more than 500,000 people filled Tiananmen Square. Two days later they numbered more than a million. From the hinterland protesters surged into the city, eager to replace those who had left after voicing their concerns. In this way the crowds constantly regenerated, meaning that the total number of protesters far exceeded the size of any day's crowd.[24]

Martial law was imposed on May 20, but to little avail. Protestors blocked police efforts to enter Tiananmen Square, and their numbers continued to swell in the days that followed. Here then was a direct challenge to the government's authority: It was one thing for agitators to demand reform, but for leaders like Deng who held fast to the notion that only the government could provide the stability necessary to keep China safe from itself, such an outright rejection of the rule of law could simply not be tolerated. As Premier Li caustically reminded the American ambassador, "No government in the world would tolerate this kind of disorder in the middle of its capital."[25]

The army moved in during the night of June 3. With equal furor throughout the country, though most famously in Beijing, Chinese troops suppressed the gatherings. Tanks rolled over protester's encampments. Fires erupted as they fought back with improvised weapons. Bullets flew indiscriminately through the air. Official government records contend that fewer than 300 people lost their lives in the violence that ensued and in the police crackdowns that subsequently ferreted out leading voices in the protest movement. Outside observers— including the Chinese Red Cross—put the death toll at ten times that number. Deng remained in charge, though at great cost. As journalist James Mann notes of the international implications of the hardline crackdown, "In a single night, the Chinese leadership altered irrevocably the American perceptions of a steady reforming China and the friendly relationship that had been so carefully nurtured since the days of Richard Nixon."[26]

Twenty years later, as Chen Jian argues in this book, China remains ruled by that same government, willing to violently suppress reformers who question its right to rule, trading the guarantee of prosperity for limited popular participation in the political process. The underlying rationale behind this Faustian bargain clearly has grown out of the lesson Chinese leaders drew from their tumultuous 1989, which in turn was the result of earlier experiences. For Deng and the generation of Chinese leaders that has followed, stability is society's fundamental plank, demanding continuity of government and power even if nearly all other aspects of Chinese life transform around it. Reformers who questioned the government's right to rule were crushed in 1989. Those who followed in their wake enjoy greater economic opportunity and access to a wider world—so long as they refrain from questioning the regime's fundamental authority.

In the weeks after Tiananmen, the world struggled to digest the horrific images televised from Beijing. As China turned inward, foreign heads of state—especially the recently inaugurated George H. W. Bush—balanced outward statements of condemnation with private overtures designed to retain some semblance of a working international relationship with the Chinese government. "China is back on track a little with the Soviets," Bush mused in his diary, "and they could indeed come back in much stronger if we move unilaterally against them and cut them off from the West." Bush and senior American officials were already on record as having endorsed the protestors, whom they considered to be upholding Western traditions of democracy and liberal protest. More to the point, the Americans directly linked Chinese crowds with similar protest movements that were already a frequent sight behind Europe's iron curtain. "They may have that name [Gorbachev] on their lips," Secretary of State James Baker said in late May, just as the Soviet leader was visiting Beijing, "but they have the policies of the West in mind. It is the philosophy of the West that they are advancing, and it is the values of the West that they are seeking." Bush went even further in considering events in China and those in Eastern Europe as part of the same global phenomenon. "Glasnost and the Beijing demonstrations proved that the democratic way is on the march," he publicly declared, "and it is not going to be stopped." Deng, for one, proved willing to stop such movements in his own country, leading Michael Dobbs, the *Washington Post*'s Moscow bureau chief, to warn ominously that the Tiananmen crackdown "reminds us how readily communist leaders can still resort to brute force when their power is threatened."[27]

Soviet leaders refused such violent prescriptions. Confronted with reformist impulses in Eastern Europe and within their own borders—reforms unleashed to a great extent by Gorbachev's own efforts to improve and thereby save the very Soviet society he cherished—they refused to fire on their own people or to condone allied leaders who retained power through violence. Whereas Beijing retained control, Moscow therefore witnessed its Eastern European empire fall. The force of the collapse ultimately toppled the Soviet Union itself. Poland voted its Communist government out of power in June, strikingly on the same day tanks overran Tiananmen Square. Hungarians too stripped Communists from power, followed in short order by the Bulgarians, Czechoslovakians, and Romanians. As Alexis de Tocqueville, the nineteenth century's great observer of democracy, wrote of the period before 1789, the last moment of change comparable to that explored in this book: "The most dangerous time for a bad government is when it starts to reform itself." Once the spigot of real transformational change is opened, 1989 seems to suggest, it can only be closed with the utmost of force.[28]

While Poland's electoral turn from socialism presented the first major chink in the Soviet bloc's armor, later events in Berlin demonstrated the profound emotions and dramatic consequences of these events. On November 9, the once unthinkable occurred: the Berlin Wall fell, not to a conquering army, but to the regime's own citizens. First erected in 1961, the Wall symbolized the permanency of the Cold War divide. Dozens had lost their lives in the intervening years in vain attempts to cross its iron and wire in search of a better life on the other side. The Wall did more than divide East from West. It also made real the notion that Europe's future offered two distinctly different paths: one socialist, the other capitalist. American presidents ritualistically travelled to the Wall when on European tours, using it as a backdrop to proclaim their personal opposition to tyranny. The images are iconic: John F. Kennedy stood above the newly constructed barrier in order to declare: "All free men, wherever they may live, are citizens of Berlin. And, therefore, as a free man, I take pride in the words, 'Ich bin ein Berliner.'" A generation later, Ronald Reagan stood before the Wall in order to call for wholesale change behind it. "General Secretary Gorbachev," Reagan thundered in 1987 (to the great dismay of his own state department, which loathed such fiery rhetoric and urged its removal from the president's prepared text), "if you seek peace—if you seek prosperity for the Soviet Union and Eastern Europe...come here to this gate, Mr. Gorbachev, open this gate, Mr. Gorbachev, tear down this wall!"[29]

For a generation of Communist leaders raised to believe that theirs was a particular claim to mankind's future, the demise of the Wall and, more broadly, the erosion of the Soviet empire were traumatic blows indeed. "We will not change our positions, our values, or our thinking," Gorbachev promised Reagan in 1985, "but we expect that with patience and wisdom we will find some ways toward solutions." Four years later, Gorbachev was largely out of solutions to the problems that plagued him. With the Soviet Union's empire in disarray, with the loss of the lands won at such great cost in the Great Patriotic War against Hitler's Germany and subsequently ruled so tightly and at such investment, the society Gorbachev longed to preserve through transformation had lost its very reason for being. As Anatoly Chernyaev, one of Gorbachev's closest advisers, admitted in the privacy of his diary: "The Berlin Wall has fallen. This entire era in the history of the socialist system is over.... This is the end of Yalta...the Stalinist legacy."[30]

European communism ended with a remarkable and surprising lack of violence. Any of the ruling regimes might have held tightly onto power in the face of rising popular unrest, employing violent measures and tactics well honed by frequent use over the previous decades. As noted previously, East Germany's ruling party was unlikely to give up without a fight the control it had held for forty years. One ranking East German official admitted only weeks after the fall of the Berlin Wall that Honecker had composed orders for a "Chinese solution" to the protestor problem. "It could have been worse than Beijing," he said. When Chinese tanks rolled over and through Tiananmen, East German officials publicly praised the way Deng's government had dealt firmly with its protestors. There was, Honecker warned in early October, as crowds began to rally against his regime, "a fundamental lesson to be learnt from the crushing of the counterrevolutionaries in Peking in June." Even Honecker's forced retirement at the hands of Egon Krenz and other East German party leaders later that month did not necessarily spell a nonviolent response to the protesters, who seemed to grow in number and volume with every passing week. As one leading West German commentator warned in response to the news that Krenz was now in charge: "On a trip to West Germany, during the Tiananmen Square massacre in Beijing, he [Krenz] openly sided with the Chinese regime. So the safest bet is that Mr. Krenz is no Gorbachev."[31]

East German leaders were not alone in suggesting their state might retain power at any cost. Romania's Nicolae Ceaușescu pleaded with Gorbachev and his fellow Communist leaders in August 1989 to deploy military force against Polish and Hungarian reformers before they could fully consolidate the fruits of their electoral victory. Ceaușescu was certainly loath to cede power. The widespread violence that marked his ouster culminated with his execution. All of Eastern Europe might have gone down the violent path chosen by Beijing and

Bucharest. Certainly, Western leaders looked on with apprehension every time protesters turned out by the thousands in order to face down government security forces unsure of orders or the right path to take. As Kohl told Solidarity's Lech Walesa—in a conversation emblematic of the way leaders across the once-formidable iron curtain worked together to forge a safe course through such unchartered waters—"if one shoots, everything would be over."[32]

Left unstated was Kohl's implied realization that shooting might well erupt with little warning and to little surprise. Indeed, Czechoslovakia's Communist government suffered a fatal blow on November 19, 1989, when rumors spread rapidly throughout Prague and the surrounding countryside that police had shot and killed a student protestor. Such rumors proved false. But they were easily believed. Everyone expected such a violent showdown. When news of the supposed brutality passed not only by word of mouth but also by Radio Free Europe, crowds numbering in the tens of thousands quickly gathered, demanding an end to a regime that would kill its own children. "This is it," they chanted. "Now is the time." As historian Gale Stokes concluded, "Within just seventy-two hours, the seemingly vertical Czechoslovak domino had entered its accelerating arc of fall." On December 9, Gustav Husak resigned the presidency. The next day a coalition government of noncommunists took power. The national assembly unanimously elected the writer Václav Havel president of a new democratic regime on January 1. It was less than eight weeks after the Berlin Wall had been breached, and less than six weeks after protestors had peacefully forced the government's submission following the rumor that one of their number had been shot.[33]

Any reasonable explanation for why 1989 turned out as peacefully as it did for Eastern Europe—and any good answer to the question of why such dramatic changes occurred in the first place—must include both structural and personal reasons. On the one hand, communism had always fit Eastern Europe poorly. It was largely imposed after 1945 by occupying Soviet troops primarily concerned with ensuring a large security border following Germany's most recent invasion. Uprisings against the region's Communist regimes thus regularly appeared in the subsequent decades. In 1953 East Germans called for democratic reforms and the kind of prosperity already budding in the Western half of their divided country. In Hungary three years later open fighting erupted when—with prodding from overenthusiastic American propagandists—patriots called for removal of occupying Soviet troops. The famous Prague Spring of 1968 offered Czechoslovaks their own opportunity for change. So too did Polish workers repeatedly place their own government in the awkward position of mediating between their demands for liberalization and Moscow's need for absolute control.[34]

In retrospect, Eastern Europe might appear a bubbling cauldron of democracy, awaiting the moment when sufficient energy for change built up in advance of an inevitable eruption; however, there was always the heavy hand of Soviet rule present to clamp down on the forces of change. In 1953 Soviet troops suppressed East German protestors. In 1956 it was Hungary's turn. In 1968, the Red Army led a coalition of socialist states determined to halt change. In 1981 the Kremlin forced Polish leaders to impose martial law as a means of limiting Solidarity's growing power, threatening that if Warsaw could not keep its house in order the Red Army would. There can be no doubt that without Gorbachev's presence, 1989 would not have happened in Eastern Europe. At the least, it would not have occurred the way it did. As the events of 1989 unfolded, there always remained the option for the Soviets to put down protesters with force. After all, previous Soviet leaders had done just that.

Gorbachev, and with him the story of the Soviet Empire leading to the events of 1989, therefore demands attention. He came to power in 1985 fully aware that his state was in trouble and its future was in no way assured. At the same time he hardly hoped to see the Soviet Union dissolve around him. Lest we think of Gorbachev as the father of a new Europe or of a new Russia, we should recall that his desires for reform, no matter how sincere, were born out of necessity and the realization that change was needed to preserve the communist system he staunchly embraced. "On taking office as General Secretary," he recounted in his memoirs, "I was immediately faced with an avalanche of problems." This was an extreme understatement. Soviet economic growth had slowed to a crawl in the previous fifteen years, from an enviable annual growth rate of nearly 5 percent at the end of the 1960s to an anemic 1 percent by 1985. By some estimates, the Soviet economy in fact shrank during the early 1980s, burdened by expensive commitments not only to its own nearby empire in Eastern Europe and to an increasingly unpopular war in Afghanistan, but also to the support of far-off regimes, ranging from Cuba to Vietnam. Declining global oil prices eroded the value of Soviet exports, and a country once envied for its agricultural potential was forced to import food from abroad, further draining hard currency reserves already in deficit. During the 1970s Soviet leaders had devoted more than 30 percent of their total state investment to the agricultural sector. It had progressed a mere 1.2 percent as a result, less than the population had grown. Moreover the Soviet Union had largely been on a wartime footing since Stalin's day, with military expenditures consuming upwards of one-third the state's budget by the 1980s. By comparison, American officials routinely spent a far smaller percentage of their own far larger gross national product on defense. Soviet military prowess was impressive to be sure, highlighted by thousands of nuclear weapons. Its military had recently suffered in Afghanistan, but such a defeat, while painful, resembled American difficulties in Southeast Asia. Each superpower failed to halt dissent and revolution in the far reaches of their respective Cold War empires; each was indisputably a global power whose only real peer was the other.[35]

Still the Soviet Union was clearly slipping by the 1980s. Always rampant, alcoholism was once more on the rise, as was infant mortality. Average life expectancy was declining at an alarming rate throughout the Soviet state. The series of infirm and aged leaders who occupied the Kremlin in rapid succession in the 1980s—from the octogenarian Leonid Brezhnev, to the terminally ill Yuri Andropov, to the severely asthmatic and medicated Konstantin Chernenko—made the Soviet state appear not only weak, but devoid of new ideas. As Gorbachev told his wife on the eve of his assuming power, "We can't go on living like this." To his mind, "The system was dying away; its sluggish senile blood no longer contained any vital juices."[36]

Gorbachev set out to save socialism and the Soviet Union. Aware that military spending eroded his ability to deal with economic stagnation at home, he repeatedly offered Western leaders the chance to join Moscow not only in reducing military tensions in Europe—where more than a million Soviet troops expensively stood watch outside their country's borders—but ultimately in eliminating the scourge of nuclear weapons as well. "Never before has such a terrible danger hung over the heads of humanity in our times," he told the Central Committee that elected him. "The only rational way out of the current situation is for the opposing forces to agree to immediately stop the arms race—above all, the nuclear arms race." At home he promised *glastnost* and *perestroika,* terms not easily translated in their full meaning into English, but which meant in essence "transparency" and "reform." A more transparent state and economy would further unleash socialism's potential, he argued, making it more democratic and thus more equitable. A reformed state would be more economically efficient, more politically open, and thus more able to embrace the future without forsaking its most cherished values. Even before taking power he had spoken of the need for "deep transformations" within the Soviet economy and of the need for "wide, prompt, and frank information" as a fundamental key to opening Soviet society to change. Looking back on his time in power, he reflected that "we started everything in the first place—so a human being can feel normal, can feel good, in a socialist state."[37]

To save Soviet society, and the Soviet Union itself, from its internal problems, Gorbachev first had to alter the country's international position. The arms race was financially unsustainable. American plans for a new Strategic

Defense Initiative (colloquially called "Star Wars") threatened to impose an additional financial burden for Soviet military officials determined to maintain strategic parity with the West. Unable to keep pace, Gorbachev instead decided to change the rules of the game, proposing to transform the Soviet Union from a combative presence outside of Europe to a state fully enmeshed within that increasingly vibrant continent. "We understood that if nothing was changed in our foreign policy," Anatoli Chernyaev, one of Gorbachev's central diplomatic advisers concluded, "we would get nowhere with regard to the internal changes we had in mind."[38]

One of Gorbachev's first steps was therefore to convince Europe and the wider world that Soviet forces no longer posed an existential threat. In power only a few months, he spoke increasingly of a "common security" plan for Europe and of "equal security," wherein each side might draw back their military posture to a safer—and less expensive—level. In July 1985 he announced a unilateral moratorium on Soviet nuclear testing. "In order to carry out its large-scale plans," newly appointed foreign minister Eduard Shevardnadze told an international conference that same month, "the Soviet Union needs a lasting peace in Europe, [and] a lasting peace all over the world." Having replaced the long-serving and hawkish Andrei Gromyko only weeks before, Shevardnadze's very presence symbolized a new dawn for Soviet diplomacy. Gorbachev told a French audience that same year that domestic concerns came first in his mind, as he prioritized developing "the economy, social relations, and democracy." Because we "live in the same [European] house," he said, "we need to cooperate."[39]

Gorbachev hoped to save the Soviet Union not only by decreasing its military posture in Europe, but also by further integrating it with the prosperous Europe that lay just beyond the iron curtain. Eastern Europe had long been a financial burden for Moscow. He reasoned that opening trade and fostering connections between Europe's two halves would turn this liability into an asset. Democratic changes and liberalization of communist economies foreshadowed a new era of European history in which socialists and capitalists might coexist in some new society distilled from the best qualities each system had to offer. "I will not deny that I also hoped that a positive international response to my programme would strengthen my position," he later reflected, "and help overcome the growing resistance to change inside the Soviet Union."[40]

Europe was more than a source of markets and money, it was an ideal. Long wracked by war and strife, the continent—its Western half in particular— had undergone a fundamental existential transformation since 1945. The age of exploration and imperialism had allowed European leaders to export their conflicts throughout the world, making their wars truly global in nature and subjecting countless millions to their social, political, and religious struggles. By 1945, as James Sheehan eloquently demonstrates within this book, European societies had had enough. Exhausted, defeated, fearful of the new atomic future, and (most importantly) with their own internal squabbles constrained by the larger superpower conflict that pitted Moscow and Washington in a struggle for global domination, postwar European leaders developed a comprehensive prescription for long-term peace and prosperity based on democratic rule, social justice, and collective transnational government. When Gorbachev unleashed pent-up forces of reform within the Soviet empire, promising further connections with the West, he inadvertently provided Eastern Europeans and his own Soviet citizens a means of escape, but also a place to escape to.

For the men and women who built a European Union out of the ashes of global war and Holocaust, the largely peaceful revolutions of 1989 seemed the perfect validation not only of their own wisdom, but also of their system's broad appeal. As Sheehan, William Taubman, and Svetlana Savranskaya argue in this book, the fact that Eastern Europeans and Soviet citizens cried out to join Europe as often as they pleaded for "freedom" or "democracy" seemed proof to Western Europeans that theirs was the best melding of freedom and democracy—Washington's favorite catchall terms—with communism's ongoing proclamations of concern for social justice. "The linking of the German question to pan-European developments which takes account of the interests of all concerned," Kohl promised in late 1989, once the Berlin Wall was down, "paves the way for peaceful development in freedom, which is our objective." The European Council, comprised of the countries that were already in the late stages of forming a European Union, responded in kind: "We seek the strengthening of the state of peace in Europe in which the German people will regain its unity through free self-determination." Germany could reunite, despite all the horrors of a unified Germany's modern past, they concluded, so long as it was "placed in the perspective of European integration." Modern Europe was born from the ashes of World War II. But 1989, which in many ways marked the real end to World War II, was similarly modern Europe's true coming of age, as leaders throughout the continent agreed that democracy could lead to a peaceful and prosperous future, so long as the nationalism that had spurred so many past wars was properly constrained by a transnational union. When nationalism again ran amuck in the ensuing breakup of Yugoslavia, the violent specters of Europe's past returned with a vengeance.[41]

Gorbachev eventually realized, to his great dismay, that Western Europe was not as open to East-West integration as he had hoped. In 1987 he argued that "perestroika in the USSR was only a part of some kind of global perestroika, the birth of a new world order." A year later he proclaimed the dawn of a new world system in a much-celebrated speech to the United Nations. "It should be an anti-Fulton—Fulton in reverse," he instructed his speechwriters, referencing Winston Churchill's famous 1946 "Iron Curtain" speech in Fulton, Missouri, considered by many an opening salvo in the Cold War. "We should present our worldview and philosophy based on the results of the last three years," he said. "We should stress demilitarization and the humanization of our thinking."[42]

Gorbachev's most profound promise, made not only at the United Nations in 1988 but repeated both publicly and privately over the next two years, was his rejection of Moscow's right to dictate affairs throughout the Soviet bloc. Previous leaders in the Kremlin had readily used force throughout Eastern Europe whenever Communist regimes appeared in danger. In 1968 they proclaimed their undying right to intervene. "When external and internal forces hostile to socialism try to turn the developing of a given socialist country in the direction of restoration of the capitalist system," Leonid Brezhnev announced in a doctrine that would bear his name, "it is the concern of all socialist countries." Moscow would not concede its empire in 1968, Soviet leaders declared, nor would it cede its right to dictate affairs within its allies.

Gorbachev abandoned the Brezhnev Doctrine. Speaking to the United Nations in 1988, he urged all states to follow Moscow's lead in renouncing "the use of force in the international arena." More directly, he told his eager audience that "freedom of choice is a universal principle. It knows no exceptions." He said the same privately to Honecker and Ceauşescu when they pleaded for military salvation from Moscow. He said the same publicly only a fortnight before the Berlin Wall finally fell, telling the world through a spokesman that "I think the Brezhnev Doctrine is dead." In order to further transform Europe into a continent willing and able to accept full Soviet participation, he first had to relinquish absolute control over the region between the iron curtain and the Soviet border. The changes that occurred in Eastern Europe before and especially during 1989 were therefore simply and most profoundly a case of indigenous leaders and movements taking him at his word.[43]

Yet even as Eastern Europe cried out for change and for freedom from Soviet rule, neither Europe nor the United States seemed to want full Russian participation after all. German leaders negotiated with Moscow, paying its debts in 1990 and after, but only in order to win the Kremlin's reluctant approval of a unified German fatherland, fully integrated with the West and fully a part of NATO. During Ronald Reagan's second term in particular, American leaders embraced Gorbachev primarily because his reforms promised the demise of their long-term enemy. Within his own country, moreover, the democratic impulses Gorbachev unleashed threatened to undermine the very socialism he longed to preserve. His government was lauded abroad but assailed at home. Its promises of change appealed to Europe and the West—even as they terrified Chinese leaders—but for Soviet citizens facing mounting food shortages and the steady erosion of their economy and political system, Gorbachev's lack of responsiveness seemed the greater problem. There was, quite simply, no solution capable of retaining Soviet power at home and simultaneously integrating the Soviet state with Europe. Seeking to make a virtue out of the necessity of change, Soviet leaders ultimately lost control over the very centrifugal forces of change they had unleashed. Rejected by American and European leaders, even as they publicly lauded his reforms and praised his new vision, Gorbachev eventually realized that Moscow would have to go it alone. The Americans want "to see us get stuck, to fail," a fatigued Gorbachev confided to a confidant, following a failed Soviet-American summit in 1986. "There is no other option left for our generation but to restructure the country" on our own. "Our task is to learn how to lead 280 million people to socialism" alone, he said. Once the Wall was down three years later, however, he realized history had progressed too far to stop. He turned, as Taubman and Savranskaya note in this book, toward Europe not as an ideal or as a partner, but instead as a paymaster to a charity, hoping to win sufficient credits and time to save the Soviet Union. By 1991, his state would be no more. Subsequent Russian strategists would be loath to trust Western promises again.[44]

Though the Soviet Union collapsed from within, and Eastern Europe revolted in hope of joining the promising European society budding just across the iron curtain, Americans imbibed the heady lessons of 1989 most dramatically of all. For them, as Melvyn Leffler observes in this book's final chapter, the Cold War was not survived, but transcended. Drawing heavily from Reagan's harsh anti-Soviet rhetoric and concurrent military buildup during his first term, which coincided with the erosion of Soviet legitimacy at home and a steep decline in Soviet prosperity, subsequent American policymakers found causation in correlation. Washington strategists, especially those on the political right, came to believe that communism was actively defeated with a recipe for geostrategic success easily applied to other conflicts throughout the world. Strength, resilience, and conviction were enough to carry the United States through any struggle, the nation's leaders largely came to believe, because the benefits of the American system required only time to become evident even to its harshest opponents. It had taken only a little more than forty years for even a nuclear superpower such as the Soviet Union to fall before the seemingly obvious flaws of its communist system. So long as Americans remained vigilant, strong, and true to their convictions, the lesson seemed to be, no other system could match them. Moreover, the story of 1989 as understood in Washington confirmed the long-standing American mantra that their system was universally appealing. After all, crowds behind the iron curtain called out for "democracy," "freedom," and "choice." Because they employed such terms themselves, American leaders reflexively believed that Eastern Europe's surging masses meant those terms in the American context. Europe was their more likely model. For American leaders raised on the central national tenet that the future could be won and controlled through the force and energy of American will, however, a self-serving explanation for communism's eventual collapse emerged: the capitalist world's economic might, a vital plank in their conception of a free society, had in time ground its adversary to dust.

According to Leffler, American policymakers largely perceived that their vision of freedom, validated by 1989, could surmount even the most difficult of international quandaries. As George H. W. Bush declared in his inaugural address in January 1989: "We know what works: Freedom works. We know what's right: Freedom is right. We know how to secure a more just and prosperous life for man on Earth: through free markets, free speech, free elections, and the exercise of free will unhampered by the state." American foreign policy in the decades to follow can largely be explained as an extensive effort to replicate this successful strategy throughout the world. Disaster was frequently the result.[45]

Frequently forgotten in this celebratory story of 1989 as an American victory is the Bush administration's abiding fear that the Cold War was anything but over only months before the iron curtain collapsed. Bush had never been as keen as Reagan to embrace Gorbachev. Whereas Reagan in his first term famously called the Soviet Union an "evil empire," five years later he candidly told reporters, "I was talking about another time and another era." His trust in Gorbachev made all the difference, Reagan said. "I think that a great deal of it [the prospect of change] is due to the General Secretary, who I have found different than previous Soviet leaders." Bush, not privy to one-on-one conversations between Reagan and Gorbachev, was not so easily swayed. "I don't think that we know enough to say that there is that kind of fundamental change," he told reporters in June 1988. Carefully distancing himself from Reagan, he concluded that when it came to the sincerity of Gorbachev's reforms, "My view is, the jury is still out." Later that year he repeated the charge in a televised presidential debate, arguing, "I think the jury is still out on the Soviet experiment" with reform. Even his choice of the word *experiment* emphasized his fundamental view that Gorbachev's promises were temporary at best, insincere at worst.[46]

Much of Bush's more strident posture toward the prospect of change behind the iron curtain can be attributed to his desire to hew to the right in his campaign for the White House against the seemingly more dovish Michael Dukakis. Behind Bush's cautionary campaign rhetoric, however, lay a significant dose of pessimistic caution from his closest foreign policy advisers. Neither Robert Gates nor Dick Cheney believed the Soviets could be fully trusted. Both men argued that the merits of Moscow's reforms should be weighed less by Soviet words than by actions. Bush's most intimate advisers, National Security Adviser Brent Scowcroft and Secretary of State James Baker, similarly argued for a "pause" in Soviet-American relations as the new administration took power in January 1989; such pause would give policymakers time to review the record of the past eight years, unburdened by bureaucratic pressure. The review took months to complete, but skepticism with Soviet sincerity—tinged not coincidentally with a strong desire on the part of Bush's team to distance themselves from their immediate predecessors—suffused the entire process. "I think the Cold War is not over," Scowcroft publicly admitted only two days after Bush took the oath of office; Gorbachev "badly needs a period of stability, if not definite improvement in the [East-West] relationship so he can face the awesome problem he has at home." More dramatically, Scowcroft said he also thought Gorbachev was "interested in making trouble within the Western alliance, and I think he believes the best way to do it is a peace offensive, rather than to bluster the way some of his predecessors have."[47]

Convinced that the Cold War still raged, despite Soviet overtures to the contrary, Bush and his administration gave little evidence that they embraced a general relaxation of tensions. They simply did not trust Gorbachev at his word, believing his proclamations of reform belied a more sinister strategy to preserve Soviet strength. In hindsight, they were both right and wrong. Gorbachev was sincere in his desire for reform; so too did he hope that reforming the Soviet state might save it from destruction. "What were they waiting for?" Gorbachev privately fumed at the height of Bush's pause. The new president "wasn't drawing the proper conclusions from his U.N. speech," Chernyaev recorded Gorbachev as complaining, "and even has in mind a Western effort to undermine the Soviet Union's international initiatives." Bush eventually ended his administration's self-imposed pause in May 1989 by promising to move "beyond containment." No longer would Washington reflexively view every Soviet advance as cause for confrontation, he promised. Still, he warned, "the United States will challenge the Soviet Union step by step, issue by issue and institution by institution to behave in accordance with the higher standards that the Soviet leadership itself has enunciated." Weeks later he reminded another audience, this time with French president François Mitterrand at his side, that "though hope is now running high for a more peaceful continent, the history of this century teaches Americans and Europeans to remain prepared." Bush concluded, "In an era of extraordinary change, we have an obligation to temper optimism—and I am optimistic—with prudence," because "it is clear that Soviet 'new thinking' has not yet totally overcome the old." As Soviet expert Condoleezza Rice advised, "We need a track record" for Soviet progress, because "we have been burned before." Even if Gorbachev's desire for reforms proved legitimate, one Central Intelligence Agency estimate presciently cautioned in April 1989, that "a growing perception within the leadership that reforms are threatening the stability of the regime could lead to a conservative reaction." As Scowcroft succinctly put it, "Dying empires rarely go out peacefully."[48]

The new administration of George Bush thus spent its first months in office weighing its options, while surging forward with a level of anticommunist rhetoric more akin to previous Cold War presidencies. Gorbachev might be worth the risk, Bush seemed to be stating, but there is no similar need to reconsider the wisdom of the broad American embrace of free markets and political freedom. In late May Bush made his first visit to Europe as president. He sounded less like a man devoted to prudence than a disciple of Reagan's hawkish first term. "Nowhere is the division between East and West seen more clearly than in Berlin," Bush declared. "There, a brutal wall cuts neighbor from neighbor and brother from brother. That wall stands as a monument to the failure of communism. It must come down!" Later that summer, when presented with a piece of barbed wire from the now-dismantled Hungarian portion of the iron curtain, Bush enthusiastically declared, "Let Berlin be next!" He had earlier told Poles while visiting their country that "democracy has captured the spirit of our times.... [It is] the destiny of man."[49]

Bush in time realized the full power his words conveyed. Events in China changed his thinking, revealing not only the lengths Communist leaders would go to retain control, but also the very impotence of even an American president, the most powerful man in the world, to truly control events half-a-world away. Bush returned home from his trip to Eastern Europe in July, fearful that events in that region might lead to the kind of violence seared into his memory through television images from Beijing and convinced of the need to reach out to Gorbachev so that they, and other European leaders, might somehow massage and manage the change swirling around them. There could still be more Tiananmens, he realized. He therefore implored Gorbachev to meet "without thousands of assistants hovering over our shoulders." As Bush further explained, "I just want to reduce the chance that there could be misunderstanding between us."[50]

The two men met in Malta later that year, after the Berlin Wall was already down. "The most contentious issues were discussed without rancor," Bush reported to Kohl when the summit was over. "This could have been a shouting match, but it was very calm." No doubt the serenity of the meeting had been enhanced by Bush's earlier decision to tone down his own rhetoric when discussing events in Eastern Europe. When crowds of Germans swarmed the despised Berlin Wall, Bush refused to celebrate along with them. "Gorbachev talks about a common home," Bush told reporters ushered into his Oval Office as news reports told of the momentous and largely unexpected collapse of the East German regime. They did not know he had just spoken to the Soviet leader, ending the call with a promise that he would do nothing to destabilize further an already precarious situation. "Is it a step towards that?" he offered with a shrug of his shoulders, "probably so." Even as the world celebrated, Bush later reflected, his mind "kept racing over a possible Soviet crackdown, turning all that happiness to tragedy."[51]

The Berlin Wall fell, Eastern Europe strove towards democracy, and pro-testors in China assembled and were disbanded, all without direct American action. It is true that the United States, by heading the great anticommunist coalition of the previous four decades, had enabled the forces of change to foment behind the iron curtain. It is surely true that American-led military pressure forced the Soviets to spend more on defense than they could afford. Reagan's first-term promise of Star Wars threatened an already impoverished Kremlin leadership with even more of the same. But at the same time, very little the Americans actively did or chose in 1989 led directly to the events that transformed the world throughout that year. Policymakers in Washington reacted to those changes; they surely helped manage the reunification of Germany that marked the reunion of Europe in 1990 and after; they strove to maintain some positive relationship with Beijing in order to keep China enmeshed in the international system; and they most surely provided a magnet of stability in a post–Cold War world, dangerously liable to spin into anarchy. But 1989 was hardly an American product.

So too was the West's Cold War victory more the product of long-term structural forces than the active achievement of a single philosophy. The triumphalist interpretation of a Reaganesque American victory predicated on the strategies of his first term—including harsh rhetoric, unyielding determination to confront perceived evils in the world, and military might that underlies the entire project—neglects the more open spirit of Reagan's second term, in which he embraced the possibility of change Gorbachev embodied. So too did Bush's quick conversion from Cold War hawk to cautious manager of stability and order allow pro-Western moderates such as Boris Yeltsin room to outmaneuver the conservative backlash that culminated in the coup against Gorbachev in 1991. "The magnitude of change we sense around the world," Bush declared in 1989, "compels us to look within ourselves and our God to forge a rare alloy of courage and restraint." American leadership was critical in determining how the world reacted to 1989 and the end of the Cold War. It was critical for shepherding the transition to peace. But the catalyst for change is best sought elsewhere, beyond Washington.[52]

Everything changed in 1989—but not only because the world map appeared fundamentally different by the close of the year. Everything changed because the four principal geostrategic players of that year drew four fundamentally different conclusions about why change had occurred. As the chapters in this book collectively argue, each strategic conclusion brought its own prescription for future success. Chinese leaders continued to value stability and prosperity above political liberalization. Russian leaders learned that the Western powers they yearned to join were neither willing to accept full Russian participation nor easily trusted with Russian weakness. European leaders came to believe multilateral unity built on a foundation of economic integration offered the best hope for continued peace and prosperity. American leaders came to believe, as in many ways American leaders always had, that their system was divinely inspired and unquestionably superior, universally appealing to any people wise enough to understand its evident benefits and free from those despots who denied these benefits to them. World War II and the Cold War each ended for all practical purposes in 1989, even if the twentieth century that spawned each would not fully end until September 11, 2001. "The past must never be repeated," Soviet Foreign Minister Eduard Shevardnadze warned, only a week after the Berlin Wall was breached. "Europe and the world paid a high price for past mistakes," he said in obvious reference to the pains of Germany's militaristic history. "The Soviet people have not forgotten and never will forget history's lesson." Neither, he implied, would Moscow allow its whole world to crumble without a fight—or so it was feared in Western capitals. As Bush had earlier cautioned, "As we wait for history to render judgment, a prudent skepticism is in order."[53]

NOTES

1. Surveys of the Cold War, including its end, abound. For useful primers written largely from an American perspective, see John Lewis Gaddis, *The Cold War: A New History* (New York: Penguin, 2006); Walter LaFeber, *America, Russia, and the Cold War, 1946–2006* (New York: McGraw-Hill, 2006); and Melvyn Leffler, *For the Soul of Mankind: The United*

States, the Soviet Union, and the Cold War (New York: Hill and Wang, 2007). For Europe, see William I. Hitchcock, *The Struggle for Europe: The Turbulent History of a Divided Continent* (New York: Doubleday, 2002), and Tony Judt, *Postwar: A History of Europe since 1945* (New York: Penguin Books, 2005). For a history of the Cold War as seen from Moscow, see Vladislav Zubok, *A Failed Empire: The Soviet Union in the Cold War from Stalin to Gorbachev* (Chapel Hill: University of North Carolina Press, 2007). For China's perspective, see Chen Jian, *Mao's China and the Cold War* (Chapel Hill: University of North Carolina Press, 2000), and Lorenz Luthi, *The Sino-Soviet Split: Cold War in the Communist World* (Princeton, N.J.: Princeton University Press, 2008). The conflict was also global—see Odd Arne Westad, *The Global Cold War: Third World Interventions and the Making of Our Time* (New York: Cambridge University Press, 2007).

2. Don Oberdorfer, "Thatcher Says Cold War Has Come to an End," *The Washington Post,* November 18, 1988, A1. For a similar look at international relations though the lens of a single year, see Jeremi Suri, *Power and Protest: Global Revolution and the Rise of Détente* (Cambridge, Mass.: Harvard University Press, 2005). Readers of this book, published on the twentieth anniversary of the fall of the Berlin Wall, might find interesting Sorin Antohi and Vladimir Tismaneanu, *Between Past and Future: The Revolution of 1989 and Their Aftermath* (New York: Central European University Press, 2000), developed for the tenth anniversary.

3. "Remarks at the Swearing-in Ceremony for Richard B. Cheney as Secretary of Defense," March 21, 1989," *Public Papers of the Presidents of the United States: George Bush,* Vol. 1 (Washington: US Government Printing Office, 1990), 275–278. Hereafter *PPP, GHWB.* Robert M. Gates, *From the Shadows: The Ultimate Insider's Story of Five Presidents and How They Won the Cold War* (New York: Simon and Schuster, 1996), 449 (emphasis in original).

4. For a history of China, with particular attention to the Cultural Revolution, which loomed so large in the thinking of policy makers in 1989, see John King Fairbank and Merle Goldman, *China: A New History* (Cambridge, Mass.: Belknap Press, 2006), and Kenneth Lieberthal, *Governing China: From Revolution to Reform* (New York: W. W. Norton, 2006); Roderick MacFarquhar, *The Politics of China: The Eras of Mao and Deng* (New York: Cambridge University Press, 1997); Roderick MacFarquhar and Michael Schoenhals, *Mao's Last Revolution* (Cambridge, Mass: Belknap Press, 2006); and Jonathan Spence, *The Search for Modern China* (New York: W. W. Norton, 1999). See also the bibliographic essay and introduction to Jeffrey A. Engel, *The China Diary of George H. W. Bush* (Princeton, N.J.: Princeton University Press, 2008).

5. Thatcher quoted in Christopher Maynard, *Out of the Shadow: George H. W. Bush and the End of the Cold War* (College Station: Texas A&M University Press, 2008), 56. Mitterrand quoted in Judt, *Postwar,* 637.

6. Judt, *Postwar,* 630.

7. Hitchcock, *Struggle for Europe,* 359.

8. Timothy Garton Ash has astutely coined the term "refolution" to describe the political seachange in Eastern Europe in 1989, considering it as much the product of

domestic reform as outright revolution. See Ash, *In Europe's Name: Germany and the Divided Continent* (New York: Vintage Books, 1993), 344. For a survey of 1989 behind the iron curtain, see Charles Maier, *Dissolution: The Crisis of Communism and the End of East Germany* (Princeton, N.J.: Princeton University Press, 1997); Padraic Kenney, *A Carnival of Revolution:* (Princeton, N.J.: Princeton University Press, 2002); Daniel Chirot, ed., *The Crisis of Leninism and the Decline of the Left* (Seattle: University of Washington Press, 1992); Ken Jowitt, *New World Disorder: The Leninist Extinction* (Berkeley: University of California Press, 1992); and Gale Stokes, *The Walls Came Tumbling Down: The Collapse of Communism in Eastern Europe* (New York: Oxford University Press, 1993). See also the provocative introduction to Charles Maier, ed., *The Cold War in Europe: Era of a Divided Continent* (Princeton, N.J.: Markus Wiener Publishers, 1996). For longer-term structural trends, see Valerie Bunce, *Subversive Institutions: The Design and Destruction of Socialism and the* State (New York: Cambridge University Press, 1999).

9. Frederick Taylor, *The Berlin Wall* (London: Bloomsbury, 2006), 400.

10. Hungary's foreign minister quoted in Taylor, *Berlin Wall,* 406. East German crowds quoted in Stokes, *Walls Came Tumbling Down,* 256.

11. Judt, *Postwar,* 622.

12. George H. W. Bush, "Remarks to the Polish National Assembly in Warsaw," July 10, 1989, PPP, GHWB, 1989, II, 920–24.

13. East German crowds quoted in Judt, *Postwar,* 603. Rakowski quoted in Gale Stokes, *From Stalinism to Pluralism: A Documentary History of Eastern Europe since 1945* (New York: Oxford University Press, 1996), 256.

14. James A. Baker, *The Politics of Diplomacy* (New York: Putnam, 1995), 97.

15. For a recent discussion of NATO's expansion, whose disputed origins from this period continue to confound contemporary Russian relations with Europe and the United States, see Mark Kramer, "The Myth of a No-NATO-Enlargement," *The Washington Quarterly* 32.2 (April 2009): 39–61.

16. Francis Fukuyama, *The End of History and the Last Man* (New York: Free Press, 2006). For discussion and refutation of the democratic peace theory, see Michael E. Brown et al., *Debating the Democratic Peace* (Cambridge, Mass: MIT Press, 1996). For the related argument that democracies typically triumph in war, see Michael C. Desch, *Power and Military Effectiveness: The Fallacy of Democratic Triumphalism* (Baltimore, Md.: Johns Hopkins University Press, 2008).

17. Chinese officials quoted in chapter 4, this volume, by Chen Jian, p. 158.

18. A useful discussion of Deng's political philosophy is Maurice Meisner, *The Deng Xiaoping Era* (New York: Hill and Wang, 1996).

19. Orville Schell, *Mandate of Heaven: The Legacy of Tiananmen Square and the Next Generation of China's Leaders* (New York: Simon and Schuster, 1995), 354.

20. Beijing students quoted in Binyan Liu, *Tell the World: What Happened in China and Why* (New York: Pantheon Books, 1989): 8. Lilley quoted in Randy Kluver, "Rhetorical Trajectories of Tiananmen Square," *Diplomatic History* (forthcoming, January 2010, Vol. 34(1); unpublished manuscript in author's possession.

21. James Lilley, *China Hands: Nine Decades of Adventure, Espionage, and Diplomacy in Asia* (New York: Public Affairs, 2004), 300. Readers should note the recent publication of Zhao Ziyang's recent memoir, secretly recorded following his house-arrest. See *Prisoner of the State: The Secret Journal of Premier Zhao Ziyang* (New York: Simon and Schuster, 2009).

22. Student signs quoted in Lilley, *China Hands,* 301. For the "New May Fourth Manifesto," see Han Minzu [pseud.], *Cries for Democracy: Writings and Speeches from the 1989 Chinese Democracy Movement* (Princeton, N.J.: Princeton University Press, 1990), 135.

23. Manifesto and poster quoted in Han, *Cries for Democracy,* 135, 159. For earlier examples of this sort of public communication, see Lincoln Cushing and Ann Tompkins, *Chinese Posters: Art from the Great Proletarian Cultural Revolution* (New York: Chronicle Books, 2007).

24. *Renmin ribao* editorial quoted in Liang Zhang et al., *The Tiananmen Papers* (New York: Public Affairs, 2001), 71. Deng quoted in Han, *Cries for Democracy,* 370. Li Peng quoted in Lilley, *China Hands,* 300.

25. Lilley, *China Hands,* 300.

26. James Mann, *About Face: A History of America's Curious Relationship with China, from Nixon to Clinton* (New York: Vintage Books, 2000), 192. See also Mann's more polemical *The China Fantasy: How Our Leaders Explain Away Chinese Repression* (New York: Viking, 2007).

27. For the Bush diary, see George H. W. Bush and Brent Scowcroft, *A World Transformed* (New York: Vintage Books, 1999), 98. Baker quoted in Kluver, "Rhetorical Trajectories" (forthcoming). Bush quoted in Martin Walker, "NATO Is a Winner, Says Upbeat Bush," *The Guardian* (London), May 24, 1989. Michael Dobbs, "The Great Global Shake-up," *The Washington Post,* June 11, 1989, C1.

28. Tocqueville quoted in Gates, *From the Shadows,* 439.

29. For discussion of U.S. presidents and the Wall, see the aforementioned Taylor, *Berlin Wall,* as well as the following: A. James Adams, *Germany Divided: From the Wall to Reunification* (Princeton, N.J.: Princeton University Press, 1993); Michael Beschloss, *The Crisis Years: Kennedy and Khrushchev, 1960–1963* (New York: HarperCollins, 1991); William F. Buckley, *The Fall of the Berlin Wall* (New York: Wiley, 2004); Mary Fulbrook, *The People's State: East Germany Society from Hitler to Honecker* (New Haven, Conn.: Yale University Press, 2005); John Lewis Gaddis, *We Now Know: Rethinking Cold War History* (New York: Oxford University Press, 1997); Norman Gelb, *The Berlin Wall: Kennedy, Khrushchev, and a Showdown in the Heart of Europe* (New York: Dorset Press, 1986); Serge Schmeman, *When the Wall Came Down* (New York: Kingfisher, 2006); and Peter Schweizer, *The Fall of the Berlin Wall* (Palo Alto, Calif.: Hoover Institution Press, 2000). Peter Robinson, author of Reagan's famous speech, describes its creation in *How Ronald Reagan Changed My Life* (New York: Regan Books, 2003), 85–113.

30. Gorbachev and Chernyaev quoted in Leffler, *For the Soul of Mankind,* 385, 436.

31. For Honecker, see Richard Bassett, "East Berlin Warns on Reform Protests," *The Times* (London), October 10, 1989. For West German commentor, see Joseph Joffe, "Who's Egon Krenz? He's No Gorbachev," *The New York Times,* October 19, 1989, A29.

32. Leffler, *For the Soul of Mankind,* 434.

33. Chanting Prague crowds quoted in Gale Stokes, *Three Eras of Political Change in Eastern Europe* (New York: Oxford University Press, 1997), 177. Stokes, *Walls Came Tumbling Down,* 156. For a first-hand account of these events, see Timothy Garten Ash, *The Magic Lantern: The Revolution of '89 Witnessed in Warsaw, Budapest, Berlin, and Prague* (New York: Vintage Books, 1993). See also his *In Europe's Name: Germany and the Divided Continent* (New York: Random House, 1993).

34. Christian Ostermann, "This is Not a Politburo, But a Madhouse." [Cold War International History Project] *Bulletin* 10 (March 1998). For Hungary, see Mark Kramer, "The Soviet Union and the 1956 Crises in Hungary and Poland: Reassessments and New Findings," *Journal of Contemporary History* 33.2 (1998): 163–214. For Czechoslovakia, see Mark Kramer, "The Czechoslovak Crisis and the Brezhnev Doctrine," in *1968: The World Transformed,* edited by Carol Fink et al. (New York: Cambridge University Press, 1998); H. Gordon Skilling, *Czechoslovakia's Interrupted Revolution* (Princeton, N.J.: Princeton University Press, 1976); and Kieran Williams, *The Prague Spring and its Aftermath* (New York: Cambridge University Press, 1997). For the American response to these Soviet moves, see Bennett Kovrig, *Of Walls and Bridges: The United States and Eastern Europe* (New York: New York University Press, 1991).

35. For Gorbachev, see his own *Memoirs* (New York: Doubleday, 1995), and also the following works: Archie Brown, *The Gorbachev Factor* (New York: Oxford University Press, 1996); Robert G. Kaiser, *Why Gorbachev Happened: His Triumphs and His Failure* (New York: Simon and Schuster, 1991); David Remnick, *Lenin's Tomb: The Last Days of the Soviet Empire* (New York: Vintage Books, 1994); and Stephen White, *After Gorbachev* (Cambridge: Cambridge University Press, 1993). For Soviet economic decline, see Zubok, *Failed Empire,* 298–300. For a first-hand American perspective on Gorbachev and this period, see Jack F. Matlock, *Autopsy on an Empire* (New York: Random House, 1995).

36. Leffler, *For the Soul of Mankind,* 374.

37. Gorbachev quoted in Leffler, *For the Soul of Mankind,* 375, and Stokes, *Walls Came Tumbling Down,* 68, 72.

38. Anatoly Chernyaev, *My Six Years with Gorbachev* (University Park: Pennsylvania State University Press, 2000), 55.

39. Leffler, *For the Soul of Mankind,* 380.

40. James Mann, *The Rebellion of Ronald Reagan: A History of the End of the Cold War* (New York: Viking, 2009), 317. See also Gorbachev, *Memoirs,* 459.

41. Kohl and the European Council quoted in chapter 2, this volume, by James J. Sheehan, p. 84.

42. Gorbachev quoted in Zubok, *Failed Empire,* 310, and Mann, *Rebellion of Ronald Reagan,* 317.

43. Hitchcock, *Struggle for Europe,* 358.

44. Gorbachev quoted in Leffler, *For the Soul of Mankind,* 396.

45. Bush, "Inaugural Address," January 20, 1989, PPP, GHWB, 1989, I, 1–4.

46. Reagan and Bush quoted in Mann, *Rebellion of Ronald Reagan,* 304–6.

47. David Hoffman, "Gorbachev Seen as Trying to Buy Time for Reform," *The Washington Post,* January 23, 1989, A1.

48. Gorbachev, *Memoirs,* 496–97. Chernyaev, *My Six Years,* 215. For quotations from Bush and a discussion of his administration's strategic pause and subsequent policy of moving "beyond containment," see Maynard, *Out of the Shadow,* 1–26. Rice quoted in Hal Brands, *From Berlin to Baghdad* (Lexington: University of Kentucky Press, 2008), 24. Scowcroft quoted in Maynard, *Out of the Shadow,* 39.

49. Bush, "Remarks to the Polish National Assembly in Warsaw," July 10, 1989, and "Remarks to the Citizens in Mainz, Federal Republic of Germany," May 31, 1989.

50. See Bush and Scowcroft, *World Transformed,* 131, and Bush, *All the Best My Life in Letters and Other Writings* (New York: Scribner, 1999), 433.

51. Bush quoted in Brands, *From Berlin to Baghdad,* 25; Bush, "Remarks and Question-and-Answer Session with Reporters on the Relaxation of East German Border Controls," November 9, 1989, PPP, GHWB, 1989, II, 1488–1490 and Stokes, *From Stalinism to Pluralism,* 266–67.

52. Bush, "Remarks to the Polish National Assembly in Warsaw," July 10, 1989, PPP, GHWB, 1989, II, 920–24.

53. Shevardnadze quoted in Leffler, *For the Soul of Mankind,* 438. Bush quoted in Maynard, *Out of the Shadow,* 15.

Chapter 2

THE TRANSFORMATION OF EUROPE AND THE END OF THE COLD WAR

James J. Sheehan

There is no question about Europe's importance for the Cold War. It was in Europe that the Cold War began, when the grand alliance against Nazi Germany dissolved because of disputes over the continent's political future. Europe was the only place in the world where the ground forces of the superpowers directly confronted one another, deployed along a fortified line between the two Germanies that was densely packed with the largest concentration of lethal hardware in human history. The potential perils in this confrontation were high, but so were the stakes: any significant geopolitical shift within Europe would surely have had enormous consequences. Indeed, Europe may have been the only place where the global balance of power between East and West might have been fundamentally altered. And, of course, it was in Europe where the final chapter in the story of the Cold War began, its eventual outcome most powerfully symbolized by the opening of the Berlin Wall on November 9, 1989. The Soviet Union did not survive the loss of its European imperium.

The Cold War in Europe is most often viewed from the perspectives of the United States and of the Soviet Union. "Europe between the Superpowers," the title of A. W. Deporte's fine book, first published in 1979, captures the way scholars conventionally saw European international history in the decades after 1945.[1] And no wonder: The superpowers' antagonism both caused and sustained the continent's division. Like those great rivalries in the past—Athens and Sparta, Rome and Carthage, England and Spain—the struggle between the

United States and the Soviet Union shaped historians' grand narrative from the Cold War's contested origins to its extraordinary climax. Most observers, therefore, have looked for answers to questions about the war's sources and outcome in Washington or Moscow. Who was responsible for the Cold War? Was it forced on a reluctant United States by Russian aggression or, as revisionist historians claimed, was it the result of American political ambitions and economic interests? And who can take credit for the victory of the West in 1989–90? Is the protagonist of this story Mikhail Gorbachev, whose efforts at reforming the system inadvertently led to its collapse? Or was the hero Ronald Reagan, whose moral vision and military spending initiated the crisis that led to Communism's demise?

There have, of course, always been critics of this bipolar vision. Recently, what is regarded as American triumphalism about the end of Cold War has become the target of sharp attacks. Michael Cox of the London School of Economics, for example, goes so far as to link Cold War triumphalism with the Gulf War: Iraq, he wrote in a collection published in 2008, "is the by-product of an American mind-set that never for once questioned the assertion that the United States—and the United States alone—won the Cold War a decade and a half earlier."[2] Cox insists that in addition to the United States, individual European decision makers—Kohl, Mitterrand, and Thatcher—and the European Community as a whole played important roles in ending the Cold War.

I will not attempt to determine the relative impact of individuals on what happened in 1989–90, nor do I speculate about how this might have influenced American foreign policy fifteen years later. There is, I think, an important element of truth in the superpower perspective: with the significant exception of Helmut Kohl, the most important figures in 1989 were in Washington and Moscow. But while individual Europeans may have played marginal roles, "Europe," as an idea, an aspiration, and a historical example, was of great importance. My central point, therefore, is suggested by the order of items in my title: "The Transformation of Europe and the End of the Cold War." My subject is not how the end of the Cold War transformed Europe after 1989, but rather how the transformation of Europe after 1945 affected the timing and character of the Cold War's end. At the heart of this transformation, I shall argue, were two inseparable developments: first, the discrediting and eventual abandonment of war as a political instrument by the European society of states; second, the creation of new international institutions, centered in the European Economic Community but including a variety of other modes of cooperation and mutual support.[3] When, how, and why the Soviet empire collapsed are closely connected to these two developments, at once their result and their reaffirmation.

The chapter begins with a discussion of how the European states—concentrating on Britain, France, and the Federal Republic of Germany (FRG)—learned to live with the Cold War, each seeking to manage a triangular relationship with the Soviet Union, the United States, and one another. It then examines the dramatic changes that occurred after 1985, when Mikhail Gorbachev became the leader of the Soviet Union and the process of European integration entered a new phase. Finally, it will analyze the European role in the end of the Cold War and especially in resolving that quintessential Cold War issue, the German question.

LIVING WITH THE COLD WAR

The Cold War was a necessary cause of Europe's transformation after 1945 because, if it had not been for the global conflict with the Soviet Union, the United States would never have become so deeply and persistently engaged with European affairs. Although its effect has sometimes been overestimated, American aid was an important impetus to Europe's economic recovery as well as to its first step towards intracontinental cooperation. More significant was the American contribution to the formation of a security architecture that promoted peaceful and stable relations among traditional antagonists in Western Europe. The United States, together with France and Britain, continued to maintain troops in the Federal Republic as the first line of defense against Soviet expansion and also as a guarantee of the republic's political stability. By anchoring the United States in Europe and containing a revitalized and rearmed Germany, the Atlantic alliance seemed to solve the problem of Germany's place in Europe, which had been the central issue in European international relations since 1914 and perhaps, as some have argued, since 1871. After two catastrophic wars, Europeans could have no illusions about the dangers of international conflict, but only after the German question had been resolved, could they begin to take peace for granted.[4]

American engagement in Europe is so prominent a part of postwar history that its historically unprecedented character can be too easily overlooked. In 1941, when they reluctantly abandoned their deeply rooted isolationism to enter the war, few Americans could have imagined that they were to remain actively involved in European affairs and that, seven decades later, there would still be substantial American forces stationed on the continent. From the European perspective, American involvement was equally unprecedented: When have rich, well-organized states, each with its own formidable military tradition, ever entrusted their security to another power thousands of miles away?

After 1945, each European state pursued its self-interest within a triangle marked by three sets of relationships: with the Communist states of Eastern Europe, especially the Soviet Union; with the United States; and finally with its European neighbors. The relative importance of these vectors was often a matter of intense domestic debate. Emphasis on one or another changed as each state sought to defend its position within the international system according to its own history, geography, and political alignments. But each vector was essential, and all were closely connected: because of the Soviet threat, Europeans needed both the Americans and one another. Throughout the postwar era, therefore, Western European states sought an effective equilibrium between the imperatives of solidarity and independence, community and autonomy. In their search for this equilibrium, states did not give up the pursuit of their own security and self-interest. The Cold War—to borrow a distinction from the great Prussian strategist Carl von Clausewitz—changed the grammar, not the logic of European statecraft.

Every European state saw its place in the postwar world through the lens of its experiences in the Second World War. British statesmen, for example, knew that they could not have survived the war without the United States. Viewed from London, the Atlantic alliance seemed to provide the foundation for British security in the new struggle against the Soviet Union, just as it had in the old battle against Hitler's Germany. The British accepted their role as America's partner—a junior partner, to be sure, but nonetheless a partner whose experience and strategic position would give them ample opportunities for influence. The vector of Britain's relationship to Europe was less strong, since it was qualified by her commitments to the United States, to the Commonwealth, and to what remained of her imperial aspirations. Nor were the British as concerned with the German question as most other Europeans: after all, the Channel that had saved them in 1940 was still there. Moreover, from London, a divided Germany within a divided Europe looked very much like that diffusion of power on the continent that had always been a goal of British diplomacy. Among the major European states, therefore, Britain was most unambiguously in favor of the continental order created by the Cold War. As one senior foreign policy official wrote in the summer of 1971, "I have never been convinced that instability within the Soviet empire would necessarily work out to the advantage of the West; and I have never thought that attempts actively to promote instability added up to a prudent long term policy for the West."[5] This commitment to stability and therefore to the status quo continued to guide British policy until the end of the Cold War.

Like Britain, France defined its postwar interests in the light of the Second World War. But France's wartime experience was substantially more painful:

Britain had suffered and survived in 1940; France had been invaded, defeated, and occupied. The British had been America's valued ally; the French had to choose between Vichy and the Resistance, that is, between being Germany's collaborator or the allies' marginal and often ignored client. The war's lessons for French policy, therefore, were elusive and contradictory. France's security, like Britain's, was dependent on others, particularly the United States; but France bore this dependency with less confidence and grace, never forgetting her wartime humiliations. The underlying problem of French diplomacy was to find the proper balance between solidarity and independence. Neither alternative could be pursued consistently: to cooperate too closely with her allies would make France's security dependent on the whims of distant and unreliable foreigners, while to be too independent would bring isolation and vulnerability. This meant that France's triangle of relations—with the Soviet bloc, the United States, and the rest of Europe—was inherently unstable; the relative strength of each vector constantly changed as France made and unmade accommodations that seemed best suited to preserve her security and enhance her independence.[6]

Charles DeGaulle, whose political views continued to be marked by his unhappy experiences with the "Anglo-Saxons" during the war, returned to power in 1958 with the goal of restoring France's proper place in Europe. He came to believe that this could only be done by dissolving the blocs that had frozen the status quo, creating a new Europe from the Channel to the Urals, and thus permanently ending American influence in European affairs. To break the web of dependent relationships that limited French autonomy, he vetoed Britain's entry into the European Community, derailed moves towards political integration within the community itself, pulled France out of the North Atlantic Treaty Organization (NATO), and began a diplomatic offensive in Eastern Europe.[7]

Far from dismantling the "Yalta system," however, DeGaulle's efforts demonstrated the tensile strength of the bonds within both the Eastern and Western blocs and the magnitude of the gap separating them. None of DeGaulle's bold moves paid off. Britain eventually joined the European Community, the impulse for stronger political cooperation among Europeans returned, and American leadership in NATO remained. "Western cohesion [is] indispensable," a senior French diplomat admitted in 1982, but the alliance should not merely serve American interests.[8] Western cohesion remained indispensable because French efforts to shake Soviet control in Eastern Europe had failed miserably: When DeGaulle visited Poland in 1967, his hosts greeted him warmly but ignored his suggestions that they loosen their ties to Moscow; a year later the Soviets' violent repression of the Prague Spring demonstrated the limits of autonomy within the bloc. Despite the failure of the general's assault on the Cold War order, his vision of a French leadership in a transformed Europe never entirely faded from the minds of French policy makers. It would reappear in 1989 when François Mitterrand suggested the creation of a European confederation embracing both East and West.

DeGaulle's nightmare was a repeat of his days in wartime London, when the Americans and British had so often ignored his obdurate assertion of French interests. Konrad Adenauer, the Federal Republic's first chancellor, also had a nightmare, and it too was a product of the Second World War: "Its name," he told a journalist in 1953, "is Potsdam. The threat of a joint policy of the great powers that would be to Germany's disadvantage has existed since 1945 and continued to exist even after the founding of the Federal Republic."[9] DeGaulle could dream of dissolving the division of Europe so that France might have greater flexibility and influence. Adenauer had no such longings because he knew that close ties to the West were Germany's only chance to recover some measure of control over its own destiny.

In his very first meeting with the Allied High Commission in September 1949, Adenauer established the two guiding principles of his foreign policy.[10] One was the recovery of German sovereignty, which had been lost in 1945 and was now, after the foundation of the Federal Republic, only tentatively and incompletely restored. Without questioning the legitimacy or substance of the new Occupation Statute, which had made the creation of his state possible, Adenauer immediately pressed for revisions that would grant greater autonomy. This would remain a structural characteristic of German diplomacy, which constantly endeavored to pursue change within rather than against the status quo.

The second foundational principle of West German foreign policy was closely intertwined with the first. Adenauer insisted on the need to rethink the whole concept of sovereignty in the light of Europe's—and especially Germany's—tragic past. In practice, this meant closer cooperation with the Western powers: first in the administration of the Ruhr; then in the European Coal and Steel Community; and finally and most significantly in the European Economic Community, established by the Treaty of Rome in 1957. Paralleling the creation of a European common market, parliament, and judicial system was NATO, whose structure was altered in order to contain the new German army that Adenauer, against strong domestic opposition, regarded as both strategically and symbolically essential for German statehood. The stronger West Germany became, the more important these Western ties were, both to enhance German power and to make it acceptable to its former antagonists. This too remained a structural characteristic of German international policy and was very much in evidence as the Cold War came to its dramatic conclusion.

The Federal Republic's remarkable recovery, indeed its very existence as a state, depended on the Cold War; neither would have been possible without the support provided by the Americans and the threat posed by the Soviets. Recovery's price was the continued division of Europe and therefore of Germany—a price that Adenauer, in contrast to his critics on the left and right, had been willing to pay, even though he tried to obscure the costs with talk about "positions of strength" and the "rollback" of Soviet power.

For the first two decades of its existence, the Federal Republic insisted that because it was the only legitimate German state, it would not recognize the German Democratic Republic (GDR) or any state that did so (with the exception of the Soviet Union). By the 1960s, the bankruptcy of this policy was apparent: national unification was no closer than it had been in 1949, and the GDR seemed strong and stable, its citizens totally cut off from the West by the Wall erected in Berlin in August 1961. No one, least of all the cautious and commercially oriented West Germans, imagined that this situation could be challenged by the threat of force, much less by force itself. Indeed the fear of an armed conflict between the superpowers (which neither German state would survive) was never far from the Germans' political imagination. Stability was essential for a peaceful European order and a precondition of Germany's existence. Nor were most West Germans prepared to challenge the status quo by seeking to create a united, neutral nation outside of the two blocs. Adenauer's integration with the West had worked too well for that: membership in NATO and the European communities, in addition to thousands of institutional and personal relationships, had created a dense web of connections between the Federal Republic and the West. By comparison, practical and sentimental ties between the two Germanies had steadily weakened, as was reflected in the declining place of unification on West Germans' political agenda and the shrinking number of ties between the two states. By 1988, for example, 84 percent of West Germans had no contacts with East Germans.[11]

The question West German policymakers faced in the 1960s was how to manage their relationship with the Soviet bloc and especially with the German Democratic Republic without disturbing the peace and stability of the European order or threatening their ties to the West, both of which were enduring elements in postwar Germany's approach to international relations. The answer to this question was what came to be called *Ostpolitik*. Here it might be worth recalling that *Politik* has a somewhat broader meaning than the English word *politics* since its includes theory and practice, programs and policies. Ostpolitik, therefore, refers both to ideas about West Germany's relationship to East Germany and to efforts to implement these ideas.

The theoretical roots of Ostpolitik are usually traced to a brief speech delivered at the Protestant Academy in Tutzing in the summer of 1963 by Egon Bahr, an advisor to Willy Brandt, then the Social Democratic mayor of Berlin. Like Adenauer in 1949, Bahr proposed changing the status quo by accepting it and then, step by step, seeking to overcome it. This would require cooperation with the Soviet Union, encouraging economic growth in East Germany ("A material improvement would be bound to have a tension-relaxing effect in the Zone"), and gradually establishing closer ties between the two German states, producing—in what would be the most famous phrase from Bahr's speech—"Wandel durch Annährung," change through rapprochement.[12] It would take another decade before the program Bahr sketched at Tutzing changed German-German relations, but gradually the Federal Republic abandoned its self-imposed separation from the other Germany, eventually signing treaties with the Soviets, then Poland, and finally the German Democratic Republic itself. The currency that moved from west to east was hard, but the words describing their new relationship were often vague and elusive. Despite their closer ties, the two German states stopped short of full recognition; for example, instead of embassies, they exchanged permanent representations—*Ständige Vertretungen* (the term survives as the name of a pub near Berlin's Friedrichstrasse train station).

Ostpolitik was the German version of a broader policy of détente conducted by every European state in order to reduce the possibility that the Cold War might produce a great-power war that Europe would not survive.[13] The most elaborate articulation of this policy was the set of accords signed by thirty-three European states, the United States, and Canada in Helsinki in August 1975. The agreements consisted of three "baskets": the first recognized the postwar borders, including the German-German border, although—at the insistence of the West Germans—it retained the possibility of "peaceful change"; the second created a number of cultural and economic exchanges, largely benefiting the East Europeans; and the third guaranteed civil rights and political liberties. We can see in these agreements the inherent tension between stability and reform that was at the core of détente. Like détente as a whole, Helsinki was an agreement that, at least some of the signers hoped, might have implications for the *peoples* of Eastern Europe.[14]

Détente meant different things to different participants. For American policymakers, it was one among many ways to manage the global contest with the Soviet Union and its proxies. By the time the Helsinki Accords were signed, interest in détente had already begun to ebb in Washington; within a few years, it gave way to a new era of tension and recrimination between the superpowers.[15] The leaders of the Soviet Union also saw détente as a strategic option, a source of legitimacy and much-needed material assistance and, therefore, a way of consolidating their power and defending the European status quo. Only a small, embattled minority of dissidents in Eastern Europe hoped that détente might provide the possibility of peaceful change. In Czechoslovakia, for instance, when a diverse group calling itself Charter 77 petitioned for civil liberties, it based its claim on the Helsinki Accords, which their government had signed.[16]

In most of Western Europe, détente seemed to be an indispensable way of living with the two superpowers, one of them politically estranged but geographically contiguous, the other politically sympathetic but geographically distant. Although each Western European state adopted its own particular brand of détente, all had the main goal of avoiding conflict by encouraging peaceful change—and therefore greater stability—in the East. In essence, this approach to détente applied to Europeans' relations with the East the same principles and practices that had worked so brilliantly in overcoming international animosities in the West. In both détente and Western European integration, the point of departure was a renunciation of force as an instrument of foreign policy and the adoption of incremental, largely economic modes of international collaboration. This is how the German foreign minister, Hans-Dietrich Genscher, summarized the ends and means of détente in 1987: "Through deepened co-operation, lying in the interests of both sides, an irreversible, system-opening process must be shaped."[17] The echo of Robert Schuman's description of the Coal and Steel Community is unmistakable: "Europe," Schuman had announced in May 1950, "will not be made all at once or according to a single plan. It will be built through concrete achievements which first create a de facto solidarity."[18]

There was, of course, one significant and apparently insurmountable difference between the implication of these ideas in the West and the East. Schuman's "de facto solidarity" had emerged in Western Europe because the superpowers created and enforced a stable security system; within this system, traditional antagonists like France and Germany could afford to share resources, adopt common laws, and open their frontiers. In Eastern Europe, the power of the Soviet Union and its allies stood firmly in the way of Genscher's "irreversible, system-opening process"; there could be cooperation aplenty—particularly when it involved the eastward flow of resources—but the basic division between the two blocs remained, as did the heavy hand of internal repression. A decade after the signing of the Helsinki Accords, therefore, reformers in Eastern Europe were scattered and at risk, their institutions fragile, their popular appeal uncertain. Although few realized it, this situation began to change in 1985, when Mikhail Gorbachev became general secretary of the Communist Party.

EUROPE AND GORBACHEV, GORBACHEV AND EUROPE

It was of great significance that Mikhail Gorbachev's campaign to reform the Soviet system coincided with efforts to quicken the pace of Western European integration. The emergence of perestroika and the renewal of the European project are usually told as separate stories, but they are connected in at least two important ways. First, the integration process encouraged a peaceful, consensual solution to the German question by facilitating key compromises between the Federal Republic and France. Had the movement towards greater European unity not gathered so much momentum by 1989, it is likely that the absorption of a unified Germany into the international system would have been more difficult and disruptive. The second connection was indirect and less easily documented, but perhaps even more significant. By reaffirming Europeans' extraordinary success in constructing a prosperous and peaceful world, the reinvigorated European Community encouraged Gorbachev to imagine an extended system of relationships, what he would call "a common European home," in which a reformed Soviet Union might find security and sustenance. As Svetlana Savranskaya and William Taubman's contribution to this volume demonstrates, this—ultimately illusory—vision of a new Europe increased Gorbachev's willingness to make the dramatic concessions that opened the way for the Cold War's peaceful conclusion.

A new chapter in the history of European integration began in January 1985 when—just three months before Gorbachev came to power in the Soviet Union—Jacques Delors became president of the European Commission. In June, the European Commission issued a white paper outlining an ambitious program to create an internal market; France, Germany, Belgium, Luxembourg, and the Netherlands signed the Schengen Agreement, which would gradually eliminate border controls; the council set up an intergovernmental conference on treaty revision; and the European Community expanded to include Spain and Portugal, thus raising the number of members to twelve. A year later, members signed the Single European Act, which called for a common currency, common social legislation, and greater political cooperation. In December 1989, the

European Community's council agreed to the formation of an economic and monetary union. Yet another year later, intergovernmental conferences began to work on the details of a monetary union and political reform. A new treaty establishing the European Union (EU) was accepted by the council in December 1991 and signed by the members' heads of state in Maastricht the following February. Taken together, these steps greatly strengthened the connections between each European state and its neighbors, just as the relations between East and West were being transformed.[19]

Few if any Europeans recognized the seeds of transformation in Gorbachev's selection as general secretary. Most of them hoped that he would return to the policy of détente that had been threatened in the late 1970s and early 1980s by the Soviet invasion of Afghanistan, by the imposition of martial law in Poland, and especially by the bruising debates over the stationing of medium-range missiles in Western Europe. Ronald Reagan's forceful rhetoric and expansive arms program may have been designed to intimidate the Soviets, but they also frightened a significant number of Europeans, straining relations throughout the Atlantic alliance. The young, vigorous new Soviet leader seemed eager to overcome these difficulties, improve relations with the United States, and reach out to Western Europe. The result would stabilize rather than overturn the division between East and West. As Egon Bahr, the architect of Ostpolitik, wrote in "Towards a European Peace: An Answer to Gorbachev," published in 1988, "European security and cooperation can only be achieved through stability within today's borders."[20] People like Bahr welcomed Gorbachev not as harbinger of change, but as an instrument of peace and order.

The first European leader to assess Gorbachev was Prime Minister Margaret Thatcher, who met him in December 1984, before he became general secretary. Her impression was favorable: "I like Mr. Gorbachev," she famously remarked; "We can do business together." In fact, this odd couple got along extremely well, combining genuine personal warmth with sometimes sharp disagreements. They would meet frequently over the next several years, often at critical junctures in the final stages of the Cold War. Not only did Thatcher's positive impression provide the basis for improving Anglo-Soviet relations, it also helped smooth Gorbachev's relations with President Reagan, who naturally distrusted any leader of what he had once called the "evil empire." Because of her unassailable anticommunist credentials and warm personal relationship with Reagan, Thatcher was Washington's favorite European leader. "The president," Secretary of State Shultz recalled, "had immense confidence in her, and her views carried great weight."[21] In the crisis of 1989, as we will see, Thatcher's position was substantially weakened by her failure to achieve the same influence over Reagan's successor, George H. W. Bush.

President François Mitterrand also welcomed Gorbachev as a partner. Immediately after his election in 1981, Mitterrand had strengthened France's relationship with the West in the face of new Cold War tensions; he feared that the missile controversy, which had activated powerful anti-American sentiment among many Germans, would dislodge the Federal Republic from the alliance, thus leaving France exposed to Soviet expansion. But at the same time, Mitterrand did not abandon the old Gaullist idea of transcending European divisions with a new opening to the East: "All that will help leaving Yalta is good," he declared at the end of 1982.[22] Two years later, he visited Moscow and proclaimed the continued value of détente, which Gorbachev's selection in 1985 seemed to underscore. France, Mitterrand hoped, might once again play a critical role as mediator between the Western alliance, on which her security still depended, and the East, where new initiatives were now possible. In October 1985, Gorbachev chose Paris for his first official visit to the West; ten months later, Mitterrand was in Moscow, where he and Gorbachev seemed to agree on a range of issues, including a renewal of détente. Between 1986 and 1988, however, Mitterrand's foreign political activities were inhibited by his uncomfortable "cohabitation" with Prime Minister Jacques Chirac, who had a much sterner view of the Soviet Union and was more pessimistic about Gorbachev's willingness and ability to change.

Among the leaders of the major European states, Chancellor Helmut Kohl was initially the most skeptical about Gorbachev. Chancellor since 1982, Kohl had reaffirmed the Federal Republic's commitment to NATO and defied leftwing opposition by accepting the stationing of American midrange missiles on German soil. Many in Kohl's Christian Democratic Party had bitterly opposed Ostpolitik and had voted against the treaties that put it into practice, but by the 1980s, a broad consensus had emerged that this was the best, perhaps the only, way for the Federal Republic to live peacefully and comfortably with its unpleasant neighbor to the east. In a long letter to Gorbachev in January 1986, Kohl emphasized the continued significance of Ostpolitik as the basis for German-German relations. "I am convinced," he wrote in the cautious and elusive prose so characteristic of the German version of détente, "that life in a common European home with fewer tensions will only be possible when relations between the two German states, too, are constantly stimulated as a stabilizing element in the context of the overall process of development between east and west."[23] When the West German foreign minister, Hans-Dietrich Genscher, visited Moscow that July, he found Gorbachev ready "to open a new page" in the complex and often tragic story of Russian-German relations.

These relations were severely strained in October 1986, when Kohl gave an interview to *Newsweek* magazine in which he compared Gorbachev to Joseph Goebbels, Hitler's infamous propaganda minister.[24] This was, of course, an example of the monumental tactlessness to which the usually prudent chancellor occasionally succumbed. But it may also have reflected Kohl's genuine anxiety about Gorbachev's seductive powers. Faced with national elections in January 1987, Kohl had reason to fear that Gorbachev's enormous popularity might enable him to persuade unwary Germans to abandon their true interests, leading them to forsake solidarity with the West for a dangerous neutrality. Whatever his motives, Kohl's unfortunate remarks lead to a coolness between the two men that lasted for more than a year.

Although they might have differed in their perceptions of what Gorbachev wanted to do, European policymakers had no doubt about his significance. Less certain is how important Europe seemed to the new general secretary. His own direct contacts with Europe and Europeans were limited. In 1972 he had visited Belgium, but according to Anatoly Chernyaev, who would eventually become part of his inner circle, Gorbachev had not been much interested in what he saw there; his mind and his heart remained back in Stavropol, where he was the local party leader.[25] Eleven years later, now established in Moscow and rising swiftly in the Soviet hierarchy, Gorbachev led a delegation to Canada, where its general prosperity and agricultural productivity greatly impressed him. More significant, at least in retrospect, was Gorbachev's trip to Italy in June 1984 as the head of the Soviet delegation to the funeral of Enrico Berlinguer, the leader of the Italian Communist Party. In ways that often infuriated Moscow, Berlinguer had led his party away from ideological orthodoxy and political isolation, converting it into a party of the democratic left that was prepared to work within the existing political order. Gorbachev seems to have been deeply impressed both by Berlinguer's personal popularity and the Italian Communist Party's apparent vitality.[26]

Over the next five years, Gorbachev continued to maintain his ties to the Italian Communist leadership. When Berlinguer's successor, Alessandro Natta, visited the Soviet Union in January 1986, he was given the kind of reception usually accorded heads of state. In addition to Natta and other prominent Western European Communists, Gorbachev cultivated Democratic Socialists, whom Moscow had traditionally viewed with distrust and hostility. Socialist representatives attended the seventieth anniversary celebration of the October Revolution in 1987, where they were accepted as part of an extended European left.[27] Gorbachev also received socialist politicians like the Swedish prime minister, Olof Palme, and the former German chancellor Willy Brandt, who, as the president of the Socialist International, was European socialism's elder statesman. Gorbachev was particularly drawn to the Spanish socialist leader, Felipe González, who had been part of a peaceful revolution that transformed an authoritarian regime into a politically stable and economically vibrant democracy. Like the Italian Communists, González personified a flexible, open, energetic left in which, as Gorbachev would come to believe, many sorts of socialism, including the Soviet variety, might find a place.[28]

During his first two years in office, Gorbachev continued to meet regularly with European visitors, but he concentrated his attention on Soviet-American relations. The United States, he was convinced, represented the only real threat to the Soviet Union. To diminish this threat and to reduce the extraordinary defense spending it required was a stable foundation for national security and a prerequisite for economic reform—for Gorbachev, two centrally important and essentially inseparable goals. Until late 1987, Gorbachev tended to view his relations with European statesmen in terms of their usefulness in dealing with the Americans. Thus he valued Margaret Thatcher as a mediator with Ronald Reagan. Washington was also fixated on superpower negotiations in which Europe played little or no role. There was, for example, no mention of either Western or Eastern Europe in the briefing book prepared for Reagan's summit meeting in Reykjavik in October 1986.[29]

In 1987–88, Gorbachev became increasingly interested in European affairs. In part this was due to his difficulties at home, in part to a shift in political alignments in the West. Reagan, with whom Gorbachev had developed a good working relationship, was nearing the end of his term. His successor, George H. W. Bush, was getting conflicting advice about how much to trust Gorbachev's reforms. A cautious man, for whom prudence was a cardinal virtue, Bush wanted to review his options carefully before extending Reagan's policies; unlike most Europeans, Bush and his advisors were not unambiguously committed to returning to the hopeful years of détente. As a result, Soviet-American relations were put on hold during the first year of the Bush presidency. Meanwhile, the political climate in Europe was changing. In early 1987, Helmut Kohl had secured his political position with an electoral victory and was now ready to repair his tattered bonds with Moscow. Mitterrand, reelected president in 1988 and also freed from his "cohabitation" with Chirac, began a diplomatic offensive in the East. In January 1987, the Soviet Union began direct negotiations with the European Community, laying the groundwork for a bilateral trade agreement that was finally signed two years later. In early 1988, the importance of Europe for Soviet policy was underscored by the foundation of an Institute for Europe under the direction of the Academy of Sciences. That June, the European Community and the Council of Mutual Economic Assistance, the Eastern bloc's economic organization, recognized each other as bargaining partners.[30]

Although Gorbachev did not travel to Western Europe again until the spring of 1989, he continued to entertain a large number of prominent politicians and the major European heads of government, including Thatcher, Mitterrand, and Kohl. Of these, the German chancellor was the most important. Gorbachev had always recognized the Federal Republic's special significance among the European powers, but his relations with Kohl remained cool, especially after that disastrous *Newsweek* interview. Other German leaders did go to Moscow, including President von Weizsäcker and Foreign Minister Genscher, who made five trips there in a somewhat desperate effort to blow some life into the embers of détente. Finally, Kohl himself arrived in October 1988. Even though the visit was correct rather than excessively cordial, Anatoly Chernyaev, Gorbachev's foreign policy advisor, regarded it as a significant turning point. "I felt physically that we were entering a new world," he wrote in his diary, "where class struggle, ideology, and in general, polarity and enmity are no longer decisive."[31] The path to better German-Soviet relations was cleared with a number of economic agreements, including a 3 billion deutsche mark line of credit—the first but by no means the last in a series of financial transfusions from the Federal Republic to the Soviet Union's anemic economy.

Increasingly frustrated by domestic resistance to his reform program, far more popular abroad than at home, Gorbachev grew closer to the prominent Europeans who paraded through his office, where they listened respectfully to his ideas and applauded his efforts. These Westerners became, in the historian Vladislav Zubok's words, "his most important reference group."[32] Gorbachev solicited their support, was warmed by their approval, and, most importantly, began to see the world through their eyes—that is, in the light of their experience in the transformed Europe that was now enjoying a new period of institutional growth. This Europe was both the basis and the audience for two extraordinary speeches that Gorbachev delivered, the first to the U.N. General Assembly in December 1988, the second to the European Parliament in July 1989.

At the United Nations, Gorbachev began by evoking the French and Russian Revolutions, which had changed the course of history and which, each in its own way, had "given a gigantic impetus to man's progress." The age of violent revolution is over and a new world is taking shape, "a mutually connected and integral world" in which violence has no place. "It is evident...that force and the threat of force can no longer be, and should not be instruments of foreign policy....Freedom of choice is a universal principle to which there should be no exceptions." And while he continued to speak in terms of capitalist and socialist systems, he recognized the variety of social and political institutions within each. The Soviet Union will not surrender its convictions, he continued, nor does it expect others to give up theirs, but "we are not going to shut ourselves up within the range of our values."[33] As evidence of this openness and willingness to change, he pointed to the process of reform going on within the Soviet Union, announced substantial reductions in conventional forces, and called for new efforts at limiting strategic weapons.

When Gorbachev repeated these themes in Strasbourg six months later, he gave them a distinctively European formulation. It is now time, he began, to rethink what European unity does and does not mean. It cannot require "the overcoming of socialism," which is "a course toward confrontation, if not worse." The European states belong to different systems, a fact which must be recognized and accepted by all. "Any interference in domestic affairs and any attempts to restrict the sovereignty of states—friends, allies, or any others—are inadmissible." Competition among states is healthy, provided that it aims at "creating better material and spiritual living conditions for all people." Now that the Soviet Union has been reformed, it is ready to participate in this competition, putting the "intrinsic strengths of our social system...to use for the benefit of ourselves and for the benefit of Europe."[34]

This last sentence captured Gorbachev's conception of a "common European home." In its original formulation—Andrei Gromyko had used the phrase as early as 1972, and Brezhnev repeated it in 1981—the notion had been part of the Soviets' repeated attempt to disrupt the Atlantic alliance by drawing Europeans away from the United States. This tactic had evidently also been on Gorbachev's mind when he employed the phrase for the first time during his trip to London in 1984—another reason why some policymakers in Washington viewed perestroika as a tactical move rather than as an authentic effort to change the system. Increasingly, however, Gorbachev's idea of a European home, a new kind of European community, took on a life of its own outside the conventional rivalries of the Cold War. This Europe would expand the West's peaceful community to include both socialist and capitalist states, which could live together in a rich variety of mutually beneficial ways. Gorbachev's "common European home," therefore, shared the essential assumptions of European détente: a rejection of war as a political instrument and a belief in the primacy of economic growth and material progress. And like détente, it uneasily combined a deep commitment to continental stability with the recognition that change might be possible.[35]

"To put it simply," Zubok once remarked, "Gorbachev took ideas too seriously." As the Cold War's endgame approached, these ideas were an unstable mixture of East and West, shaped by both his earlier commitments and current experience. Gorbachev retained his belief in the superiority of socialism as well as a Leninist faith in the ability of a great leader to impose his ideas on history. But while Lenin had ruthlessly used force to seize power and remained committed to a strategy of violent revolution, Gorbachev believed that force was anachronistic and violence unproductive. Lenin had seen a world sharply divided between communism and its enemies; Gorbachev was prepared to tolerate different systems. Lenin preached class struggle; Gorbachev advocated a gradual transformation of social and political life through economic growth.[36]

Like Lenin, Gorbachev believed that the survival of the Soviet Union required that it join a reorganized Europe. Lenin had assumed that the success of the revolution in Russia depended on a Communist victory in the more advanced West. In Gorbachev's Europe, however, communism and capitalism, East and West, would coexist, each learning from and strengthening the other. This Europe would contain the two "systems," enabling them to be freer, more flexible, and better able to compete peacefully and cooperate fruitfully in a common quest for material progress and individual well being. Finding a place for the Soviet Union in this redefined European community was now Gorbachev's overriding goal, for which he was prepared to sacrifice everything else.

THE GERMAN QUESTION AND THE END OF THE COLD WAR

In what was probably its final appearance on the global stage, the German question dominated international politics from the fall of 1989 through the summer of 1990.[37] As it had for more than a century, the German question blended international and domestic issues, combining questions about Germany's place in Europe with questions about Germany's political identity. Gorbachev's reforms activated both dimensions of the German question: How would perestroika affect the domestic politics of the German Democratic Republic and therefore the foreign relations of the two German states? If, as Gorbachev told the United Nations, freedom of choice was, without exception, the principle of the new Europe, what would happen if Germans chose to live in a unified state? How would this state be governed? And where would it fit into the new European Community that was taking shape in the West? In Germany, therefore, the two developments of the late 1980s—reform in the East and greater integration in the West—intersected. And, as had always been the case, while these questions could be posed in Germany, they had to be answered in Europe as a whole.

In June 1989, as part of his new engagement with European affairs, Gorbachev visited Bonn in order to deepen the personal relationship with Helmut Kohl that had begun in Moscow the preceding October. Amid an outpouring of the extraordinary popular enthusiasm that greeted the Soviet leader wherever he traveled in the West, the two men signed a series of cultural and economic agreements and, on June 13, issued a joint declaration that can be seen as a kind of prologue to the great historical drama about to unfold. After the conventional evocation of the declaration's importance for the future of humanity, the two leaders rejected war as a political instrument, called for greater international cooperation, especially in Europe, and underscored the significance of economic growth and material progress. Perhaps the most striking passage was the one that endorsed "the right of all peoples and states freely to determine their destiny and their sovereign right to shape their relationships to one another on the basis of international law."[38] This linkage of *Völker und Staaten*, peoples and states, recalls the tension between stability and change that was coiled at the heart of détente. Although easy enough to join in a phrase, the rights of peoples and states had very different implications, especially when applied to the German situation. The right of peoples to determine their destiny was potentially transformative—nowhere more so than in the two Germanies. The right of states was implicitly conservative, if one assumed that it would be defined by a government as hostile to change as that of the German Democratic Republic. Whose rights, then, did the chancellor and his guest seek to proclaim: the German people's right to self-determination or the two German states' sovereign right to exist? By the time Gorbachev and Kohl were enjoying the early summer days on the Rhine, the peoples of Eastern Europe had begun to shape a new future both for themselves and for their states.[39]

Poland was the first and most significant site of revolutionary change in the east and also the best example of the political implications of Gorbachev's rejection of force. A dense and overlapping set of religious, national, and political antagonisms had always made the Poles reluctant participants in a Soviet empire. In 1979, following a triumphant visit by the newly elected Polish pope, John Paul II, Poland had enjoyed a brief but intense rebirth of popular politics, most dramatically represented by Solidarity, an organization of workers and intellectuals. In December 1981, the government imposed martial law, arrested or drove underground dissidents, and eventually dissolved Solidarity. But while the regime was still powerful enough to prevent change from below, its authority was severely limited by the waning of its own ideological self-confidence and its manifest failure to solve Poland's chronic economic difficulties. Increasingly unwilling and perhaps unable to repress popular dissent with violence, the government tried a series of increasingly desperate compromises. Finally, in February 1989, it recognized and began negotiating with the Solidarity Citizens Committee that had been formed two months before. Free elections in June produced a resounding defeat for Communist candidates. Gorbachev, whose curious lack of concern for Eastern European affairs is analyzed in this book's chapter by Taubman and Savranskaya, made clear that the government had no choice but to accept the verdict of the electorate. In September, Poland's first noncommunist government in the postwar era took office. The Communist regime, imported with the Red Army in 1944, imposed with violence, and frequently defended at great cost, left the historical stage with astonishing speed and remarkable restraint.

In the course of 1989, the various East European states followed different paths to similar destinations. The process of reform in Czechoslovakia was haunted by the memories of 1968, when efforts to create a new kind of communism were crushed by the overwhelming power of the Soviet Union and its allies. In the late 1970s, a few brave men and women tried—in the words of Václav Havel—"to speak truth to power," but they were easily repressed. While Havel himself was well known abroad, he was isolated and largely ignored at home. As perestrokia unfolded in the Soviet Union, dissent in the Czech lands grew. Popular demonstrations, including a dramatic appearance by Alexander Dubček, the hero of the Prague Spring, tested the regime's will and undermined its legitimacy. In November 1989, the government fell in the face of nonviolent but nonetheless resolute protests; on the first day of 1990, Václav Havel became president under a new constitutional order.

In Hungary, the dynamics of dissent worked within, rather than against, the Communist Party. For more than a decade, the Hungarian party had been relatively easygoing, and a shadow economy allowed the intrusion of private enterprise into what came to be called "goulash communism." With Gorbachev's example in mind, a number of younger Communists became impatient with the pace of change and the possibilities of reform. In May 1988, the long-serving leader of the party, János Kádár, was replaced. In October 1989, the Hungarian Communist Party became the Hungarian Socialists. That November, political parties appeared; open debate became possible; and free elections were scheduled. A few months later, the Hungarian People's Republic disappeared.

Events in Hungary provided the link between the crises within the Soviet bloc and the German question. As early as May the Hungarian government had begun to dismantle the barriers along its frontier with Austria. As the reformers in Budapest gained ground, their willingness to seal their borders declined. In early September, Hungary announced that it would allow East Germans to cross freely into Austria, from where they could go to the Federal Republic. Meanwhile, citizens of the German Democratic Republic crowded into the west German embassies in Prague, Warsaw, and East Berlin, seeking permission to emigrate. A clear sign that the eastern bloc was unraveling, the opening of the Hungarian border put to the test Gorbachev's promise not to interfere in the affairs of other states. Continuing to display what often seemed like remarkable indifference to the deepening unrest all along his western frontier, the general secretary made no effort to stop the Hungarians or to assist other Communist governments as they confronted and eventually yielded to pressures for reform.[40]

To understand the distinctive character of events in the German Democratic Republic, we must keep in mind two movements. The first was a movement of dissidents, Communist reformers, and opportunists, who saw in perestroika a chance to change but not necessarily to transform their social, economic, and political institutions. This movement started rather slowly in East Germany, then gathered momentum both within the inner circles of the ruling party and in the streets, especially in Leipzig where Monday-evening protest demonstrations became larger and bolder. Paralleling this domestic activity, which was similar to protest movements throughout the Soviets' European empire, was another *movement* that was uniquely German. It was composed of those who seized the opportunity to flee the German Democratic Republic and settle in the West. Not surprisingly, the East Germans who left were precisely those people a society can least afford to lose—the young, energetic, and skilled. This demographic hemorrhage did not diminish in October, when a reformist government under Egon Krenz replaced the stubbornly orthodox Erich Honecker. In East Germany, therefore, widespread dissent not only pushed for regime change, but by threatening the very existence of the state, called into question the stability of the international order.[41]

Few people realized the depth of the East German crisis at the beginning of November 1989. After all, popular demonstrations in East German cities remained peaceful; the regime seemed, if somewhat belatedly and half-heartedly, prepared to introduce reforms. Moreover, hundreds of thousands of Soviet troops remained deployed on German soil, living proof that memories of the Second World War and anxieties about a rebirth of German power continued to haunt Russian foreign policy. It was easy to underestimate the disruptive potential of the steady westward stream of East Germans, both for the German Democratic Republic and for the Federal Republic. Nor did people—including Gorbachev himself—grasp the implications of the Soviet Union's apparent unwillingness to come to the East Germans' aid, either by closing the frontier or by helping to repress internal dissent. On November 1, Gorbachev, who remained skeptical about Krenz's competence and convictions, was not ready to offer the new East German leadership much help, but he could assure them that the Soviet Union remained firmly committed to the existence of two German states and that "all serious political figures" agreed.[42] Gorbachev, in other words, still saw a solution to the German question—and to the growing unrest within Eastern Europe—in the light of his hopes for a common European home, which would have room for a variety of reformed socialist regimes, including the German Democratic Republic.

The slow, uncertain response of West German policy makers to the terminal crisis of the German Democratic Republic suggests the extent to which their view of international politics continued to be shaped by the emphasis on stability that was the heart and soul of Ostpolitik. Writing in *Der Spiegel* on September 25, Foreign Minister Genscher declared that the Federal Republic "did not wish, now or in the future, to destabilize the German Democratic Republic." The architecture of détente, including the guarantees in the Helsinki Accords, remained the basis of Western policy. Four days later, Theo Sommer, the well-informed and usually astute editor of *Die Zeit,* downplayed the significance of what was happening on the other side of the Wall: "We are not," he concluded, "an inch closer to reunification than a year ago, or five or ten years ago...."[43] Six weeks later, as the situation in the east further deteriorated, Chancellor Kohl, while recognizing the East German *people's* rights of self-determination, still thought in terms of encouraging reform in East German *state*. This was, he told the Bundestag on November 8, "a national task," necessary to make it possible for people to remain in the east with the expectations of more freedom and economic progress. Following an intense debate on these issues, the chancellor and his party left for a long-planned state visit to Poland.[44]

The next day all this began to change when, as the result of a miscommunication among the Communist Party leadership, the border posts in the Wall dividing East Berlin and West Berlin were opened. The immediate impact of this decision flashed on television screens around the world: peaceful, celebratory, and cheerful crowds breaching this ugly symbol of the Cold War division. While people everywhere were stirred by what was happening in Berlin, many did not see its full significance: In the Federal Republic, for example, public opinion polls taken in late November showed that while 30 percent of the respondents expected to see national unification in their lifetime (as opposed to just 3 percent two years before), 46 percent did not. In Moscow, Anatoly Chernyaev immediately grasped the implications of these events. "The Berlin Wall has collapsed," he wrote in his diary on November 10; "The entire era in the history of the Soviet system is over.... This is the end of Yalta."[45]

West European policy makers, who had invested so much effort in learning to live with the international order created at Yalta by managing its tensions and avoiding destabilizing surprises, watched this festive revolution with decidedly mixed feelings. Détente in all its forms had included the idea of change, but it was supposed to be slow, cumulative, and carefully controlled by governments. Few prominent Europeans were prepared to say that the people in East Germany did not have the right to self-determination, but most—including an important part of the West German public—hoped that they would exercise this right without destroying the East German state and thus threatening the European peace. The need for caution, the importance of consultation, and the value of stability—these were the themes that reverberated throughout the public and private communications of European leaders as they began to assess what Europe would be like without the Wall. Everyone seemed to agree that they should do all they could to slow the process down and thus avoid any precipitous actions that might provoke a crisis.[46]

The tempo of events, especially at moments of crisis, is the most difficult thing for any policy maker to control. It was in Bonn that the quickened pace of change created the most potent sense of opportunity and danger, the two elements of which all crises are composed. The opportunities were obvious: the opening of the Wall had made a new solution to the German question possible for the first time since 1945. Seizing this historic opportunity would be difficult at best and impossible without Gorbachev, whose renunciation of force was a prerequisite for any peaceful unification of the two states. This raised the dangers of which German statesmen were increasingly aware: What might happen if Gorbachev's hold on power weakened? Or if he were deposed by those in the Soviet Union who did not share his distaste for violence? Equally disquieting were the problems created by the flood of refugees, unchecked either by the desperate decision to open the border or by the formation of a new East German government under Hans Modrow on November 13. The number of refugees not only challenged West Germans' capacity to absorb new arrivals, it also underscored the fragility of the political and social order in East Germany. What would happen if the Communist regime were to collapse? Could the West allow chaos to engulf the German Democratic Republic? Would the Soviets simply stand by while their client disintegrated?[47]

Stability—the lodestar of Ostpolitik—remained the primary goal of West German policy makers. But some of them gradually, and often reluctantly, realized that the path to stability had changed. In early November, Genscher's advisor, Frank Elbe, told an American official that the movement towards German unity should not endanger European stability; a month later he said that without unity, stability was at risk.[48] It was easy for policy makers in Washington, London, Paris, and Moscow to talk about the slow forces of historical change, but it would be in Bonn where the price of hesitation and passivity would have to be paid. And that price might be what West Germans feared above all: political disorder, social unrest, and the danger of international conflict—in other words, the return of those terrible forces that still haunted Germans' historical imagination.

The key figure in this transformation of German policy was Helmut Kohl, who, much sooner and far more clearly than most other members of the German political elite, began to see what the fall of the Wall meant for Germany and Europe. A cautious, deliberate politician, whose success came from diligence and resolve rather than eloquence or imagination, Kohl was both unnerved and inspired by events in East Germany. He decided that he had no choice but to seize the initiative. Gathering a small group of old friends and confidants under his national security advisor, Horst Teltschik, Kohl began drafting a new, comprehensive statement on the German situation. The group worked in secret; no one, including Bonn's allies and Foreign Minister Genscher, knew what the chancellor had in mind until he delivered his famous "Ten Point Program for Overcoming the Division of Germany and Europe" to the Bundestag on November 28.[49]

Kohl's speech represented a clear break with Ostpolitik. First and most important, the chancellor's emphasis was on the East German *Volk,* not their state. He began by praising the population's civil courage and commitment to liberty, including the right to self-determination: "The credit for the present transformation goes primarily to the people, who are so impressively demonstrating their will for freedom." He did not exclude further assistance to the East German state nor did he reject Modrow's idea of confederation between the two Germanies. But neither aid nor confederation would become a way of propping up a failed East German regime. The Federal Republic's relations with the German Democratic Republic would depend on radical democratic reforms that ensured it was an authentic representative of the popular will: Kohl's program, therefore, pointed towards transforming, not stabilizing the regime. Change was a precondition for rapprochement, not, as in Egon Bahr's famous formulation, the reverse.

Within the context of Kohl's remarks, his restatement of the Federal Republic's commitment to national unification became more than a conventional and largely empty aspiration. The chancellor left no doubt that German unity was now a real possibility. However, he qualified his national aspirations in two significant ways. First, he insisted once again that German unification was only possible or desirable if it could be achieved in consultation with Germany's European neighbors and as part of a broader process of European integration. Second, he did not mention a timetable. "The linking of the German Question to pan-European developments and east-west relations....will allow a natural development which takes account of the interests of all concerned and paves the way for peaceful development in freedom, which is our objective." The chancellor said nothing about how long this might take. Few, including Kohl himself, realized that it would happen so swiftly.[50]

The weeks that followed Kohl's "Ten Point" speech witnessed intense activity on the three axes that defined European diplomacy: relations among the European states themselves and variously between the Europeans and the two superpowers. On December 1–2, Bush and Gorbachev met at Malta. Two days later there was a NATO summit in Brussels. During the rest of that month, Mitterrand and Gorbachev met in Kiev on December 6; a European Council meeting was held in Strasbourg on December 8–9; a four-power meeting on Germany was convened on December 11; U.S. Secretary of State Baker met with with Kohl and Genscher in Berlin on December 12; Mitterrand met with Bush on St. Martin on December 16; Kohl met with Modrow in Dresden on December 19; and Mitterrand made an official visit to East Germany on December 20–22. In addition to these formal gatherings, there were numerous conversations between heads of states and intense consultations among their advisors.[51]

For our purposes, the most important of these international gatherings was the European Council meeting in Strasbourg on December 8–9. Helmut Kohl, who had spent the past ten days listening to European (including many German) attacks on his ten-point program, was nonetheless astonished at the hostility and mistrust that confronted him when the council's deliberations began. With only González and the Irish premier Charles Haughey coming to his defense, Kohl faced "tribunal like interrogations" about German ambitions. But despite some very unpleasant moments, the Strasbourg meeting represented a success for Kohl and an important step in the European absorption of a new German state. Margaret Thatcher's efforts to forge an Anglo-French alliance against unification failed. Mitterrand's uneasiness about the German situation was mollified by Kohl's support, promised during their meeting in November, for an intergovernmental conference to work on monetary union and other European Community reforms, thus opening the way for the agreement signed at Maastricht two years later. Moreover, with only Thatcher in opposition, the council passed a new social charter, committing the community to the protection of workers' rights. On the German question, the council essentially accepted Kohl's position: "We seek the strengthening of the state of peace in Europe in which the German people will regain its unity through free self-determination." This process, the council declared, should be democratic and peaceful, "in full respect of the relevant agreements and treaties [and] in a context of dialogue and East-West cooperation. It has also to be placed in the perspective of European integration."[52]

While European leaders deliberated, the German Democratic Republic continued to deteriorate. On January 11, the Modrow government issued a bleak report on the economy, whose deplorable condition had been concealed by fraudulent statistics, foreign subsidies, and a protected East European market. Four days later, an angry crowd of Berliners occupied the headquarters of the state security apparatus, the infamous Stasi, whose ruthless ubiquity had been a foundation of the regime. Although this demonstration was disorderly rather than violent, it did reveal the volatility and potential for chaos that existed in the country. Equally important, the migration out of the German Democratic Republic swelled as more and more East Germans expressed their distrust of the government's willingness and ability to reform. Unless the two states united, people joked, German unification might take place within the Federal Republic. By the end of January, Gorbachev recognized that the German Democratic Republic would not survive. This assessment was confirmed by the East German elections held in March that returned a clear majority favoring unity. Fewer than 17 percent voted to retain some version of an East German state.[53]

By the time the East German people made clear that self-determination would mean unification, Mitterrand had become reconciled to the idea of a united Germany. Throughout November, French policy had been opaque and inconsistent. On a visit to Bonn at the beginning of the month, the president declared that he did not fear unification, but added rather cryptically that French policy would be dictated by her own and European interests. As the crisis deepened, Mitterrand continued to support unity in general terms, but apparently hoped—as did Margaret Thatcher—that Gorbachev would slow down and perhaps even stop the process. In the meantime, he managed to get Kohl's agreement to the creation of the monetary union, which was a principle achievement of the Strasbourg meeting. At the end of December, Mitterrand attempted to provide a new framework for thinking about East-West relations by proposing a European confederation, a new version of the Gaullist dream of a Europe from the Channel to the Urals in which France would have a new and more influential role. Although he would return to this confederation proposal several times in the next year, the pressure of events made a decision on the German question unavoidable. In the first weeks of 1990, with Gorbachev's willingness to support the German Democratic Republic clearly ebbing and with Kohl's commitment to Europe apparently secure, Mitterrand dropped the qualifications on his support for German self-determination and therefore unification.[54]

Only Margaret Thatcher continued to take a clear and decisive stand against German unification. She had never liked Helmut Kohl and had always distrusted the Federal Republic. Germany, she believed, "is by its very nature a destabilizing rather than a stabilizing force in Europe."[55] For a while, she had great hopes that Gorbachev shared her views: that was, at least, the impression she took away from their meeting in September 1989, when the crisis in Germany was just beginning to gather momentum. She also hoped that an Anglo-French agreement (recreating the alliance of 1914 and 1939) might block German efforts. But Gorbachev remained indecisive and elusive and Mitterrand proved unreliable. Indeed, the French decision to use European integration as a way of containing Germany simply strengthened the kind of European "federalism" that the prime minister regarded as a threat to British sovereignty. In a last, somewhat desperate attempt to mobilize European opinion against Germany, Thatcher tried to use the specter of the German past to prevent unification. This made some people angry and others uneasy, but had no impact on the outcome. With uncharacteristic candor about her own shortcomings, Thatcher would later admit that her German policy was an "unambiguous failure."[56]

By the time of the March elections in East Germany, it was no longer a question of *whether* the two German states would unite, but rather *when, how,* and *under what conditions.* That a new Germany would be firmly tied to the European Community was clear: this had been Kohl's central theme from the start of the crisis, and it was achieved, without difficulty, in 1990.[57] Much more complicated was Germany's place in the European security system. Even when they recognized that unification was inevitable, Soviet leaders had insisted that the new nation could not be a member of NATO, as both Bonn and Washington demanded. In the end, after long and complex negotiations, Gorbachev swallowed this bitter medicine, washed down with a great deal of West German economic assistance. Once again, the value of stability prevailed. Despite strong opposition from some of his inner circle, Gorbachev eventually concluded that membership in the Atlantic alliance was the best way to make Germany a predictable and reliable part of the European order. This historic concession, announced rather offhandedly at news conference in July 1990, marked the final resolution of the German question and, in many ways, the end of the Cold War.[58]

Throughout 1989–90, European leaders' responses to the German situation reflected their personalities and values, but also their states' historical experiences and geopolitical positions. Even in this period of rapid change, therefore, certain continuities are apparent. Kohl, like Adenauer, recognized that German power had to be defined and confined within a broader institutional frame, including an integrated Europe and an Atlantic security system. In the end, Kohl was able to persuade France and most other Europeans that Germany's commitment to these institutions was sincere and sufficient. France's German policy was characteristically ambivalent. Although Mitterrand eventually accepted unification, he continued to look for ways to give France more flexibility and autonomy in a new European confederation. Continuities were also apparent in Margaret Thatcher's obdurate resistance to German unity. Like generations of British leaders, she feared a concentration of power in Europe and thus recognized the value of a divided Germany and, for that matter, a divided continent. As so often in the past, it was not possible for Britain to defend this vision of Europe without the support of the United States. Unable to prevail in Washington, the prime minister tried to enlist Gorbachev to stand in the way of German unification. This too failed.

There were many reasons why Gorbachev did not play the role of spoiler, as both Mitterrand and Thatcher hoped and expected; of these, perhaps the most important were his perceptions of Europe—both of its past, which proved accurate, and of its future, which proved illusory. Gorbachev correctly saw that Germany within a transformed Europe did not represent a serious threat to Soviet security. The Germans, he realized, had fully accepted the premise on which postwar European domestic and international politics rested: for them, violence was no longer a legitimate political instrument. His misperception of Europe's future came from his failure to see what this eclipse of violence would mean for Communist regimes in general and for the Soviet Union in particular. Without the power of coercion, the Soviet empire collapsed, brought down by popular movements that began in the allied states of Eastern Europe and then finally shattered the Soviet Union itself. The Soviet system, therefore, was destroyed by the same historical processes that Gorbachev hoped would save it: the eclipse of violence in the European society of states, the development of new forms of international cooperation, and the political primacy of economic issues. There was indeed a common European home, but there was no room in it for the Soviet Union.[59]

That virtually everyone was surprised by the revolutions of 1989 did not dissuade observers from trying to predict what the unification of Germany would mean for Europe's future. In one particularly fanciful flight of geopolitical imagination, A. M. Rosenthal informed the readers of the *New York Times* that a united Germany would be the most powerful country on earth. He was, needless to say, deeply concerned about how this new superpower would behave. On the other side of the Atlantic, Conor Cruise O'Brien's column in the *London Times* was even more hysterical. We are, he asserted, "on the road to the Fourth Reich," in which racial science would flourish once again and intellectuals would express pride rather than guilt over the Holocaust. Like Rosenthal, O'Brien foresaw a dramatic expansion of German power, including economic hegemony from the Aran Islands to Vladivostok. Charles Krauthammer's assessment, published by the *New Republic* in March 1990, was much more sober and sensible. But he too worried about a revival of German power, not because a new Bismarck or Hitler would conquer Europe, but rather because "the birth of a new giant in the middle of the continent will arrest Europe's great confederational project" and put in its place "the kind of international system of the late nineteenth and early twentieth centuries that ended in catastrophe." The danger, in other words, was a return of sovereignty, not the rebirth of nazism.[60] The American political scientist John Mearsheimer made much the same point in an article appropriately entitled "Back to the Future."[61]

None of these predictions—neither intemperate ones like Rosenthal's and O'Brien's nor thoughtful and theoretically informed ones like Krauthammer's and Mearsheimer's—turned out to be accurate. Statues of Hitler did not reappear in German town squares, the European project did not collapse, sovereignty in its traditional form did not return. Instead, the European Union created at Maastricht was renewed by the Treaty of Amsterdam. In 1995, the union expanded to include three former neutrals, Austria, Finland, and Sweden; in 2004, ten additional states joined the EU, including former Soviet satellites and the three Baltic republics; two years later, Bulgaria and Romania followed, bringing the total of member states to twenty-seven. The forces that had transformed European domestic and international politics after 1945 were too deeply embedded to be uprooted by the end of the Cold War or by the unification of the two postwar German states.

In Eastern Europe, the events of 1989–90 were a genuine revolution, one of those rare occasions when a massive transfer of power has occurred without extensive violence. In the West, the end of the Cold War altered but did not destroy the existing order. Western European states' relations with one another were reaffirmed by the creation of the EU, but are still a complex blend of interdependence and self-interest; remarkably enough, the Atlantic alliance has also survived, since European security remains, uneasily but irresistibly, tied to the United States; and finally, the relationship between Europe and what was once the Soviet Union continues to be unsettled. The Soviet superpower is gone; the threat of tank armies rushing through the Fulda Gap is past. But the Russian Republic and the other states of the former Soviet Union are politically unstable; their relations with one another and with the West are still fraught with unfulfilled ambitions and unresolved conflicts. These problems are potent legacies of the Cold War and of Gorbachev's failed vision of a common European home.

NOTES

1. For a good selection from the immense literature on the Cold War in Europe, see the articles collected by Charles Maier in *The Cold War in Europe: Era of a Divided Continent*, 3rd edition (Princeton, N.J.: Princeton University Press, 1996), and by Odd Arne Westad in *Reviewing the Cold War: Approaches, Interpretations, Theory* (London: Frank Cass, 2000).

2. Michael Cox, "Who Won the Cold War in Europe? A Historiographical Overview," in *Europe and the End of the Cold War: A Reappraisal*, edited by Frederic Bozo et al. (London: Frank Cass, 2008), 18. This is the best collection of recent work on the subject. For a further elaboration of Cox's views, see "Another Transatlantic Split? American and European Narratives and the End of the Cold War," *Cold War History* 7.1 (February 2007): 121–46, and the comment by Edwina Campbell, *Cold War History* 8.1 (February 2008): 103–13. These issues are addressed in chapter 5, this volume, by Melvyn Leffler.

3. This is the subject of my book, *Where Have All the Soldiers Gone? The Transformation of Modern Europe* (Boston: Houghton Mifflin, 2008).

4. See Klaus Schwabe, "The Cold War and European Integration, 1947–1963," *Diplomacy and Statecraft* 12.4 (2001): 18–34, and the essays in N. Piers Ludlow, ed., *European Integration and the Cold War: Ostpolitik-Westpolitik, 1965–1973* (London: Routledge, 2007).

5. Sean Greenwood, "Helping to Open the Door? Britain in the Last Decade of the Cold War," in *The Last Decade of the Cold War: From Conflict Escalation to Conflict Transformation*, edited by Olav Njølstad (London: Frank Cass, 2004), 323. See also Luca Ratti, "Britain, the German Question and the Transformation of Europe: From Ostpolitik to the Helsinki Conference, 1963–1975," in *Helsinki 1975 and the Transformation of Europe*, edited by O. Bange and G. Niedhart (New York: Berghan Books, 2008), 83–97.

6. On the structure of French diplomacy, see the various works of Frederic Bozo, especially "Before the Wall: French Diplomacy and the Last Decade of the Cold War," in *The Last Decade of the Cold War: From Conflict Escalation to Conflict Transformation*, edited by Olav Njølstad (London: Frank Cass, 2004), 288–316, and *Mitterrand, la Fin de la Guerre Froide et l'unification allemande de Yalta à Maastricht* (Paris: Jacob, 2005). Also of value are the essays in Helga Haftendorn et al., eds., *The Strategic Triangle: France, Germany, and the United States in the Shaping of the New Europe* (Washington, D.C.: Woodrow Wilson Center Press, 2006), and Georges-Henri Soutou, *L'Alliance incertaine: Les rapports politico-stratégiques Franco-allemande, 1954–1996* (Paris: Fayard, 1996).

7. See Georges-Henri Soutou's "France and the Cold War, 1944–1963," *Diplomacy and Statecraft* 12.4 (2001): 35–52, and "The Linkage between European Integration and Détente. The Contrasting Approaches of deGaulle and Pompidou, 1965–1974," in *European Integration and the Cold War: Ostpolitik-Westpolitik, 1965–1973,* edited by N. Piers Ludlow (London: Routledge, 2007), 11–35.

8. Quoted in Bozo, "Before the Wall," 292.

9. Quoted in Wilfried Loth, "Germany in the Cold War: Strategies and Decisions," in *Reviewing the Cold War: Approaches, Interpretations, Theory,* edited by Odd Arne Westad (London: Frank Cass, 2000), 249.

10. R. Blasius (Munich: Oldenbourg Verlag, 1997), 3–6.

11. Timothy Garton Ash, *In Europe's Name: Germany and the Divided Continent* (New York: Vintage Books, 1993), 208. In the 1950s and 1960s, between 35 and 45 percent of West Germans regarded unification as the most important foreign policy issue; after the mid-1970s, it was around 1 percent (Ash, *In Europe's Name,* 134).

12. Garton Ash's *In Europe's Name* remains the best single book on Ostpolitik. For Bahr's role, see his memoirs, *Zu meiner Zeit* (Munich: K. Blessing, 1996).

13. See the essays on various countries in Richard Davy, ed., *European Détente: A Reappraisal* (London: Sage Publications, 1992).

14. O. Bange and G. Niedhart, eds., *Helsinki 1975 and the Transformation of Europe* (New York: Berghan Books, 2008).

15. See, for example, Henry Kissinger's brief discussion of Helsinki in *Diplomacy* (New York: Simon and Schuster, 1994), 757.

16. Gale Stokes, *The Walls Came Tumbling Down: The Collapse of Communism in Eastern Europe* (New York: Oxford University Press, 1993), 23.

17. Garton Ash, *In Europe's Name,* 268.

18. Pascale Fontaine, *A New Idea for Europe: The Schuman Declaration, 1950–2000,* 2nd edition (Luxembourg: Office for Official Publications of the European Communities, 2000), 14.

19. See John Gillingham, *European Integration, 1950–2003* (Cambridge: Cambridge University Press, 2003), for an introduction to these developments.

20. Egon Bahr, *Zum Europäischen Frieden. Eine Antwort auf Gorbatschow* (Berlin: Seidler, 1988), 42.

21. Archie Brown, *The Gorbachev Factor* (New York: Oxford University Press, 1996), 77.

22. Bozo, *Mitterrand,* 6.

23. Garton Ash, *In Europe's Name,* 106. For a survey of German policy, see Hans-Hermann Hertle, "Germany in the Last Decade of the Cold War," in *The Last Decade of the Cold War: From Conflict Escalation to Conflict Transformation,* edited by Olav Njølstad (London: Frank Cass, 2004), 365–87.

24. Kohl's attempts to explain this blunder are in his *Erinnerungen 1982–1990* (Munich: Droemer Knaur, 2005), 450–51.

25. Chernyaev, *My Six Years with Gorbachev* (University Park: Penn State University Press, 2000), 3–4.

26. Chernyaev, *My Six Years,* 10, and the very interesting account in Antonio Rubbi, *Incontri con Gorbaciov. I Colloqui di Natta e Occhetto con il leader sovietico 1984–1989* (Rome: Editori Reuniti, 1990), 17. On the background of the Italian Communist Party's relationship with the Soviet Union, see Jacques Levesque, *Italian Communists versus the Soviet Union: The PCI Charts a New Foreign Policy* (Berkeley: University of California Press, 1987), which emphasizes the Italians' changing attitudes towards violence as a political instrument.

27. Chernyaev, *My Six Years,* 23; Rubbi, *Incontri con Gorbaciov,* 38ff, 74ff, and 130ff.

28. Brown, *Gorbachev Factor,* 119–20 and 242–43. See also Robert English, *Russia and the Idea of the West: Gorbachev, Intellectuals and the End of the Cold War* (New York: Columbia University Press, 2000).

29. Printed in V. Zubok et al., eds., *Understanding the End of the Cold War: Reagan/Gorbachev Years* (Providence, R.I., 1998).

30. On the growing importance of Europe for Gorbachev, see J. Van Oudenaren, "Gorbachev and His Predecessors: Two Faces of the New Thinking," in *New Thinking and Old Realities: America, Europe, and Russia,* edited by M. Clark and S. Serfaty (Washington, D.C.: Seven Locks Press, 1991), 2–28; Jacques Lévesque, *The Enigma of 1989: The USSR and the Liberation of Eastern Europe* (Berkeley: University of California Press, 1997); Svetlana Savranskaya, "In the Name of Europe: Soviet Withdrawal from Eastern Europe," in *Europe and the End of the Cold War: A Reappraisal,* edited by Frederic Bozo et al. (London: Frank Cass, 2008), 36–48.

31. Chernyaev's diary, quoted in [Cold War International History Project] *Bulletin* 12/13 (Fall/Winter 2001): 16.

32. Zubok, "Gorbachev and the End of the Cold War: Perspectives on History and Personality," *Cold War History* 2.2 (January 2002): 79–80.

33. M. S. Gorbachev, *A Road to the Future....Address to the United Nations General Assembly, in New York, Wednesday, December 7, 1988* (Santa Fe, N.M.: Ocean Tree Books, 1990).

34. *The New York Times,* July 7, 1989.

35. See Savranskaya, "In the Name of Europe," and Marie-Pierre Rey, "'Europe is our Common Home': A Study of Gorbachev's Diplomatic Concept," *Cold War History,* 4.2 (2004): 33–65.

36. Zubok, "Gorbachev and the End of the Cold War," 67. For Gorbachev and Lenin, see Jacques Lévesque, "The Messianic Character of 'New Thinking': Why and What For?" in *The Last Decade of the Cold War: From Conflict Escalation to Conflict Transformation,* edited by Olav Njølstad (London: Frank Cass, 2004), 159–76.

37. For an astute statement of Germany's central importance for the postwar order, see J. Joffe, "The 'Revisionists': Germany and Russia in a Post-Bipolar World," in *New Thinking and Old Realities: America, Europe, and Russia,* edited by M. Clark and S. Serfaty (Washington, D.C.: Seven Locks Press, 1991), 95–125. On the historical background, see Peter Alter, *The German Question and Europe* (New York: Hodder Arnold, 2000). The most complete collection of evidence on German foreign policy in 1989–90 is in Hans Jürgen

Kuesters and Daniel Hofmann, eds., *Dokumente zur Deutschlandspolitik. Deutsche Einheit Sonderedition aus den Akten des Bundeskanzleramtes 1989/90* (Munich: Oldenbourg Verlag, 1998).

38. See Garton Ash, *In Europe's Name,* 112ff. Useful materials on this meeting are Kuesters and Hoffmann, *Dokumente zur Deutschlandspolitik,* 276–98.

39. There is a good summary of events in East Europe in Stokes, *Walls Came Tumbling Down.* I am also grateful for Professor Stokes's comments on an earlier version of this paper in which he correctly emphasized the importance of events in Eastern Europe for the end of the Cold War. A fascinating collection of documents, mostly from the Soviet perspective, can be found in Svetlana Savranskaya, Thomas Blanton and Vlad Zubok, *Masterpieces of History: The Soviet Peaceful Withdrawal from Eastern Europe, 1989* (Budapest: Central European University Press, forthcoming 2009).

40. For more on Gorbachev's attitudes towards Eastern Europe, see chapter 3, this volume, by Taubman and Savranskaya.

41. On the East German situation, see Manfried Görtemaker, *Unifying Germany* (New York: St. Martin's Press, 1994); Charles Maier, *Dissolution: The Crisis of Communism and the End of East Germany* (Princeton, N.J.: Princeton University Press, 1997); and Konrad Jarausch, *The Rush to German Unity* (New York: Oxford University Press, 1994).

42. [Cold War International History Project] *Bulletin* 12/13 (Fall/Winter 2001): 18–19.

43. Quotations in Görtemaker, *Unifying Germany,* 65–66.

44. Ibid., 86–87.

45. Poll numbers from P. Merkl, *German Unification in the European Context* (University Park: Penn State University Press, 1993), 125; Chernyaev's diary in [Cold War International History Project] *Bulletin* 12/13 (Fall/Winter 2001): 20. In chapter 3, this volume, Taubman and Savranskaya show that, unlike Chernyaev, most Soviet policymakers did not recognize the full significance of November 9.

46. For the impact of the opening of the Wall, see Görtemaker, *Unifying Germany,* 92ff; Bozo, *Mitterrand,* 129ff; and Philip Zelikow and Condoleezza Rice, *Germany Unified and Europe Transformed* (Cambridge, Mass.: Harvard University Press, 1995), chapter 4.

47. These anxieties are clearly reflected in Horst Teltschik's excellent record from Kohl's inner circle: *329 Tage: Innenausichten der Einigung* (Berlin: Siedler, 1993).

48. Elbe quoted in Zelikow and Rice, *Germany Unified,* 148.

49. On the origins of the "ten point" speech, see Teltschik, *329 Tage,* 48–58, and Kohl, *Erinnerungen,* 990ff.

50. There is a translation of Kohl's speech in Harold James and Marla Stone, eds, *When the Wall Came Down: Reactions to German Unification* (New York: Routledge, 1992), 33–41.

51. There is a good summary of this diplomatic activity in Bozo, *Mitterrand,* 129. Zelikow and Rice, *Germany Unified,* chapter 4, has a great deal of excellent material, especially on the American side. Kuesters and Hofmann, *Dokumente zur Deutschlandspolitik,* 567ff., is the best source for the German perspective.

52. The official transcript is published by the European Council, *Strasbourg 8 and 9 December. Bulletin of the European Communities,* no. 12 (1989). For Kohl's view, see *Erinnerungen,* 1011ff., and Kuesters and Hofman, *Dokumente zur Deutschlandspolitik,* 628. For a different view of this meeting, see Thatcher, *Downing Street,* 796–97.

53. For a concise summary, see Jarausch, *Rush to German Unity,* chapters 4–6.

54. Frederic Bozo, "Mitterrand's France, the End of the Cold War, and German Unification: A Reappraisal," *Cold War History,* 7.4 (November, 2007): 455–78. See also the material in Mitterrand's posthumously published *De l'Allemagne, de la France* (Paris: Odile Jacob, 1996), and Soutou, *L'Alliance incertaine.*

55. Thatcher, *Downing Street,* 791.

56. Ibid., 813. For a view of the prime minister's policy by a critical insider, see Douglas Hurd, *Memoirs* (London: Little, Brown, 2003), 384ff. In an effort to activate fears of resurgent German power, Thatcher summoned a group of British and American historians to her country residence, Chequers, in March 1990. A distorted view of their discussion was published soon thereafter and quickly became the subject of brief but intense public debate: see the articles by Charles Powell and Timothy Garton Ash, reprinted in James and Stone, *When the Wall Came Down,* especially 233ff. and 242ff., and the account by George Urban, one of the participants: *Diplomacy and Disillusion at the Court of Margaret Thatcher* (New York: St. Martin's Press, 1996). There is a good analysis of British policy in Louise Richardson, "British State Strategies after the Cold War," in *After the Cold War,* edited by Robert Keohane (Cambridge, Mass: Harvard University Press, 1993), 148–69.

57. Commission of the European Communities, *The European Community and German Unification, Bulletin: Supplement* 4/90 (Luxembourg: European Commission, 1990).

58. Michael Beschloss and Strobe Talbott, *At the Highest Levels* (Boston: Back Bay Publishing, 1993), 238, on the news conference in Arkhyz.

59. See Hannes Adomeit, "Gorbachev's Consent to United Germany's Membership in NATO," in *Europe and the End of the Cold War: A Reappraisal,* edited by Frederic Bozo et al. (London: Frank Cass, 2008), 107–18.

60. These articles are reprinted in James and Stone, *When the Wall Came Down,* 168, 221–22, and 177.

61. John Mearsheimer, "Back to the Future: Instability in Europe after the Cold War," *International Security* 15.1 (Summer 1990): 5–56. On the theoretical implications for the end of the Cold War, see William Wohlforth, "Reality Check: Revising Theories of International Relations in Response to the End of the Cold War," *World Politics* 50.4 (July 1998): 650–80.

Chapter 3

IF A WALL FELL IN BERLIN AND MOSCOW HARDLY NOTICED, WOULD IT STILL MAKE A NOISE?

William Taubman and Svetlana Savranskaya

On November 10, 1989, the day after the Berlin Wall fell, Anatoly Chernyaev, chief foreign policy adviser to Soviet leader Mikhail Gorbachev, wrote the following in his diary:

> The Berlin Wall has fallen. This entire era in the history of the social-ist system is over. After the [Polish and Hungarian leaders] went [Eric] Honecker. Today we received messages about the "retirement" of Deng Xiaopeng and Todor Zhivkov. Only our "best friends"—[Fidel] Castro, [Nicolae] Ceauşescu, and Kim Il Sung—are still around, people who hate our guts.
>
> But the main thing is the GDR, the Berlin Wall. For it has to do not only with "socialism," but with the shift in the world balance of forces. This is the end of Yalta...the Stalinist legacy....
>
> That is what Gorbachev has done. He has indeed turned out to be a great leader. He has sensed the pace of history and helped history to find a natural channel.[1]

Chernyaev saw the future—an end to the division of Europe that took shape after World War II. He welcomed that change in the hope that it would lead to a unified continent that included the Soviet Union. Although he had worked in the Communist Party's Central Committee for years, Chernyaev had long become disillusioned with Marxist-Leninist ideology.

What did Gorbachev think on November 10? Did he share Chernyaev's view? Or, like all his postwar predecessors as Soviet leader, did he fear that the Wall's fall would doom Communist rule in Eastern Europe, depriving Moscow of what it had won at great cost in the Great Patriotic War, a realm that helped to legitimize communism and protect the Soviet Union from Western threats?

If we look for evidence of Gorbachev's thinking, we encounter puzzles. The first is that Soviet leadership did not anticipate the fall—although, as other chapters in this book show, neither did American, Chinese, and even European leaders.

Nor did Gorbachev pay immediate attention to the Wall's fate. The party's ruling Politburo did not even discuss the situation in Germany on November 9. It focused instead on the domestic Soviet economy and especially on the situation in the Baltic republics. Prime Minister Nikolai Ryzhkov was on the verge of panic—not about Germany, but about the Baltics: "Everything [there] is aimed at preparations for secession. All these discussions with us are just for show, for buying time. As soon as they win elections, they will adopt a decision to leave. What should be done? ... What we should fear is not the Baltics, but Russia and Ukraine. I smell an overall collapse."[2]

In the Soviet scheme of government, the Politburo decided not only matters of the greatest importance, but minor ones as well, and yet it didn't even bother to meet right after the Wall fell. And on November 11, in a conversation with West German chancellor Helmut Kohl, Gorbachev didn't sound very concerned, perhaps because he trusted Kohl's pledge not to destabilize the German Democratic Republic (GDR). Said Gorbachev: "That is why I take the words you have spoken in our conversation today very seriously. And I hope that you will use your authority, your political weight and influence to keep others within limits that are adequate for the time being and for the requirements of our time."[3]

Why did Gorbachev react this way, neither rejoicing at the fall of the Wall nor recoiling from the possibility that it might lead, as in fact it did, to the reunification of Germany on Western terms and to the new Germany's entry into NATO? This question is important because, like all the leaders examined in this book (Bush, Kohl, Thatcher, Mitterrand, and Deng), Gorbachev played a crucial role in 1989—even more so, in fact, than the others. His were the reforms in the Soviet Union that encouraged ferment in Eastern Europe, not only in East Germany but in Poland, Hungary, and elsewhere. And it was he who allowed that turmoil to take its own course. Initially, Western leaders expected him to fight to keep Eastern Europe, especially East Germany, in the Communist camp—perhaps even to try to crush East European unrest as Deng had smashed Chinese demonstrators in Tiananmen Square on June 4, 1989. Instead, it was the Soviet leader who liberated the "Soviet satellites" from Soviet rule.

The enigma of the peaceful end of the Cold War, of the Soviet Union's seeming indifference to the fate of Eastern Europe, has been widely discussed in the scholarly literature. Most studies come to the conclusion that by 1989 the use of force by Moscow was not an option because it would undermine the entire project of perestroika both domestically and in foreign policy.[4] However, these studies lack a comprehensive analysis of documentary evidence, as presented in this chapter, that have only recently become available from Russian, American and German archives.

The German issue—why Moscow acquiesced in German unification and entry into NATO—is particularly puzzling because the sizable Soviet military presence on East German soil offered Moscow various methods of pressure, diplomatic as well as military, had Gorbachev chosen to use them. Yet, German events also proceeded with very little Soviet interference.

Our short answer to the mystery of Gorbachev's behavior has two parts. The first is that he and his Kremlin colleagues were mightily *distracted* by disturbing domestic developments in the Soviet Union The second is that he was guided, or perhaps misguided, by a new set of foreign policy priorities that made the Wall's fall seem less significant than in fact it would turn out to be.

To understand these distractions and priorities, we need to remember how far Gorbachev had come between 1985 and 1989. He had moved from trying to reform the Soviet Union to transforming it—economically, politically, and in ethnic/national affairs, by introducing perestroika, glasnost, and democratization. In foreign affairs, he had shifted from trying to ease the Cold War to ending it, to constructing a new world in which East and West would work together to pursue common aims and a new Europe in which the divided continent would come together in what he called "a common European home." This slogan may sound like Communist propaganda. In fact, Gorbachev embraced the very sorts of developments that, as James Sheehan's chapter in this volume shows, had brought peace to Western Europe and undergirded a new European Community: "a rejection of war as a political instrument and a belief in the primacy of economic growth and material progress" (51).

The domestic transformation Gorbachev was trying to achieve was unprecedented. So too was his transformation of Soviet foreign policy. Put them together and you have an overwhelming set of challenges and opportunities—in the blinding light of which the fall of the Wall paled in comparison.

To a first-time reader interested in Gorbachev's European policy in 1989, the minutes of Soviet Politburo sessions seem quite puzzling.[5] It is as if European policy and foreign policy in general weren't of great interest to the highest Soviet decision-making body. The main reason for this was that in 1989 domestic problems dominated the Soviet leadership's agenda and were of primary concern to Soviet society as a whole. Governmental revenues were plummeting as the result of falling oil prices and of Gorbachev's unsuccessful anti-alcohol campaign, which deprived the treasury of vast sums raised by the tax on vodka. This fall-off undermined the already struggling Soviet economy, while glasnost—the new set of freedoms Gorbachev had granted the press and the population—allowed increasing protests, thus intensifying the impression of an impending crisis.

By 1989 Gorbachev's reforms included a Law on Enterprises (1987), which granted more autonomy to their directors, and a Law on Cooperatives (1988), which encouraged nonstate entrepreneurship. Both innovations were supposed to yield greater efficiency and output, but the results were disappointing. According to Gorbachev associate Vadim Medvedev, "The program of economic reforms of 1987 was in effect buried; people recalled it less and less. The main issue was we had lost control over the money mass, over the monetary income of the population, and that gave a major push to...an inflationary spiral that everyday became more difficult to stop."[6]

January and February 1989 were consumed by preparations for a Central Committee plenum on agriculture that took place in mid-March. Agricultural reform was the hardest part of Gorbachev's agenda to advance because of deeply collectivist attitudes in the leadership and the country. Aggravating the problem was the fact that the Central Committee's secretary for agriculture, Yegor Ligachev, was Gorbachev's main opponent in the Politburo. On March 2, Gorbachev spent his birthday, from early morning to late at night, wrestling with "agro-industrial issues." According to his aide, Georgy Shakhnazarov, Gorbachev was "passionately" in favor of radical reform in agriculture, including renting land to farmers; but these reforms, too, either were never carried out or failed to live up to their promise.[7]

The Soviet economic situation began to deteriorate very quickly at the end of 1988. In addition to falling oil prices, a drop in oil production due to crumbling infrastructure was to blame for the crisis. Both developments constitute an often overlooked story that influenced Soviet policy toward Germany. Oil prices had started to decline in 1986, but central planning gave the illusion that the government could cushion the blow by printing more money. Few in the Soviet leadership understood the depth of the crisis. One person who sounded the alarm early and often, but was rarely heard, was Prime Minister Ryzhkov. The Politburo session that finally awakened the leadership took place on February 16, 1989. At that meeting, Ryzhkov presented the following grim statistics:

> In three years of perestroika, government spending exceeded budget revenue by 133 billion rubles. Losses due to the decline in oil prices constitute 40 billion rubles, and losses due to reduced sales of vodka reached 34 billion rubles.... The industrial surplus increased by 10 billion rubles. But in agriculture, we lost 15 billion rubles. Chernobyl took away 8 billion rubles. Monetary emission over the course of three years was 21 billion rubles, 11 billion in 1988 alone, more than in any year after the war.[8]

The effect of all this was to create a huge monetary overhang—some 40 billion rubles chasing nonexistent consumer goods—thus producing an acute feeling of deficits and shortages among the population. Only 11 percent of consumer goods that were theoretically available were actually in Soviet stores at the beginning of 1989.[9] During Gorbachev's meetings with workers, he was subjected to open criticism. Miners' strikes erupted in the spring and summer. Throughout the year, the Central Committee received angry letters from workers complaining about acute shortages of food and other basic goods. In July 1989 the Central Committee's agriculture department reported that food supplies were dwindling even in favored Moscow.[10]

Soviet economic straits had international implications. Moscow increasingly saw the answer in building direct ties between enterprises in the Soviet Union and Eastern Europe, in expanding trade with the West, and especially in attracting Western investment and obtaining credits with which to purchase consumer goods. While the United States at first dragged its feet, one other rich and powerful country was interested—West Germany.

Beginning in the early 1970s, after the two sides signed the Moscow Treaty normalizing their relations, the Federal Republic of Germany (FRG) was the most important Soviet trade partner in the capitalist world. The Soviet Union purchased one-third of all imported machinery and equipment for industry from the FRG; on the export side, it sold over 35 percent of its exported natural gas, 20 percent of its exported oil and petroleum products, and also timber, gold, and precious stones to the FRG. West Germany also offered access to technology and scientific information from the West. The Soviet ambassador to West Germany, Yuli Kvitsinsky, recalls that by the summer of 1989 his main concern was to develop economic relations, especially direct contacts with the biggest West German industrial enterprises and banks and that he was continually playing the role of a supplicant for credits and investment.[11]

Upon taking office in January 1989, President George H. W. Bush declared "a pause" in U.S.-Soviet relations to assess the seriousness of Gorbachev's reforms and whether Soviet foreign policy had really changed. (See chapter 5, this volume, by Melvyn P. Leffler.) After that, Gorbachev came to see West Germany as his main hope for the kind of financial help that might prevent a domestic explosion in the Soviet Union. But to realize that hope, Soviet leaders had to be flexible about East German–West German relations and, eventually, about the issue of German unification. Inside the Central Committee it was thought that Gorbachev should request as much as $100 billion from West Germans.[12] After Gorbachev's June 1989 visit to West Germany, the issue of credits was at the center of practically every conversation he had with West German interlocutors.

The year 1989 also witnessed the first democratic elections to the new Soviet legislature—the Congress of People's Deputies. The long-debated decision to hold contested elections was made at the nineteenth party conference in the summer of 1988. According to the agreed-upon procedure, two-thirds of the deputies were to be elected from territorial constituencies and one-third from "public organizations," with one hundred of the latter seats allocated to the Communist Party. The coming elections and the process of selecting and nominating deputies were at the center of Politburo discussions through the end of March. Gorbachev hoped that the new elections would rid him of the conservative majority of the Supreme Soviet and attract new reformers to his coalition, allowing him to play the more progressive legislature against the intransigent party bureaucracy.

Although Gorbachev and his supporters anticipated electoral losses among Communists, the results of the elections came as a shock. Some 85 percent of elected deputies were members of the Communist Party of the Soviet Union (CPSU), but key party apparatchiki lost. All the top party leaders in Moscow and Leningrad were voted out—even in the districts where they ran unopposed! Throughout the rest of the country, 20 percent of party secretaries were defeated. On March 28, the Politburo engaged in collective soul-searching. Anatoly Lukyanov blamed it on the economic crisis and the destructive influence of new "informal" organizations like the Memorial Society, which devoted itself to unearthing the full truth about Stalin's terror. Yegor Ligachev condemned the mass media, unleashed by glasnost, and its coverage of negative aspects of party history. He pointed out that in Hungary and Czechoslovakia, where Moscow had crushed reforms with tanks (in 1956 and 1968, respectively), "everything began with mass media."[13]

These electoral results were not easy for Gorbachev to swallow. Even though they removed many conservatives from the Supreme Soviet, they gave an over-whelming victory to his main rival, Boris Yeltsin, who ran for the Moscow at-large seat; and they brought many radicals to the legislature, such as prominent human rights activist and nuclear physicist Andrei Sakharov. Instead of using the new legislature as leverage against the party, Gorbachev would have to battle the parliamentary opposition that would form around Yeltsin. "March 26 was a turning point," said Ryzhkov. "We got a realistic picture of what is going on in the society. It is one thing when we make speeches, and another when people cast secret ballots."[14]

The congress began its work with an investigation of Gorbachev's involvement, if any, in the tragic events in Tbilisi on April 9. Troops had killed twenty demonstrators demanding Georgian independence and injured hundreds of others. This bloodshed was but one manifestation of another development with direct implications for Soviet relations with the West—growing discontent in the union republics, which started in the Baltics and soon reached Georgia and Ukraine. Deteriorating economic conditions exacerbated simmering ethnic tensions. Many republics began demanding economic self-sufficiency. The Baltic republics, reflecting their special history of independence between the wars, followed by brutal Soviet occupation, led the way. On January 30, the Politburo adopted a resolution on "extremist and anti-Soviet groups and organizations in the Baltics," but that didn't deter Lithuanian rallies demanding independence on February 15 and 16, after which the Politburo Commission on the Baltics held a special session on February 18.[15] Gorbachev believed in persuasion and applying economic leverage. He agreed to allow the three Baltic republics to embark on economic self-sufficiency beginning January 1, 1990.[16] He was convinced that they could not survive economically outside the Soviet Union and that they would eventually decide to remain in union. He was wrong on both scores.

Gorbachev and most members of the Politburo were blind to the dangers of nationalism, having grown up believing Soviet propaganda about harmonious relations between nationalities in the Soviet Union. In a poignant passage of his diary, on December 10, 1988, Chernyaev described a conversation with Gorbachev about the Baltics: "Gorbachev asked me and, as I learned, asked Shakhnazarov and [Aleksandr] Yakovlev: Is it really true that the Baltic people want to secede? I told him: I believe they do....Then he told me (Was he mocking me or does he seriously think so?), They will perish when they cut themselves off from the rest of the Union. What self-delusion and naiveté!"[17]

Practically every month in 1989 brought more fires to put out in the republics. After bloody Azerbaijani pogroms in 1988 against Armenians living in Sumgait, the two republics' fight for control of Nagorny Karabakh—part of Azerbaijan but claimed by Armenia—became so explosive that the region had to be ruled directly from Moscow. In May and June, the Fergana Valley of Uzbekistan erupted with violence against the Meskhetian Turks, who were deported to Central Asia from Georgia by Stalin. Most politically damaging to Gorbachev was the suppression of the rallies in Tbilisi. The troops, ordered into action by Georgia party leader Jumber Patiashvili, used gas and wielded shovels to disperse the demonstrators. But despite the casualties, Gorbachev did not condemn the use of force decisively, which led to accusations of his complicity and dealt a serious blow to his reputation. But he drew a crucial lesson, which later had a decisive effect on the outcome in Eastern Europe. On May 11, during a Politburo discussion of the Baltics, Gorbachev declared: "Use of force is excluded. We excluded it in foreign policy, thus it is even more inadmissible to [use it] against our own peoples."[18]

By September 1989, the wave of nationalism had reached Ukraine, the second most populous Soviet republic, with the first congress of the Ukrainian nationalist movement Rukh proclaiming Ukrainian independence to be its ultimate goal and mass rallies of Ukrainian Catholics. Ukrainian Communist leader Vladimir Scherbitsky resigned. Suddenly, the issue of preserving the Soviet Union as a federal entity assumed overriding priority. Compared to that, preservation of the external empire in Eastern Europe was secondary.

Gorbachev's dilemma was this: He could not use force and continue to be viewed as legitimate, either by the West or his own people. Neither could he maintain control without the use of force. In China (as shown in chapter 4, this volume, by Chen Jian) Deng managed to achieve a political trifecta—using force against his own people, maintaining legitimacy, and eventually reestablishing business as usual with the West. But Gorbachev had visited Tiananmen Square shortly before the crackdown, and even though he had failed to condemn it outright (so as to keep the budding Sino-Soviet détente on track), he was determined not to follow Deng's example. Instead he hoped to solve his country's problems by integrating the Soviet Union into Europe as quickly as possible and attracting foreign credits and investments along the way.

For Soviet foreign policy, 1989 really began on December 7, 1988, when Gorbachev delivered a stunning address to the U.N. General Assembly. In it he publicly tied together for the first time the elements of his "new thinking" that marked a fundamental break with bolshevism. He came out against the use or threat of force to resolve international issues; in favor of deideologizing relations among states; for a universal rather than Marxist-Leninist class view of human rights; and for basing government on the consent of the governed. Gorbachev believed these things. But documents from the Gorbachev Foundation reveal an additional rationale behind the address: to break the emerging stalemate on arms control after the Reagan administration failed to conclude a strategic arms control agreement (START), as well as to impress European public opinion by beginning to dismantle the Soviet conventional arms superiority in Europe. For Gorbachev the speech also offered the opportunity to meet with the U.S. president-elect, George H. W. Bush, thus affirming continuity in U.S.-Soviet relations and laying a foundation for a 50 percent reduction in strategic offensive weapons when the new administration entered the White House.[19]

Given deepening economic and ethnic problems in the Soviet Union, writes speechwriter/adviser-turned-biographer, Andrei Grachev, Gorbachev badly needed "a show of success, and this could be produced by foreign policy. With hopes rapidly fading for any quick, spectacular achievements on the home front, it was the mission of diplomacy to play the role of perestroika's political safety belt."[20] However, the calculation that the U.N. speech would become a "watershed" did not bear fruit. Instead, the incoming Bush administration informed Gorbachev that it needed "space" to reassess U.S.-Soviet relations, even though Bush had personally helped to formulate U.S.-Soviet policy as vice president in the Reagan White House.[21]

Three of Bush's most senior advisers—National Security Adviser Brent Scowcroft, Scowcroft's deputy Robert Gates, and Secretary of Defense Dick Cheney— shared a hard-line position towards the Soviet Union. In their judgment, the Cold War was not over; Gorbachev had not yet proved that his reforms were fundamental; and even his U.N. speech could be viewed as propaganda. For them, U.S. policy in Europe was designed not to help Gorbachev build a "common European home," but to compete with him, to prevent him from upstaging the new president, especially in Europe.[22]

Because Moscow wanted to move very fast on arms control and other issues, President Bush's pause and seeming indecisiveness in the first months of 1989 greatly frustrated Gorbachev, even leading him to suspect that the administration was trying to undermine perestroika.[23] However, this lack of U.S.-Soviet progress made Europe seem even more important to Gorbachev.

Another pressing issue in 1989 was Afghanistan. The Soviet Union started pulling out its troops in May 1988 and was scheduled to complete the withdrawal by February 15, 1989. But the Soviet-installed president of Afghanistan, Najibullah, pressed Moscow for additional reinforcements and military operations to strengthen the Afghan army as the deadline approached. Soviet negotiators at Geneva sought a compromise under which both the Soviet Union and the United States would stop supplying weapons to Afghan warring parties, but Washington rejected this and continued to provide the mujahadeen with arms and cash through the Pakistani intelligence service, ISI. Gorbachev called Afghanistan a "bleeding wound" in his address to the Twenty-seventh Party Congress in 1986. On December 26, 1988, Gorbachev's close colleague Aleksandr Yakovlev complained to U.S. Ambassador Jack Matlock that the United States was preventing a faster resolution of the conflict.[24] Meanwhile, the Soviet leadership itself was split, with some wanting to strengthen Najibullah's regime as a guarantor of stability against religious fundamentalists on the southern Soviet borders. In particular, Foreign Minister Eduard Shevardnadze, who backed Gorbachev on virtually all other issues, sided with Najibullah and lobbied for more military aid after the Soviet army's departure.[25] Even after the last Soviet soldier crossed back into the Soviet territory on February 15, Afghanistan remained a major concern of the Gorbachev leadership.

It wasn't Afghanistan, however, but Europe that was at the top of Gorbachev's agenda. Europe was the epicenter of the Cold War. To end that conflict, to reduce the terrible dangers it posed to the world and the huge burden of military spending it imposed on the Soviet Union, Gorbachev had to overcome Europe's divisions. More than that, by unifying East and West Europe, he sought to fully bind the Soviet Union itself into the family of civilized nations. "Returning to Europe" was one of the earliest ideas of perestroika. From 1986 on, the Soviet leadership accepted the idea of taking the initiative on German reunification and guiding the process so that Moscow would get the most dividends from it.[26] What Gorbachev wanted was a gradual, long-term, "all-European process," building on the existing structures of the Conference on Security and Cooperation in Europe (CSCE), leading to rapprochement between—and then dissolution of—NATO and the Warsaw Pact, and culminating in the construction of a common European home.

The phrase "common European home" was first used by Gorbachev during his visit to Britain in November 1984. The idea grew out of Soviet proposals for replacing NATO with a collective security framework in Europe, which appeared in the early 1970s during talks on détente and the CSCE process, leading to the signing of the Helsinki Final Act in 1975. But Gorbachev's version was very different from the traditional Soviet strategic vision of splitting NATO and dissolving the blocs so as to achieve European dominance. "[W]hat we have in mind," he told the European Council in Strasbourg on July 6, 1989, "is a restructuring of the international order in Europe that would put European common values in the forefront and make it possible to replace the traditional balance of forces with a balance of interests."[27] Gorbachev's predecessors had seen the CSCE mainly as an irritant because the Helsinki Final Act included a commitment to human rights. By contrast, Gorbachev gave it new attention and support almost as soon as he came to power. Foreign Minister Shevard-nadze's first foreign trip was to the CSCE review conference in Vienna, where he made an unprecedented proposal to host a CSCE conference in Moscow on the humanitarian dimension of security, including human rights. To make this possible, the Kremlin released political prisoners and put an end to the persecu-tion of prominent dissidents.[28]

Gorbachev also tried to defang the Western image of a Soviet military threat. During a May 8, 1987, Politburo discussion of Warsaw Pact military doctrine, he mentioned his conversation with Margaret Thatcher, which left a lasting impression on him: "She said they were afraid of us; that we invaded Czecho-slovakia, Hungary, and Afghanistan. This perception is widespread among the public there." The Soviet Union should stop lying about its troop strength and the size of its conventional forces in the European theater, he said. Arguing for troop reductions, he tied them directly to the need to think "about Europe: from the Atlantic to the Urals."[29] Previous Soviet leaders, too, had sought to alter the Soviet image, sometimes seeming more belligerent to intimidate the West, on other occasions trying to ease Western fears. Stalin, in a euphoric mood, might have hoped to dominate "Europe from the Atlantic to the Urals," but Gorbachev was no Stalin. In early 1988, in an effort to provide the concept of the common European home with greater substance, and to shift the intel-lectual center of gravity in Moscow toward the study of Europe, he established the Institute of Europe within the Soviet Academy of Sciences. The institute provided detailed analysis of the prospect of European integration and German unification to the Central Committee.[30]

After his December 1988 speech to the United Nations, encouraged by Europeans' enthusiastic response and discouraged by the Bush administra-tion's "reassessment pause," Gorbachev attempted to make a European break-through in his Strasbourg speech. The speech was drafted in secret, kept even from other members of the leadership. It was envisioned as "similar to the U.N. speech, only with a specific European angle."[31] Gorbachev wanted to spell out his vision of a "common European home," as well as to show how Europe could achieve that goal. The Strasbourg address was a cri de coeur, a passion-ate appeal to the West Europeans for Soviet entry into their community. He even quoted French author Victor Hugo, who in the nineteenth century had predicted that all European nations "without losing [their] distinguishing fea-tures and splendid distinctiveness [will] merge inseparably into a high-level society and form a European brotherhood." The common European home, Gorbachev explained, would combine four elements: collective security based on restraint rather than deterrence, full economic integration, environmental protection, and respect for human rights in every country. The entire edifice would be rooted in universal values. The new Europe would be based on the rule of law.[32]

Later, in 1990, Gorbachev would propose a summit of states whose leaders signed the original Helsinki Final Act in 1975. The Paris summit, which produced a charter on "Europe from Vancouver to Vladivostok," would embody Gorbachev's hope for a common European home. Virtually all discussions of Eastern Europe and Germany in the Politburo placed these issues within the framework of the all-European process. There was resistance in the Soviet establishment to the idea of dissolving military-political blocs, but not among Gorbachev's closest advisers. Georgy Shakhnazarov repeatedly pushed it in his communications with Gorbachev; he prepared a long and detailed memorandum on the issue on October 14, 1989. The memo argued that Soviet acceptance of revolutions in Eastern Europe and the withdrawal of Soviet troops from the region would logically lead to dismantling the blocs and strengthening CSCE structures as the main framework of European security. It proposed "regularizing the process of easing the military confrontation, which has already begun," and envisioned

> the liquidation of the Warsaw Treaty Organization and NATO by the end of the twentieth century. Within the framework of this process, we should define a number of interim stages, the most important of which should be the elimination of the military structures of the two blocs by 1995.[33]

Obviously, this scenario precluded any use of force to maintain Communist regimes in Eastern Europe.

Gorbachev pushed the idea of a common European home in every meeting he had with European leaders in 1989. He was convinced that they (especially French President François Mitterrand) understood and supported his vision and that they also shared his view of German unification. On the latter issue, his strongest supporter was British Prime Minister Margaret Thatcher, who rejected any early unification in a one-on-one conversation with Gorbachev in September 1989. Even President Jimmy Carter's former national security adviser, Zbigniew Brzezinski, famous for his hard-line stance on the Soviet Union, mentioned to Yakovlev his opposition to unification and spoke about the dangers it would represent to European security.[34]

As pointed out above, Gorbachev wasn't opposed to German unification per se, but envisioned it as the culmination of a gradual process, including demilitarization, dissolution of the blocs, Soviet integration into Europe, Soviet trade benefits, and a new, far-reaching environmental regime. This also meant that East European transformation would proceed in a controlled fashion, precluding instability in the region. East European governments would continue to be friendly to Moscow, even if they were to become Social Democratic regimes.

Meanwhile, however, instability was growing in Eastern Europe. Reforms in the Soviet Union were encouraging popular movements for change. Gorbachev hoped the appeal of Soviet perestroika would strengthen East European reformers while keeping the socialist system intact. Instead the reaction to Soviet reforms split the bloc's leaders into two groups, as Gorbachev himself noted in his memoirs: "I can point to the exact moment...when some leaders of socialist countries rejected Soviet perestroika. It was January 1987, the Plenum of the Central Committee of the CPSU on democratization."[35] East German leader Erich Honecker, in an unprecedented gesture, prohibited publication of plenum materials in the GDR. The leadership of Poland and Hungary, where reforms were already underway, meanwhile, cited Gorbachev's reforms to defend their own policies. The GDR, Romania, and Bulgaria, trying to block change, had the gall to claim they had already reformed—even earlier, that is, than the Soviet Union.

Poland was farthest along the road of reforms, but its economic situation was probably most critical in the mid-1980s. The Polish economy exhibited the slowest growth of all socialist bloc countries in 1980–85, experiencing a rapid decline in food supplies, a drop in investment, and an enormous debt burden, with its hard currency debt being the highest in Eastern Europe at 21.2 percent of the GDP.[36] Also unique to Poland was the existence of Solidarity, the broad movement of workers and intellectuals that was suppressed but not eliminated by the declaration of martial law in 1981. When Polish leader Wojciech Jaruzelski in 1986 established the Consultative Social Council as a forum for civil society and intelligentsia, one of its first demands was to legitimize Solidarity. Jaruzelski also had to accommodate the Catholic Church, which was particularly strong in Poland, a move that led him to visit the Vatican in early 1987, and Pope John Paul II (formerly Cardinal Karol Wojtyla) to visit Poland that summer. Gorbachev himself arrived in early July 1988; his speech to the Polish Parliament's lower house explained his concept of a common European home and pledged allegiance to universal human values, including non-use of force in international relations. The speech reverberated through Polish society, increasing pressure for change. Massive strikes the next month forced the government to contemplate roundtable talks that eventually led to free elections and coalition rule. The government opted for such negotiations in late August and early September 1988. During a conversation that fall with Joseph Czyrek, Polish Central Committee secretary, former ambassador to Moscow, and Jaruzelski's trusted envoy, Gorbachev actually encouraged them to do so.[37] In February 1989, roundtable negotiations started in Poland.

Hungary experienced not mass movements or strikes comparable to Poland, but rather an acute debate about the causes and nature of the revolution of 1956. János Kádár, whom the Soviets installed after crushing the 1956 revolt, but who himself was open to reform, kept Gorbachev informed about the Hungarian situation. Hungary, too, carried a heavy burden of external debt, which Moscow, suffering from its own economic crisis, could not help to reduce. Kádár eventually understood that he had to resign in favor of moderate reformers, lest the party lose control of the country. After consulting with Gorbachev, Kádár stepped down as general secretary in the early summer of 1988 and as president a year later. After visiting Moscow,[38] the new Hungarian leadership intensified economic and political reforms, the latter culminating in Polish-style roundtable negotiations in July 1989.

Czechoslovakia also grappled with how to retrospectively interpret its own revolution—the Prague Spring of 1968. Not only the noncommunist opposition but reformist elements in the government equated Gorbachev's reforms with those of the Prague Spring. That's why Czechoslovak society greeted his visit to Prague in April 1987 with great hopes. But Gorbachev disappointed them. He did not mention 1968 because, as Zdenek Mlynar (Gorbachev's friend at Moscow University in the early 1950s and later chief ideologist of the Prague Spring) put it, Gorbachev was still the hostage of the Brezhnev Doctrine.[39] Meanwhile, however, the Czechoslovak opposition was radicalizing, converging around the prominent dissident organization Charter 77. In November 1989, a peaceful, "velvet" revolution, featuring massive student demonstrations, brought to power Charter 77 leader Václav Havel.

East Germany was a special case due to its role in German unification and also because of Communist leader Erich Honecker's intransigence. The Stasi, the East German secret police, was second only to the Soviet KGB when it came to repressing dissent. Gorbachev understood that Honecker was a major obstacle to East German reform and to any comprehensive dialog with West Germany on unification. Yet he had very little leverage over Honecker, short of outright pressure on him to resign. Gorbachev reluctantly went to Berlin in October 1989 to celebrate the fortieth anniversary of the GDR. Young party activists marching in the parade chanted, "Gorbachev, save us one more time," right in front of the two leaders. Gorbachev warned East German communists that "where the party is lagging behind the times in theoretical and practical terms, we will harvest bitter fruit." He told Honecker's colleagues a story about miners in Ukraine who wanted to oust their leaders but "didn't dare" because they were "afraid to offend them."[40] East German Communists got the message. Ten days later they replaced Honecker with Egon Krenz, a reform-minded member of the Politburo, who enjoyed the trust of the Soviet leadership.

Not just Gorbachev, but the whole Soviet leadership knew that force wasn't a good option in Eastern Europe; even Soviet conservatives never challenged him openly about this, as they would on German unification and NATO membership. After all, even Brezhnev had refrained from military intervention in Poland to crush Solidarity in 1981. However, ambiguity remained, especially in the minds of East Europeans with strong memories of 1956 and 1968, as Gorbachev himself noted at a Politburo session on January 21, 1989: "The peoples of those countries will ask: What about the CPSU? What kind of leash will it use to keep our countries in? They simply do not know that if they pull this leash harder, it will break."[41]

In March 1989, days before fateful elections for the new Soviet legislature, in conversation with Hungarian party leader Károly Grósz, Gorbachev hinted that there were limits to what Moscow would tolerate: "The limit," he said, "is the safekeeping of socialism and assurance of stability."[42] And yet, earlier in the same month he had tacitly allowed the Hungarians to open their Austrian border when Hungarian reformer Miklós Németh had informed him of the decision to "completely remove the electronic and technological defenses from the western and southern borders of Hungary. It has outlived the need for it, and now it serves only to catch citizens from Romania and the GDR who are trying to escape illegally to the West through Hungary."[43]

In June 1989, in the first free elections in Poland, Solidarity took 99 out of 100 seats in the upper house and all 161 contested seats in the lower house. Many expected an alarmed reaction from Moscow. Instead, Gorbachev expressed his support for the elections in Poland, and later in the summer he endorsed the resulting coalition government—even though that meant that Poland might leave the Warsaw Pact. As Andrei Grachev has pointed out,

> Psychologically, the significance of an eventual Polish defection from the socialist camp was even more important than any hole it might leave in the strategic wall of Eastern bloc defenses. The failure of the Polish communists represented a spectacular setback for the East European "Gorbachevists" [and] a very tough first test for the principles of

"the new political thinking" that had been proclaimed by Gorbachev several months earlier at the United Nations.[44]

And yet, in Gorbachev's conversations with his Polish allies Jaruzelski and Mieczyslaw Rakowski, which began in the fall of 1988 and continued especially when Jaruzelski visited Moscow in April 1990, the question was not whether force would be used, but how to preserve the influence of the reform communists in the new government and keep Poland in the Warsaw Pact.[45]

Even though the Polish elections dealt a blow to Gorbachev's hopes for reform communism in Eastern Europe, he still thought events were under control. Coalition governments, even led by noncommunists, were acceptable as long as they remained within the "all-European" framework. This view came up in every one of his conversations with Western leaders. He appealed to them to avoid an "uncontrolled course of events" in Eastern Europe, maintain stability, and promote gradual transformation. He raised this concern with Thatcher in April, James Baker in May, Kohl and German President Richard von Weizsacker in June, Mitterrand in July, and Thatcher again in September.

Gorbachev's reaction was equally restrained following the reburial of Imre Nagy (the former Hungarian premier executed by the Soviets after 1956) and the start of Hungarian roundtable negotiations on June 13. Gorbachev was privately concerned but outwardly supportive. He was visiting Kohl in Bonn when Hungarian roundtable talks started. Discussing Poland and Hungary, the two men sounded like allies and friends contemplating a joint plan of action. This is how Kohl described Gorbachev's stance in a phone call to Bush immediately after Gorbachev left West Germany:

> The Chancellor emphasized Gorbachev's very close personal relationship with General Jaruzelski and their common approach toward developments in Poland. No such personal relationship exists with any one Hungarian leader, the Chancellor added, but Gorbachev also supports Hungary's reform efforts. By contrast, there is an enormous distance between Moscow and Bucharest, and also East Berlin.[46]

When Gorbachev and Kohl discussed East Germany in the same conversation on June 14, the level of communication and shared understanding of the situation was simply astonishing. Here is Kohl complaining to Gorbachev about Honecker and his wife:

> Now a couple of words about our mutual friends. I will tell you directly that Erich Honecker concerns me a great deal. His wife has just made a statement, in which she called on East German youth to take up arms

and, if necessary, defend the achievements of socialism against external enemies. She clearly implied that socialist countries which implement reforms, stimulate democratic processes, and follow their own original road, are enemies. Primarily, she had Poland and Hungary in mind.[47]

An exchange like this demonstrates how important West Germany had become to Gorbachev, how far he had gone in building ties beyond his former Communist allies, and how much he was counting on new allies to help him shape European and global developments.

Another symbolic event for the socialist bloc in 1989 took place in July. Right after Gorbachev's speech in Strasbourg, he attended a meeting of the Warsaw Pact's Political Consultative Committee in Bucharest. The speeches and the conversations there had a surreal character. The meeting really was a wake for the Warsaw Pact. Two of its members were negotiating the formation of non-communist coalition governments, and the bloc's leader had just proclaimed the supremacy of common democratic values over class interests. Gorbachev was signaling his socialist allies that if their own populations were to vote them out or rise against them, Moscow would not come to their rescue. But, as Andrei Grachev confirms in his memoir, "behind the scenes [Romanian dictator Nicolae] Ceauşescu and Honecker tried to raise the 'Polish question,' hoping to persuade their colleagues of the imperative need to render 'fraternal aid' to Poland, as in the case of the 1968 Warsaw Pact intervention in Czechoslovakia."[48]

By the summer and fall of 1989, East European leaders must have known they could no longer count on Soviet protection against their own populations. Even so, was it not in their interest to behave as if such a threat existed in order to restrain their own domestic opposition? Particularly since the opposition, especially dissidents who were not engaged in direct interactions with Soviet reformers, had only previous East European reform attempts to go by, most of which had ended tragically. Knowing the strategic value of Eastern Europe for the Soviet Union, remembering Moscow's brutal interventions in earlier years, East European oppositionists behaved very cautiously, taking care not to provoke Moscow, pledging adherence to the Warsaw Pact, as they did repeatedly during the Polish and the Hungarian roundtable discussions. This self-restraint was probably the best course for East Europeans, resulting in "velvet" revolutions that developed gradually and peacefully along the lines Gorbachev has envisaged.

During the summer and fall of 1989, Gorbachev traveled to European capitals and hosted his new partners in Moscow, looking not only for solutions to Soviet economic troubles, but for the appreciation and praise that was so lacking at home. Uncomfortable with most of his East European allies, he viewed West

European leaders as his main peer group and behaved accordingly, astonishing many of his interlocutors.[49]

Practically every conversation included three main items: a complaint about the Bush administration's "pause," a request to avoid destabilizing the situation in Eastern Europe by encouraging even faster reform, and a discussion of what would follow the end of the Cold War in Europe. Of course, German unification could happen, but Gorbachev believed it would happen slowly and that the West European leaders—especially Margaret Thatcher—shared his belief. As early as Gorbachev's visit to Britain in 1984, he and Thatcher had taken a political as well as personal liking to each other. She had helped to persuade President Reagan of Gorbachev's seriousness and trustworthiness. Later she reassured Gorbachev that the Bush administration was not seeking to exploit Soviet weakness in Eastern Europe. In 1989 she spoke in favor of gradual democratization there, praising Jaruzelski as "a prominent and honest politician, who is doing everything he can for this country at a very difficult stage in its development." She told Gorbachev that she had "repeatedly" advised leaders of Solidarity to "seek a dialogue with the government, not to limit themselves to confrontation."[50]

Gorbachev attached great importance to the fact that Thatcher opposed German unification, since he assumed her view carried special weight with the U.S. administration. But Gorbachev overestimated her willingness to act openly, partly because she unintentionally led him to do so. At a meeting in Moscow on September 23, 1989, she said this on the record: "I understand your position in the following way: you are in favor of each country's choosing its own road of development so long as the Warsaw Treaty is intact. I understand this position perfectly." Off the record, Thatcher spoke even more strongly: "Britain and Western Europe are not interested in the unification of Germany. The words written in the NATO communiqué may sound different, but disregard them! We do not want the unification of Germany." She also added,

> We are not interested in the destabilization of Eastern Europe or the dissolution of the Warsaw Treaty either.... We will not interfere and spur the decommunization of Eastern Europe. I can tell you that this is also the position of the U.S. President. He sent a telegram to me in Tokyo in which he asked me to tell you that the United States would not undertake anything that could threaten the security interests of the Soviet Union, or that could be perceived by the Soviet society as a threat. I am fulfilling his request.[51]

George Bush and James Baker also led Gorbachev astray. They didn't disagree when he spoke about the unification as a long-term process. Other

Americans, whom the Soviet leaders perceived as representing the U.S. government position, portrayed German unification as a potential threat to European security. In January, Henry Kissinger came to Moscow proposing a U.S.-Soviet condominium to prevent destabilization of Europe, citing Germany especially as the potentially unstable place.[52] Zbigniew Brzezinski, just ten days before the Wall fell, outdid Yakovlev in opposing German unification in a Moscow conversation. Yakovlev argued for disbanding European alliances while creating "a common parliament, common affairs, and trade relations; the borders will be open." Brzezinski argued that both alliances should be preserved for the time being, and that there should be no individual withdrawals from the Warsaw Pact so that the two alliances could "conduct discussions about all issues" as blocs, not individual countries. Destabilizing the Warsaw Pact would immediately raise the German issue, Brzezinski noted: "That is why I openly said that I am in favor of Poland and Hungary remaining within the Warsaw Treaty Organization. Both blocs should not be disbanded right now. I do not know what will happen if the GDR ceases to exist. There will be one Germany, united and strong. This does not correspond to either your or our interests." Yakovlev: "How would you keep the GDR? By force?" Brzezinski: "I think that is also not necessary. Political possibilities always exist."[53]

French President François Mitterrand held his cards closer to his vest. Mitterrand's position on German unification is still not entirely clear. Was he initially against it but could not say so openly? Or, as Chernyaev puts it, was he trying to slow it down by using "Gorbachev's hands"?[54] Whatever his real conviction, he convinced Gorbachev that, like Thatcher, he shared the Soviet leader's position.

As for Gorbachev's relations with Kohl, their meeting of the minds, on vivid display during Gorbachev's visit to the FRG in June 1989, sent a signal, whether intended or not, to the East Germans. According to Chernyaev, it was obvious to them, "both at the top, and at the bottom," that from now on West Germany, not East, would be Moscow's most important European partner. The conclusion that followed from that for East Germany's population was clear: "The Soviet Union was not an obstacle to unification any longer—they could act now."[55] If so, then Gorbachev's visit to West Germany accelerated the process that led to the Wall's fall. Yet, after Krenz replaced Honecker in October 1989, Gorbachev assured him that no German unification was in sight: "You must know: No serious political figure—not Thatcher, Mitterrand, Andreotti, or Jaruzelski, not even the Americans, though their position has recently exhibited some nuances—are looking forward to German unification. In today's situation that would probably be explosive. The majority of Western leaders do not want to see the dissolution of NATO or the Warsaw Treaty Organization."[56]

On October 9, 1989, exactly a month before the Wall was breached, Anatoly Chernyaev wrote in his diary that throughout Europe "everybody says in a single voice—nobody needs one Germany."[57]

When news first reached Moscow that the Berlin Wall had been breached, Soviet troops in East Germany were ordered to stay in the barracks. There was to be no bloodshed. Chancellor Kohl was in Warsaw on November 9, talking to Solidarity leader Lech Wałesa about the situation in East Germany and the effect it could have on the Polish reform. Had Honecker embarked on reform two years earlier, said Kohl, that "might have worked. But now in the face of demonstrations by 500,000 people in Leipzig, 600,000–700,000 people in Berlin, it is too late. One can no longer align with the police and tanks against such a crowd of people. Gorbachev also realizes this."[58] Upon hearing the news about the Wall, Kohl rushed back to Berlin to see it with his own eyes.

After witnessing the fall of the Wall, Kohl called Bush first:

I've just arrived from Berlin. It is like witnessing an enormous fair. It has the atmosphere of a festival. The frontiers are absolutely open. At certain points they are literally taking down the wall and building new checkpoints. At Checkpoint Charlie, thousands of people are crossing both ways. They are mainly young people who are coming over for a visit and enjoying our open way of life. I expect they will go home tonight.[59]

Next, Kohl called Gorbachev to reassure him: "I recently told you that we did not want a destabilization of the situation in the GDR. I am still of the same position." He reiterated several times that he expected East Germans to return to East Berlin. "We want the Germans to be able to build their future at home." He promised Gorbachev he'd keep in close touch and discuss new developments as they emerged.[60]

During this historic phone call, Gorbachev spoke to Kohl as partner to partner, without alarm or anxiety, referring to previous conversations and their shared understanding of the European process: "I understand that all Europeans, and not only Europeans, are closely following developments in the GDR. This is a very important point in world politics. But it is also a fact that you and I—the FRG and the Soviet Union—have even more interest in these developments both because of the history, and because of the character of our relations today."[61] For Gorbachev, Kohl's reassurance meant they still shared the goal of a common European home. Within this framework, the fall of the Wall did not appear so significant; after all, other borders had been breached—between Hungary and Austria for example—and nothing earth-shattering happened.

After talking to Kohl, Gorbachev looked forward to a summit meeting with President Bush on Malta in December. It might be that he even contemplated the idea of a U.S.-Soviet condominium to resolve the future of Eastern Europe, as his tentative mentioning of this issue during the Malta meetings have shown. In the meantime, however, while Gorbachev returned to his domestic troubles, Kohl reversed course, deciding to use the momentum produced by the Wall's fall to jump-start unification on his own terms. In secret, without even consulting with Bush, he started preparing a ten-point plan for unification. Bush wanted to talk with him before Malta, but, in an unprecedented fashion, Kohl was too busy to see the U.S. president.[62]

Kohl delivered his "ten-point" address to the Bundestag on November 28. The decisive sixth point called for the unification of Germany based on free and democratic elections rather than negotiations between FRG and GDR. The immediate shock of Kohl's program did not register with Gorbachev, who was on his way to Malta, still assuming that Bush was on his side. But at Malta Bush gently warned Gorbachev that the United States "could not be expected to oppose the German unification"; shortly afterwards, Bush expressed full support for Kohl's ten-point platform at a NATO meeting in Brussels. Meanwhile, no West European leader spoke out publicly against Kohl's program.

Gorbachev felt betrayed. At a meeting with West German Foreign Minister Hans Dietrich Genscher on December 5, the Soviet leader exploded. He had expected Kohl to consult with Moscow before announcing his ten points, but "he probably already thinks that his music is playing, a march, and that he is already marching with it." He called the ten points "an ultimatum," "interference in internal affairs," a reversal of commitments and understandings previously reached with Kohl. Shevardnadze, who was also present, referred to Hitler, and Gorbachev reminded Genscher, "You have to remember what mindless politics has led to in the past." What Kohl had done with his ten points was to "prepare a funeral for the European process." Kohl was "rushing, ... artificially stimulating the events, and by doing that, he is undermining the European process that is being developed with such difficulty."[63]

The next day Gorbachev complained bitterly to Mitterrand about what Kohl had done. Mitterrand said he would do everything to keep the European process going:

> I am true to my duty—to preserve the balance in Europe. We should not change the order of the processes. First and foremost among them should be European integration, the evolution of Eastern Europe, the all-European process, the creation of peaceful order in Europe. If the

United States participates in these processes it would give all of us additional guarantees. Kohl's speech, his ten points, has turned everything upside down. He mixed all the factors together, he is rushing. I told Genscher about it, and he did not oppose my conclusions very much.[64]

But Mitterrand wouldn't openly oppose German unification publicly either. And even Thatcher remained conveniently silent. Only now did Gorbachev appreciate the real meaning of what had happened in Berlin on November 9.

In January and February 1990, Gorbachev and Shevardnadze tried to slow the pace of German unification, arguing that haste would destabilize the continent and undermine prospects for a common European home. But what was the alternative? Gorbachev's main expert on Germany, Valentin Falin, favored a confederation of two states, but a larger group of advisers (Ryzhkov, Shevardnadze, Medvedev, KGB chief Vladimir Kryuchkov, Defense Minister Dmitry Yazov, Chief of the General Staff Sergei Akhromeev, Yakovlev, Chernyaev, and Shakhnazarov) concluded that instead of trying to revive a dying GDR, Moscow should accept a united Germany with external constraints on its behavior.[65] The main issue now, Gorbachev insisted, was to keep a united Germany out of NATO. To achieve that, he would be "prepared to suspend both Vienna negotiations on conventional arms and the U.S.-Soviet START talks" on strategic weapons.[66] When U.S. Secretary of State James Baker came to Moscow for talks on February 9, 1989, Gorbachev agreed to the 2+4 formula [two Germanies and four victorious World War II powers: Soviet Union, United States, Great Britain and France to negotiate the external aspects of German unification] but argued for the neutrality of the future German state. The Soviet leader reiterated the key point of the Soviet position that any expansion of NATO jurisdiction to the East was unacceptable to the Soviet Union, and he understood Baker to promise that, whatever the form of association between the future united Germany and NATO, there would be no further NATO expansion. As Gorbachev himself notes in his memoirs, that promise made by Baker "became the core of the formula on the basis of which the compromise on the military-political status of Germany was subsequently reached. But at that time, I was still not prepared to accept it."[67] In the light of that reassurance, however, Gorbachev began to modify his position, bracing himself to agree to German NATO membership, provided that the alliance's jurisdiction did not extend further to the east.

Meanwhile, all-German elections were held on March 18, 1990. East Germans voted overwhelmingly for Kohl's Christian Democratic Party, signaling their wish to be incorporated into West Germany. Negotiations between the two Germanies quickly culminated in the Unification Treaty, while other talks, including those between the four postwar occupying powers, produced a treaty guaranteeing full sovereignty to the newly unified German state. Throughout the spring, Gorbachev's formal position, expressed publicly and in talks with Western leaders, remained that German membership in NATO would be unacceptable. However, he "did not find much support from anybody, even from members of the Warsaw Treaty, including Poland."[68] During his visit to Washington, on May 31, 1990, Gorbachev accepted what now seemed to be inevitable. Some members of his own delegation were surprised, but he concluded that all other nonmilitary options were exhausted. In Chernyaev's words,

> When the economic situation inside the country started to deteriorate rapidly and Gorbachev realized that the whole prospect of continuing political reform was at stake, he came to the conclusion that gaining Germany—the state and a great nation, not specifically Kohl or Genscher—as a strategic ally for the future was certainly more important that to continue small disputes over formulas. This decision became part of his general determination to save perestroika.[69]

All the Soviet-German issues were finally settled during Gorbachev's meeting with Kohl in July 1990 in Arkhyz in the north Caucasus, and the final unification treaties were signed in Bonn in November.

Taken together, these developments meant the end of Gorbachev's European dream. Instead of a gradual process of reunification, West Germany swallowed the GDR. Instead of slow rapprochement between the two blocs, followed by the construction of a new all-European security system, the Warsaw Pact dissolved while NATO expanded, at first into East Germany, and later, after Gorbachev left power, all the way to the very borders of Russia itself.

For Westerners, Gorbachev's restraint added to his glory as the man who transformed communism and ended the Cold War. But his own people view him somewhat differently. In the eyes of some Russians, and not just those whose nationalism verges on fascism, Gorbachev's policies led to chaos at home and defeat abroad. They see 1989 not as a miraculous year, when peaceful revolutions transformed Europe, but as the time when the Soviet Union "lost" Eastern Europe, along with other fruits of its hard-won victory in the Great Patriotic War, without getting anything in return—no massive economic aid package, no "Marshall Plan," no integration with Western Europe. Eastern Europe, one might say, used its opportunities to the fullest in 1989. Both the West and the Soviet Union, Gorbachev would say, missed theirs—to achieve truly lasting peace and cooperation between the former Cold War adversaries by (as he put it to British Foreign Secretary Douglas Hurd in September 1991) making "irreversible the integration of this enormous country into the international community.[70]

In Russia today, many condemn Gorbachev's immediate successor, Boris Yeltsin, for deepening their "time of troubles" by administering economic "shock therapy" and acquiescing in NATO expansion in Poland, Hungary, and Czechoslovakia. Vladimir Putin, Yeltsin's successor, accepted further NATO expansion (in Eastern Europe and the Baltic states) at a time of extreme Russian weakness. But as rising oil and gas prices got Russia back on its feet, Putin emerged as a kind of anti-Gorbachev/Yeltsin, rebuilding authoritarianism domestically, turning against the West, and garnering unprecedented popularity in the process.

Could things have turned out differently? What if Gorbachev had taken advice from Honecker and Ceauşescu and used force against East European reformers? What if he had bargained harder, making the Western powers pay a higher price for German unification and entry into NATO? What if his refusal to do either of these things had led to his overthrow and replacement by those with fewer compunctions? What if instead of ending, the Cold War had turned hot?

All these are what historians call "counter-factuals," alternative scenarios of what didn't happen. What did happen was what Chernyaev foresaw on November 10, what Gorbachev initially failed fully to understand but accepted, with remarkably good grace, in the end.

NOTES

1. Anatoly S. Chernyaev Diary, November 10, 1989, translated by Anna Melyakova and Svetlana Savranskaya. Manuscript on file at the National Security Archive, Washington, D.C.

2. *V Politburo TsK KPSS...Po Zapisyam Anatoliya Chernyaeva, Vadima Medvedeva, Georgiya Shakhnazarova (1985–1991)* (Moscow: Gorbachev-Fond, 2008). All translations of Russian documents are by Svetlana Savranskaya unless otherwise noted, 557.

3. Gorbachev-Kohl conversation, November 11, 1989, Gorbachev Foundation Archive (GFA), Moscow, Fond 1, opis 1.

4. See especially Jacques Levesque, *The Enigma of 1989: The USSR and the Liberation of Eastern Europe* (Berkeley: University of California Press, 1997); Archie Brown, *The Gorbachev Factor* (Oxford: Oxford University Press, 1996); and William Wohlforth, ed., *Cold War Endgame: Oral History, Analysis, Debate* (University Park: Penn State University Press, 2003).

5. *V Politburo TsK KPSS,* 557. A full set of Politburo records is available at the Gorbachev Foundation Archive, Moscow. Subsequent references in these notes to the Gorbachev Foundation Archive in Moscow will be made using the abbreviation GFA.

6. Vadim Medvedev, *V Komande Gorbacheva* (Moscow, 1994), 103.

7. Politburo session, March 2, 1989, GFA, Shakhnazarov notes, Fond 3.

8. Politburo session, February 16, 1989, *V Politburo TsK KPSS,* 459.

9. Yegor Gaidar, *Gibel Imperii: Uroki dlya sovremennoi Rossii* (Moscow: ROSSPEN, 2006), 248.

10. Ibid., 251.

11. Yuli Kvitsinsky, *Vremya i sluchai: Zametki professionala* (Moscow: Olma-Press, 1999), 487, 543.

12. Gaidar, *Gibel Imperii,* 338.

13. Politburo session, March 28, 1989, GFA, Fond 4, opis 1.

14. Ibid.

15. Politburo Commission session, February 18, 1989, GFA, Fond 2, opis 1.

16. Politburo session, February 16, 1989, *V Politburo TsK KPSS,* 465.

17. Anatoly Chernyaev Diary, December 10, 1988.

18. Politburo session, May 11, 1989, *V Politburo TsK KPSS,* 494.

19. See Dobrynin Memorandum to Gorbachev, September 18, 1988; Gorbachev discussion with advisers, October 31, 1988; Politburo session, November 3, 1988; Anatoly Chernyaev Diary, November 3, 1988—documents on file at the National Security Archive, electronic posting EBB 261, www.nsaarchive.org.

20. Andrei Grachev, *Gorbachev's Gamble* (London: Polity, 2008), 203.

21. Memorandum of conversation, U.S. Ambassador Jack Matlock–Aleksandr Yakovlev, December 26, 1988, GARF, Fond 100063, opis 2, delo 148.

22. George H. W. Bush and Brent Scowcroft, *A World Transformed* (New York: Alfred A. Knopf, 1998), 41–44.

23. Grachev, *Gorbachev's Gamble,* 205–207.

24. Memorandum of conversation, U.S. Ambassador Jack Matlock–Aleksandr Yakovlev, December 26, 1988, GARF, Fond 100063, opis 2, delo 148.

25. Politburo session, January 24, 1989, *V Politburo TsK KPSS,* 449.

26. Memorandum from Anatoly Chernyaev to Alexander Yakovlev on Germany and Eastern Europe, March 10, 1986, GFA, Fond 2, opis 2.

27. *Vital Speeches of the Day* 55.23 (9/15/1989):706–11.

28. Yuri Kashlev, *Helsinskii Protsess 1975–2005: Svet i Teni Glazami Uchastnika,* (Moscow: Izvestia, 2005), 154–57, 172–75.

29. *V Politburo TsK KPSS,* 176–77.

30. Interview with Nikolai Shmelev, July 12, 2006, Moscow.

31. Chernyaev memorandum to Vadim Zagladin, February 4, 1989, GFA, Chernyaev notes, Fond 2, opis 2.

32. *Vital Speeches of the Day* 55.23 (9/15/1989): 706–11.

33. Georgy Shakhnazarov memorandum to Gorbachev, October 14, 1989, GFA, Fond 3, opis 1.

34. Memorandum of conversation of Mikhail Gorbachev and Margaret Thatcher, September 23, 1989 GFA, Moscow, Fond 1, opis. 1; Memorandum of conversation of Alexander Yakovlev and Zbigniew Brzezinski, October 31, 1989, GARF Fond 10063, Opis 1.

35. Mikhail Gorbachev, *Zhizn' i reform* (Moscow: Novosti Press, 1995), 2:318.

36. Karen Dawisha, *Eastern Europe, Gorbachev and Reform: The Great Challenge* (Cambridge: Cambridge University Press, 1990), 180.

37. Memorandum of conversation of Mikhail Gorbachev and Josef Czyrek, September 23, 1989, GFA, Fond 1, opis 1.

38. Summary of conversations between Karoly Grosz, Janos Berecz, Miklós Németh, Matyas Szuros, and Alexander Yakovlev, November 10–11, 1988, GARF, Fond 10063, opis 1.

39. Mlynar Zdenek on Gorbachev's visit to Prague, GFA, Shakhnazarov notes, Fond 3, opis 1.

40. Record of conversation between Mikhail Gorbachev and members of the CC SED Politburo, October 7, 1989, GFA, Chernyaev notes, Fond 2, opis 2.

41. Politburo session, January 21, 1989, GFA, Fond 2, opis 1.

42. Record of conversations between Mikhail Gorbachev and Karoly Grosz, March 23–24, 1989, MOL M-KS-288–11/4458.

43. Record of conversation between Mikhail Gorbachev and Miklós Németh, March 3, 1989, GFA, Chernyaev notes, Fond 2, opis 2.

44. Grachev, *Gorbachev's Gamble*, 203.

45. Record of Conversation between Mikhail Gorbachev and Vojciech Jaruzelski, April 13, 1990, GFA, Fond 1, opis 1.

46. Memorandum of telephone conversation between George H. W. Bush and Helmut Kohl, June 15, 1989, George Bush Presidential Library.

47. Record of third conversation between Mikhail Gorbachev and Helmut Kohl, June 14, 1989, GFA, Fond 1, opis 1.

48. Grachev, *Gorbachev's Gamble*, 205.

49. Memorandum of telephone conversation between George H. W. Bush and Helmut Kohl, June 15, 1989, George Bush Presidential Library.

50. Record of conversation between Mikhail Gorbachev and Margaret Thatcher, April 6, 1989, GFA, Fond 1, opis 1.

51. Record of conversation between Mikhail Gorbachev and Margaret Thatcher, September 23, 1989, GFA, Chernyaev notes, Fond 2, opis 2.

52. Record of conversation between Alexander Yakovlev and Henry Kissinger, January 16, 1989, GARF, Fond 10063, opis 1. Record of conversation between Mikhail Gorbachev and Henry Kissinger, January 17, 1989, GFA, Chernyaev notes, Fond 2, opis 2.

53. Memorandum of conversation of Alexander Yakovlev and Zbigniew Brzezinski, October 31, 1989, GARF, Fond 10063, opis. 1.

54. Anatoly Chernyaev, *Shest' Let s Gorbachevym* (Moscow: Progress Kultura, 1993), 246.

55. Ibid., 291.

56. Record of conversation between Mikhail Gorbachev and Egon Krenz, November 1, 1989, GFA, Fond 1, opis 1.

57. Anatoly Chernyaev Diary, October 9, 1989.

58. Record of conversation between Helmut Kohl and Lech Walesa, November 9, 1989, published as document 76 in *Dokumente zur Deutschland Politik; Deutsche Einheit: Sonderedition aus den Akten des Bundeskanzleramtes 1989/90,* edited by Hans Jurgen Kusters and Daniel Hoffmann (Munich: Oldenbourg Verlag, 1998), 492–96.

59. Record of conversation between George H. W. Bush and Helmut Kohl, November 10, 1989, George Bush Presidential Library.

60. Record of conversation between Mikhail Gorbachev and Helmut Kohl, November 11, 1989, GFA, Fond 1, opis 1.

61. Ibid.

62. Record of telephone conversation between George H. W. Bush and Helmut Kohl, November 17, 1989, George Bush Presidential Library.

63. Record of conversation between Mikhail Gorbachev and Hans Dietrich Genscher, December 5, 1989, GFA, Fond 1, opis 1.

64. Record of conversation between Mikhail Gorbachev and François Mitterrand, December 6, 1989, GFA, Fond 1, opis 1.

65. Gorbachev meeting with Central Committee members on Germany, January 26, 1990, GFA, Fond 2, opis 2.

66. Grachev, *Gorbachev's Gamble,* 153.

67. Gorbachev, *Zhizn i Reformy,* 167.

68. Mikhail Gorbachev, *Ponyat' Perestroiku…Pochemu eto vazhno seychas* (Moscow: Al'pina Biznes Buks, 2006), 249.

69. Cited in Grachev, *Gorbachev's Gamble,* 158.

70. Record of conversation between Mikhail Gorbachev and Douglas Hurd, September 10, 1991, GFA, Fond 1, opis 1.

Chapter 4

TIANANMEN AND THE FALL OF THE BERLIN WALL: CHINA'S PATH TOWARD 1989 AND BEYOND

Chen Jian

On the morning of May 16, 1989, China's paramount leader, Deng Xiaoping, arrived in high spirits at the Great Hall of the People, located at Tiananmen Square in the center of Beijing. He was there to meet Mikhail Gorbachev, the first head of the Soviet Union to visit China in thirty years. The meeting went well. Deng briefly reviewed the history of cooperation and conflict between the Chinese and Soviet parties and states. While defending Beijing's stand in the Chinese-Soviet split—mainly by emphasizing that this was caused by Beijing's consciousness that "the Chinese have not been treated as equals and thus felt humiliated"—he acknowledged that, like Moscow, Beijing also "had made some mistakes" in the Chinese-Soviet polemic leading to the split. The thrust of Deng's presentation, though, was not about the past but about the present and the future. Deng stressed that as socialist countries both China and the Soviet Union were facing critical challenges. Therefore, contended Deng, Beijing and Moscow should "close the past, open the future."[1] It seemed that Gorbachev echoed Deng's opinion, telling him that the Soviets were very pleased to see that a new and promising phase in relations between the two parties and countries was being unfolded, which would be beneficial not only to the two parties and countries but also to the cause of socialism and communism in the world.[2]

What Deng and Gorbachev had reached was a strategic consensus about enhancing Sino-Soviet relations. They certainly did not mean that Beijing and Moscow should return to the golden age of the Sino-Soviet alliance in the 1950s. Yet they clearly hoped that the Beijing-Moscow rapprochement would strengthen both countries' position in managing domestic challenges, while, at the same time, enhancing their positions in international affairs. Furthermore, the meeting also meant that for the first time since the late 1950s and early 1960s, the international Communist movement would not be burdened by the animosity and mutual exclusion of two of its most important members. Given the historical context in which this meeting was held and the multiple meanings associated with it, the Deng-Gorbachev summit should have occupied a central position in the chronicle of 1989.

However, the history of 1989 unfolded in a direction drastically different from Deng's and Gorbachev's expectations. Even as the two leaders met at the Great Hall of the People, hundreds of students from universities throughout Beijing were holding a collective hunger strike to protest widespread corruption and to strive for genuine political reforms. Four days after the Deng-Gorbachev summit, the Chinese Communist Party (CCP) leadership, headed by Deng, responded by imposing martial law in Beijing. When the student protest persisted, Deng and other CCP elders decided to use force to crush it. On June 4, People's Liberation Army (PLA) soldiers fought their way into Tiananmen Square, causing the deaths of an unknown number of students and Beijing residents.[3]

The Tiananmen tragedy stunned the world and shocked the entire Communist bloc. The summer and fall of 1989 witnessed great unrest throughout East Europe, eroding the political foundation and undermining the legitimacy of every Communist regime there. The process culminated on November 9–10, 1989, when the uprising masses brought down the Berlin Wall—the physical and symbolic dividing line of the East and the West since the early 1960s. By the end of 1989, with the execution of Romania's Communist dictator Nicolae Ceauşescu, the Communist bloc in East Europe had virtually collapsed. By the end of 1991, even the Soviet Union had ceased to exist. Along with the failure of international Communism as a twentieth-century phenomenon, the global Cold War ended in ways that neither Deng nor Gorbachev could have imagined in May 1989.

It is apparent that the Tiananmen tragedy occupies a crucial position in the chain of events of 1989, especially given the huge political and moral damage that it had inflicted on the international Communist movement, undermining the proposition that communism could provide an alternative to liberal capitalism as the preferred path toward modernity. Yet, ironically, the Chinese Communist regime survived the shockwaves of 1989. After a three-year period of stagnation, Deng used a dramatic tour of southern China in spring 1992 to regenerate the "reform and opening-up" project, initiated by Deng and the CCP leadership in the late 1970s. What has followed, as is well known today, is China's rapid economic growth—despite continuous stagnation in the country's political democratization—in the last decade of the twentieth century and entering the twenty-first century.

Why did the Tiananmen tragedy occur in 1989? What were its immediate and long-range causes as well as the domestic and international context? What position does it occupy in the shaping and unfolding of 1989 as a landmark year in world history? Why and how has the CCP and the Chinese Communist state not only survived the collapse of international Communism but also thrived, as China has steadily risen as a prominent world power? In order to understand the rich and complex meanings of 1989, these are crucial questions to answer.

Twenty years after the Tiananmen tragedy and the fall of the Berlin Wall, we have gained some perspective on those events, their causes, and their immediate consequences. Still China's story in 1989—how China shaped the specific course of that year's events and helped define the immediate aftermath— remains full of questions.[4] In China itself, 1989 has been a "forbidden zone" in press, scholarship, and classroom teaching. After twenty years, it remains inconceivable for scholars to access Chinese archival sources and many other key documents related to 1989.[5] However, we cannot allow these difficulties to block our pursuit of a more comprehensive understanding of the Chinese story of 1989—especially given the story's tremendous scholarly significance and contemporary relevance. This chapter attempts to reconstruct the Chinese story of 1989—its origins, processes, and aftermaths as viewed from both Chinese and global perspectives.

FROM THE FAILURE OF MAO'S REVOLUTION TO THE RISE OF DENG'S REFORMS

There are many different angles from which the origins of 1989 can be explored. From a historical perspective, such central events of 1989 as the Tiananmen tragedy and the fall of the Berlin Wall resulted from the accumulated legitimacy crises entangling international Communism in general and each and every Communist state in particular. In order to define and illustrate China's path toward 1989, it seems appropriate to begin by discussing how the legitimacy challenges facing the Chinese Communist state evolved.

That Mao's China had faced profound legitimacy challenges throughout the twenty-seven years of Mao's reign is a critical yet insufficiently researched issue in studies of modern China and the international Cold War. Even less studied is how, in Mao's response to the challenges, the emphasis of the legitimate foundation of the People's Republic of China (PRC) shifted from an extreme, utopian version of communism to nationalism and patriotism. This shift is of critical importance for understanding why and how the PRC was brought to 1989 and survived it.

In 1949, when the "new China" emerged, Mao announced to the whole world that "the Chinese people have stood up."[6] This was a legitimacy statement, and Mao substantiated it by establishing two fundamental missions for his "revolution after revolution": to change China into a land of universal justice, equality, and prosperity and to revive China's central position in the international community. By appealing to the Chinese people's unique "victim mentality"—a conviction that it was political incursion, economic exploitation, and military aggression by foreign imperialist countries that had undermined the historical glory of Chinese civilization and humiliated the Chinese nation—the statement reflected Mao's perception of how socialist/communist modernity should be defined while, at the same time, revealing his Chinese-centric mentality in making the definition.

In the international arena, the PRC's rise in the late 1940s had a huge impact on the ongoing global Cold War: It changed the balance of power between the Soviet Union and the United States; it helped bridge the "world proletarian revolution" and the global trend of decolonization in ways that would otherwise have been impossible; and it greatly enhanced the claim by Communists all over the world that "history is on our side." In the meantime, though, China's emergence as a revolutionary country also presented potential challenges to the international Communist movement's unified, existing structure, threatening Moscow's undisputed leadership role in the world proletarian revolution.

Like any communist design for modernization, Mao's was directed by a utopian vision. His extraordinary aspiration of overcoming China's backwardness in the shortest possible time, of transforming China into a modern power, was unable to withstand the test of the Chinese people's lived experience. Especially after the failure of the disastrous "Great Leap Forward," which caused the deaths of tens of millions of ordinary Chinese, the legitimacy of Mao's "continuous revolution" was called into serious question.

Mao responded to the challenge by further "deepening" his "continuous revolution" through even more extensive mass mobilization at home. While doing so, Mao and the CCP increasingly referred to revolutionary nationalism—epitomized in Mao's "the Chinese people have stood up" statement—for winning the Chinese people's "inner support." Within this context, Mao's and the CCP's desire to claim Chinese centrality in the world revolution collided with Moscow's leadership role in the international Communist movement. In the Sino-Soviet polemics of the 1960s, Mao asserted that socialism in the Soviet Union had been eroded by an emerging "bureaucratic capitalist class," causing the restoration of capitalism in Soviet society. In elaborating these "lessons," Mao emphasized that China also faced the danger of "restoration of capitalism." Meanwhile, Mao and the CCP claimed that Moscow had persistently exhibited great-power chauvinism toward Beijing and damaged China's independence and sovereignty. In the early and mid-1960s, with Mao's push, China's domestic politics and social life were rapidly radicalized along with the escalation of the Sino-Soviet debate, leading the country toward the "Great Proletarian Cultural Revolution."[7]

In retrospect, when Mao initiated the Cultural Revolution, he had two interrelated purposes: He hoped that it would provide him with new means to transform China's state, society, and international outlook; and he wanted to use the Cultural Revolution to enhance his much-weakened authority in the wake of the disastrous Great Leap Forward. Mao believed that his strengthened leadership role would best guarantee the success of his revolution.

Although the Cultural Revolution helped Mao destroy his opponents and the "old" party-state control system, it failed to create the new form of state power that Mao desired so much for building a new social order in China. After 1968–69, when Mao ordered the reestablishment of the party-state control system, and especially after the "Lin Biao affair"[8] in September 1971, Mao's revolutionary programs increasingly encountered people's open resistance. A society-wide "crisis of faith" began to creep into the minds of millions and millions of everyday Chinese, causing them to question the ultimate benefits of Mao's "continuous revolution" that had lasted in China for over two decades.

The fading status of Mao's revolutions at home was accompanied by a grave security situation abroad. While America's involvement in the Vietnam War placed great pressures on China's southern borders, the hostility between China and the Soviet Union culminated in March 1969, when two bloody clashes erupted between Chinese and Soviet garrisons.[9] The domestic and international conditions combined to spur Beijing to improve relations with the United States. In February 1972, during "the week that changed the world," U.S. President Richard Nixon made a historic trip to China and met with Mao in Beijing.[10]

The Chinese-American rapprochement dramatically shifted the balance of power between the United States and the Soviet Union and, more important,

Erected in 1961, the Berlin Wall physically divided a city, but more importantly separated East from West as a stark reminder of the Cold War's strategic and yet real human impact. *Library of Congress*.

A view of the wall demonstrating its stark Eastern side, including well-patrolled areas off-limits to East German residents, set against its far more colorful Western side complete with personal expressions.

When the Wall finally fell in 1989, jubilation ensued.

East German police stand watch over enthusiastic crowds in December of 1989, after the Wall had ceased to be a real East-West barrier, on the day the Brandenberg Gate officially opened to cross-border traffic.

By late May 1989, upwards of a million Chinese residents crowded Bejing's Tiananmen Square. *By permission of Armin Cantini.*

Speaking to the world as much to their nation, Chinese protests joined their counterparts in Eastern Europe in frequently speaking to global audiences. *By permission of Armin Cantini.*

The Square, only days before soldiers and police cleared it of protesters. *By permission of Armin Cantini.*

Meeting in Malta weeks after the Berlin Wall fell, George Bush and Mikhail Gobachev discussed peaceful ways to end the Cold War without disrupting the newly emerging global order. "This could have been a shouting match," Bush later noted, "but it was very calm." *George Bush Presidential Library and Museum.*

Only a month after the crackdown at Tiananmen and the electoral ouster of Poland's communist government, George Bush visited Eastern Europe to the acclaim of enthusiastic crowds, including this rain-drenched session in Budapest. *George Bush Presidential Library and Museum.*

Bush alongside Lech Walesa, leader of Poland's Solidarity trade union and political movement, in July of 1989. *George Bush Presidential Library and Museum.*

Bush came to office believing Sino-American relations stood on the verge of real progress, largely because of the personal friendship he shared with Den Xioping and other Chinese leaders. In February 1989, the recently inaugurated president visited China, and Deng. *George Bush Presidential Library and Museum.*

Bush and his wife Barbara in February 1989, on the same Tiananmen Square that would, within only a few months, be the scene of such drama and heartbreak. *George Bush Presidential Library and Museum.*

changed the essence of the Cold War. Ever since the Cold War had begun in the mid- and late 1940s, it had been characterized by a fundamental confrontation between communism and liberal capitalism. The Chinese-American rapprochement obscured the distinctions between socialist and capitalist paths toward modernity. The Sino-Soviet split buried the shared consciousness among Communists in the world that communism was the most workable solution to the problems created by the worldwide process of modernization.

It was against this backdrop that Mao introduced his "Three Worlds" theory with the hope that it would make sense of China's changed international policies while, at the same time, defending the legitimacy of his failed "continuous revolution." The Chinese chairman asserted:

> The U.S. and the Soviet Union belong to the First World. The middle elements, such as Japan, Europe, Australia and Canada, belong to the Second World. We are the Third World....The U.S. and the Soviet Union have a lot of atomic bombs, and they are richer. Europe, Japan, Australia and Canada, of the Second World, do not possess so many atomic bombs and are not so rich as the First World, but richer than the Third World....All Asian countries, except Japan, and all of Africa and also Latin America belong to the Third World.[11]

On April 10, 1974, Deng Xiaoping, head of the Chinese delegation attending U.N. General Assembly, publicly presented Mao's "Three Worlds" notion, emphasizing that the "Third World" was formed by the vast majority of *developing* countries in Asia, Africa, and Latin America.[12]

Mao's "Three Worlds" theory challenged the existing world order. But it was not a simple repetition of any of Mao's previous international statements, formatted around the discourse of "international class struggle." What formed the primary concern of the "Three Worlds" theory was the issue of economic development. As far as the theory's basic *problematique* is concerned, it already highlighted "development" as a question of fundamental importance for China.

In the meantime, with Mao's approval, a "Four Modernizations" discourse entered China's domestic affairs. At a speech to the People's Congress (the Chinese equivalent of a national parliament) in January 1975, Premier Zhou Enlai announced that China should aim to modernize its industry, agriculture, national defense, and science and technology by the end of the century.[13]

How could Mao, who had championed transforming China and the world in revolutionary ways, put forward the development-oriented "Three Worlds" theory and accept the "Four Modernizations" representation toward the end of his life? This was Mao's way of dealing with the worsening legitimacy crisis that his "continuous revolution" had been facing. Ever since Mao proclaimed, at the time of the PRC's formation, that "the Chinese people have stood up," he legitimated his "revolution after revolution" by repeatedly emphasizing how his revolutionary programs would change China into a country of "wealth and power." When the Chinese communist state was encountering an ever deepening legitimacy crisis as the result of the economic stagnation and political cruelty that resulted from Mao's revolutions, the CCP chairman embraced the "Three Worlds" and "Four Modernizations" notions to emphasize—first and foremost to the Chinese people—that his revolutions continuously play a central role in benefiting China and transforming the world. At the moment that he gave such emphasis to "development," however, Mao opened a door that he did not mean to open, and the insurmountable boundary between revolutionary China and the "outside world" began to erode.

Mao died on September 9, 1976. After a short period of political transition, with Mao's hand-picked successor Hua Guofeng as China's nominal head, Deng Xiaoping emerged as China's paramount leader. The most influential event in Deng's ascendance happened in the ideological field. After Mao's death, for the purpose of consolidating his position, Hua and some of his close associates sloganeered that "whatever policy Chairman Mao supported, we shall resolutely defend; whatever policy Chairman Mao opposed, we shall resolutely oppose." On May 11, 1978, *Guangming Daily,* a Party ideological organ, published an essay, "Practice Is the Sole Criteria to Judge Truth," which argued that whether a theory represented the truth must be tested and proven by practice. Behind those favoring "practice being the sole criteria of truth" was Deng, who supported it for breaking the restrictions that Mao and his "continuous revolution" had imposed upon China.[14] Winning the debate paved the way for Deng to introduce the "reform and opening" policies at the Third Plenary Session of the CCP's Eleventh Central Committee, held in Beijing in December 1978. China had since entered an age of "reform and opening-up," which, in retrospect, prepared conditions for China to approach 1989 and survive the challenges of that year.

PARADOXES OF DENG'S REFORMS: CHINA'S PATH TOWARD 1989

Deng's reform and opening project was first of all a de-revolutionization process, launched, on one level, for coping with the profound legitimacy crisis that the failure of Mao's revolutions had generated. The specific ways by which Deng and the CCP leadership envisioned and carried out the project, however, though easing some of the legitimacy pressure caused by the failure of Mao's revolutions, created new legitimacy challenges for the Chinese Communist state while dividing further the international Communist movement. It was the paradoxes of Deng's reforms that opened China's path toward 1989.

Unlike Mao's "continuous revolution," Deng initiated the reform and opening project without a "grand blueprint." The temporary feature of Deng's project was clearly indicated in the statement that it was like "crossing the river by stepping on one stone after another." Following his pragmatic "cat theory"—"black cat or white cat, so long as it catches mice, it is a good cat"— Deng emphasized that primacy of economics must take over that of politics. He looked to experiences of the capitalist West for defining China's path toward modernity.

The reform process first began in the Chinese countryside, and it was the peasants who started it. In 1978, peasants in one of the poorest villages in the county of Fengyang, in the province of Anhui, took the initiative to challenge the People's Communes' collective-control principles by secretly adopting a "relating production and distribution to households" practice that linked a family's income to its labor input. Although the practice encountered suppression at first, it gained recognition and support from reform-minded provincial leaders and, eventually, from Deng himself; they saw in it the prospect of significantly increasing China's agricultural production. In September 1980, the CCP leadership decided to approve the adoption of a "family-based responsibility system" in the Chinese countryside, which ultimately played the role to undermine the People's Commune system that had existed in China since the late 1950s.[15]

The reform efforts then extended to the cities, where material incentive had long been desired by ordinary workers as a force necessary for promoting productivity, yet had been suppressed by Maoist regulations. Beginning in 1979, Deng and the CCP leadership approved a series of reform measures in China's state-owned enterprises, which put increasing productivity and making profit as the enterprises' central task, opening the door for them to get out of the tight control of the state planning system. In 1979–80, with Deng's support, the CCP leadership made the decision to establish "special economic development zones" in four coastal cities, where special policies were carried out for attracting international investments. In the meantime, the Chinese government allowed privately owned business and Chinese-foreign jointly owned ventures to exist together with state-owned enterprises. In 1982, the CCP's Twelfth Congress formally accepted that "multiple forms of ownerships" should be allowed "for the promotion of socialist economic reconstruction."[16]

Within the above context, Beijing's leaders significantly broadened the scope of China's international connections through such steps as dispatching Chinese students to study abroad, promoting China's international trade with Western countries, and welcoming foreign investments. Throughout the Maoist era, markets and the pursuit of profits were viewed as values and practices alien to genuine socialism. Now, the CCP leadership adopted a more open approach toward the capitalist-dominated world market. When Deng and his fellow Chinese leaders perceived China's path toward modernity, they looked to the West for models to formulate China's own development strategy. This was a drastic departure from the Chinese experience of building socialism in the 1950s and 1960s, when China wholeheartedly embraced the Soviet model—characterized by a rigid state-controlled planning system. All of this formed a critical point of departure for China to change gradually from an outsider to an insider of the existing international system, dominated by the capitalist West.

These basic changes in China's perception and practice concerning how its path toward modernity should be defined formed the larger context in which Beijing made the strategic decisions toward the continued Cold War confrontation between the two superpowers. Deng attached new meanings to the "tacit alliance" that Beijing had entered with Washington since the Chinese-American rapprochement. The partnership with Washington remained valuable for Beijing in geopolitical and strategic senses. Yet China's tacit alliance with the United States was strategically important, from Deng's perspective, also because it was highly compatible with his new vision of looking to the West for models of modernizing China. Deng thus regarded the PRC's gaining full diplomatic recognition from the United States as a top priority goal. On January 1, 1979, formal diplomatic relations was established between Beijing and Washington.[17]

China's strengthened cooperation with the United States and the West was accompanied by heightened confrontation with the Soviet Union in the late 1970s and early 1980s. Beijing persistently regarded Moscow as its primary enemy. Even the improvement in China's relations with various Soviet bloc countries in Eastern Europe did not help mitigate the hostility between Beijing and Moscow. Beijing's rapidly deteriorating relations with Hanoi, which sunk to the lowest point when Vietnam occupied Cambodia and China waged a punitive war against the Vietnamese in early 1979, drove Beijing and Moscow to deeper suspicion and hostility.[18]

In addition to geopolitical and security considerations, underlying Beijing's Soviet and Vietnam policies were Deng's and the CCP leadership's needs to identify useful resources for coping with the new yet deepening legitimacy challenges that the Chinese Communist state was facing in the age of "reform and opening." Indeed, China's continued confrontation with Vietnam created a sustained source—one with the power to appeal to the Chinese people's patriotism and nationalistic feelings—of the CCP's domestic mobilization efforts. Throughout the 1980s, popular literature, movies, and music extolling PLA soldiers' heroic fighting against the ungrateful Vietnamese in a "war of self-defense" formed an overwhelming theme in Beijing's campaigns for promoting "love of the socialist motherland."[19] At a time when the reform and opening policies created profound economic inequality within Chinese society and, as a result, increasingly called into question the legitimacy of the Communist regime, the confrontation with Vietnam and Beijing's representation of it to the Chinese people served to retain the support of everyday Chinese for the regime in Beijing.

Beijing's partnership with Washington and confrontation with Moscow shifted the balance of power between the two superpowers continuously in favor of the United States. In a deeper sense, China's market-oriented reform and opening, together with its denunciation of the Soviet Union, further undermined the notion that communism remained a viable alternative to the capitalist path toward modernity. Consequently, the Soviet Union and its bloc experienced increasing pressures in their efforts to sustain the course of the global Cold War.

By the mid-1980s, it had become evident that the reform and opening process was indeed extraordinary in bringing about profound changes to China. In particular, it—driven by the magic forces of "market"—led to rapid growth in the Chinese economy and resulted in visible changes in Chinese society. China's agricultural and industrial products had registered significant increases; the widespread poverty that characterized everyday life in the Maoist era was in retreat; and the state's rigid control over Chinese society had been exchanged for greater flexibility in citizens' social and personal life, unprecedented in the history of the PRC.[20]

But the legacies of China's age of revolution remained deep and influential. Ever since launching the reform and opening project, Deng—a veteran Communist revolutionary himself—had repeatedly stressed that the emphasis of the reform process lay in the economic field, and he and the CCP leadership had endeavored to make politics a forbidden zone in the age of reform and opening. When the reform era began, Deng simultaneously introduced the "four basic principles," emphasizing that in no circumstances should the principles of (1) socialism, (2) the proletarian dictatorship, (3) the Communist Party's leadership role, and (4) the guidance of Marxism-Leninism and Mao's thought be compromised.[21] In early 1979, when Deng had consolidated his political power, he ordered to discontinue the "democracy wall" in Beijing. Deng and the CCP leadership repeatedly called on the whole party to fight against "bourgeois liberalization," warning ordinary Chinese that they should boycott the "spiritual pollution" of Western influence.[22]

Deng and his fellow CCP leaders also decided that they would not discard the "banner of Mao," despite the party's abandonment of the Maoist discourses since the late 1970s.[23] A party resolution on its history adopted in 1981 contended that "without Chairman Mao's leadership role, China and the Chinese revolution would have been still creeping in darkness."[24] Out of consideration of coping with the legitimacy challenges that the Chinese state had been facing, the CCP leadership presented Mao's legacies increasingly in nationalistic and patriotic terms. The greatest achievements of Mao's revolution, asserted Deng, were that it unified China, industrialized the country, and revived its greatness in world affairs.[25]

By the mid-1980s, the paradoxes of the reform process became more complex. Despite the rapid changes that the reforms had brought to China, they could not match people's expectations. Deng did everything possible to place the reforms under the CCP's control. By doing so, however, he also made the party the sole force of responsibility for all the negative effects that the reforms had produced. In particular, the increasingly rampant corruption among party and government officials, together with the widening gap between the rich and the poor (which Mao had tried to erase as China's ruler), inevitably caused millions and millions of ordinary Chinese to question the CCP's monopoly on China's political power. They were also asking a critical question: If the ideas embodied in communism were no longer in a position to define China's path toward modernity, which "-ism" (if any) could take over this constitutional mission? Failure to answer this basic question resulted in a lingering "crisis of faith" among the Chinese people, especially the younger generation.

Against this background, in late 1986, students at universities and colleges all over China—but especially in Beijing, Shanghai, and Hefei—began to protest. Attributing the spreading corruption among officials to stagnation in China's political reforms, the students held a series of demonstrations, demanding political reforms and decrying corruption. Deng regarded the demonstrations by the students as "unrest" and instructed that measures of both persuasion and, if necessary, coercion be used to bring the demonstration under control. When the protests calmed down, Hu Yaobang, the CCP general secretary who had been widely regarded as an advocate of comprehensive reforms, was forced to resign from his post.[26]

In retrospect, the student movement of 1986 presaged China's 1989 in the sense that it revealed the accumulated tension between Chinese society and the Chinese state. Although Deng succeeded in pacifying student protests, he was unable to solve any of the substantial and deeper problems they had exposed.

Within this context, the mid- and late 1980s witnessed a rising tide of "cultural fever" in China's intellectual life. Like the Chinese intellectuals of the May Fourth era of the early twentieth century, many educated Chinese became increasingly frustrated with the reality that China's "reform and opening" was restricted to economy and technology. These intellectuals used cultural criticism as a weapon to argue for "reform and opening" in politics and political culture. The political agenda of the "cultural fever" was epitomized in the television series *Heshang* (River Elegy). Tracing the origins of China's backwardness in modern times to the early development of Chinese civilization, *Heshang*'s writers emphasized the importance of transforming China's authoritarian political culture.[27] Deng sensed the crisis. He responded with a very superficial call for "exploring possible ways of conducting political reforms" in China.[28] However, no substantive action followed.

What made the situation more complicated for Deng and the CCP leadership was that since the mid-1980s, Mikhail Gorbachev, after becoming the Soviet Communist Party's general secretary, initiated perestroika and glasnost in the Soviet Union, promoting a reform and opening process that put transforming a rigid political structure at the top on its agenda. Many Chinese intellectuals and even party cadres applauded Gorbachev's efforts and called for China's own reform process to be turned to the political sphere.[29] From the beginning, Deng disapproved of Gorbachev's reform strategies. However, to deviate domestic pressure to follow Gorbachev's example—as well as in response to Washington's escalating arms sales to Taiwan, following the election of Ronald Reagan as U.S. president—Deng began seeking to improve China's relations with the Soviet Union and other Soviet bloc countries. On October 9, 1985, Deng asked the Romanian leader Nicolae Ceauşescu to convey a message to Gorbachev that "if the Soviet Union reaches agreement with us on Vietnam's withdrawal from Cambodia and takes action," he would be willing to meet with Gorbachev to discuss improving relations between the two countries.[30] Beginning in 1986, Beijing and Moscow conducted a series of political negotiations to resolve the problems between them and pave the way for a Chinese-Soviet rapprochement.

In the meantime, Deng was fully aware that the reform process was in need of a major breakthrough. Instead of conducting genuine political reforms, he decided to resort to more dramatic measures in transforming China's economic and financial structure. His vision fixed upon the price-disorder issue.

With the "market factor" being brought into the Chinese economy, a "two-way" price structure had appeared: while prices were increasingly set by the market, the prices of many commodities and services remained set with subsidies from the state and thus were much lower than their market values. This "two-way" price structure not only placed a heavy burden on the state, it also became a primary source for corruption. Zhao Ziyang, the reform-minded CCP general secretary and his associates were in favor of price reform; but they also believed that it should be carried out steadily in coordination with reforms in the political field.[31]

Deng, however, thought differently. He viewed restructuring the price system as more than just as an economic issue; for him, it was also a major political issue concerning the legitimacy of the CCP state—especially given his unwillingness to implement political reforms leading to checks and balances. Thus he pushed for the price reform to be introduced in ways that would correct the price disorder in the shortest possible time.[32] In August 1988, the CCP leadership decided to undertake price reforms. In the next five years, they planned, the state's control over and subsidies to prices in most commodities would be eliminated, and prices would thus be adjusted by the market; the price reforms would be accompanied by salary reforms so that most workers' standard of living would not be lowered.[33] When ordinary Chinese citizens learned of the decision, they immediately interpreted it as the prelude to another— and unprecedented—round of price increases. A "scare-driven purchase drive" immediately swept across China's cities and countryside. High inflation followed. China's total sum of commodity sales in August 1988 increased 38.6 percent, compared with that of August 1987, while the country's saving balance decreased by 2.6 billion yuan.[34] Consequently, the Chinese government had no other choice but to halt the price reform.

Setbacks in the price reform brought all the accumulated societal problems to the surface. Most seriously, it greatly increased the "faith crisis" among everyday Chinese by directing it toward the CCP's qualification and capacity to lead the country. China had reached the entrance of 1989.

THE TIANANMEN TRAGEDY

When 1989 began, China's society and economy were in deep disarray. A profound sense of imminent crisis hung over both political elites and everyday people. In a general sense, the majority of the population remained supportive of the reform project. Yet the widening gap between the rich and the poor, high inflation, rampant corruption, and an extraordinary sense of uncertainty concerning what the reforms would lead to created widespread frustration and fear among the people.[35] In the meantime, the division within the party leadership became more evident. Such reform-minded leaders as Zhao Ziyang and his associates were facing fierce challenges from the hard-liners among the party elders, who believed that the reform process had damaged the CCP's control of China's political power and undermined the PRC as a socialist country.[36] Deng himself was often paradoxical and even contradicted himself in describing how the reform should be carried forward. On the one hand, he persistently championed the reform project and called for "continuously emancipating our minds"; on the other, he repeatedly stressed that he firmly opposed the "bourgeoisie liberalization" tendency that the reform processes had generated, emphasizing that China's "overriding need" was "maintenance of stability."[37]

Many Chinese intellectuals, sensing that the reform process had reached a critical juncture, became profoundly worried that it would lose momentum. The most outspoken among the intellectuals began to take action. In early January, Fang Lizhi, a renowned astrophysicist, wrote to Deng to call for a general amnesty on the fortieth anniversary of the People's Republic. He particularly asked for the release of Wei Jingsheng, China's most famous dissident, who once introduced the "fifth modernization" thesis—modernization of China's political structure and institution—and had been imprisoned since 1979.[38] Deng never responded.

Spring 1989 witnessed the rapid rise of pro-democracy tides in East European countries. In the meantime, the Soviet leader Gorbachev was boldly promoting political reforms in the Soviet Union.[39] All of this formed the larger international context in which Chinese intellectuals became increasingly convinced that it was time to shift the emphasis of China's reform project to the political sphere, exploring the prospect of transforming the party-state structure and creating new political institutions with checks and balances. On February 13, thirty-three leading Chinese intellectuals sent an open letter to the People's Congress and the CCP Central Committee, endorsing a general amnesty at the PRC's fortieth anniversary and appealing for Wei Jingsheng's release.[40] On March 8, forty-two distinguished Chinese scientists issued an open letter to the Chinese leadership, contending that "in order to prevent the replay of the tragedy that citizens were punished for expressing different political viewpoints in oral and written ways, the relevant state agencies should be ordered to release all youth who have been imprisoned or placed under 'reeducation through labor' because of thought problems."[41] The Chinese leadership, however, decided to dismiss the petitions from the intellectuals. On March 14, Yuan Mu, a spokesperson of the Chinese government, announced that "since there is no political prisoner in China, there exists no such question of releasing political prisoners."[42]

Yuan's response reflected the dilemmas that the CCP leadership had been facing concerning how to cope with accumulated tensions in Chinese society. Although Deng occasionally talked about the necessity of "carrying out reforms in the political sphere," his fundamental ways of thinking, influenced by his own experience and revolutionary career, were inimical to genuine political reform in China. Deng still strongly favored carrying the reform project forward, but he firmly believed that "adherence to the Party's leadership role" was of primary importance when China's economy, state, and society were experiencing profound transformations. Thus changes in East European countries were particularly troublesome for Deng and many others in Beijing. The CCP leaders held several meetings in March 1989 to discuss "the unrest in East Europe," deciding that "every effort should be made to prevent changes in East Europe from influencing China's internal development."[43]

Since 1986, Beijing and Moscow had conducted a series of negotiations on improving Sino-Soviet relations, but the progress of these talks had been slow until early 1989. Under the huge pressure of accumulated domestic tensions and facing the prospect that international Communism was in deep crisis everywhere in the world, Deng and the CCP leadership saw the need to accelerate the process of normalizing China's state and party relations with the Soviet Union. From their perspective, a new and cooperative relationship with Moscow would help the CCP create a public image that Beijing and Moscow were joining force in reforming socialism, while, at the same time, allowing them to present it as a "great diplomatic achievement" to the Chinese people. Both effects, as Deng and his colleagues hoped, would enhance the CCP's position to deal with the deepened legitimacy crisis that it was facing. After intensive discussions, on February 6, 1989, Chinese Foreign Minister Qian Qichen and Soviet Foreign Minister Eduard Shevardnadze announced in Beijing that Gorbachev would visit China in May.[44]

In mid-April, Hu Yaobang, the reform-minded party leader who was ousted after the 1986 student protest movement, suddenly died from a heart attack. Students in Beijing turned the mourning of Hu into public expression of frustration and anger over widespread corruption and lack of political reforms in China.

Top CCP leaders were divided over how to deal with the student movement. Zhao believed that the students meant to "help the Party" to bring China's reforms to deeper levels. He favored carrying out a policy of affirming the students' motives, encouraging their "patriotic activities," and leading the demonstration by the students in a direction that would benefit reforms. But Premier Li Peng and such party elders as former PRC President Li Xiannian viewed the activities by the students as "signs of turmoil."[45]

On April 22, Hu's memorial was held at the Great Hall of the People. By that time, the majority of the students believed that they had expressed their concerns and were ready to return to their own campuses. Zhao, who left Beijing for a long-planned visit to North Korea after Hu's memorial, also believed that the students would calm down and that the main issue facing the party was how to turn the questions raised by the young people into the dynamics of carrying the reforms forward. Before leaving Beijing, Zhao shared his opinions with Li Peng, who gave Zhao the impression that he agreed with his ideas.[46]

But the situation did not develop as Zhao had expected. On April 24, the CCP Central Committee Politburo held a meeting, at which Chen Xitong and Li Ximiao, respectively mayor and party secretary of Beijing city, claimed that the students' activities were "well-planned and well-organized," which, designed for "challenging the Party and undermining socialism," had been directed by a small group of "black hands" whose purpose was to destroy the CCP's leadership role and the socialist system. With Li Peng chairing the meeting, the Politburo decided to brand the students activities as an antiparty and antisocialist "turmoil."[47]

The next day, Li Peng and others met Deng to discuss the CCP Politburo's tentative decision. Deng pointed out that what had happened in Beijing was not a normal student movement, but turmoil, which the party leadership must stop by taking "resolute action" immediately. He further contended that the turmoil was made for the purpose of "overthrowing the CCP's reign" and "making the state and the nation lose any hope for the future." In particular, he stressed that it was time to reemphasize the importance of "four principles," especially that of the "persistence in the People's Democratic Dictatorship."[48] Deng's talks were consistent with his ideas about how China's reform project should be carried out—it should be defined mainly as one to promote China's economic growth; the CCP's one-party reign in no circumstances should be weakened.

When Deng and other CCP leaders identified the student movement as a "turmoil," they had in their mind the "lessons" they had drawn from the spreading unrest in Eastern Europe. This was most clearly revealed by Yao Yilin, a CCP Politburo Standing Committee member who firmly supported Deng's judgment throughout the crisis, in an internal speech to high-ranking party cadres after the Tiananmen crackdown, in which he explained why no concession should be made to the students:

When you try to understand [Deng's judgment], you may come up with the questions such as, what if we took a step back by admitting that the student movement was a patriotic and democratic movement, and legalizing their organizations. I know that many comrades here may have this question in mind. As a matter of fact, we have pondered this question ourselves many times. If we took a step back, then opposition parties would appear in China.... If we made concessions along this line, our country would take the same path as Poland. What happened in Poland and Hungary was a combined result of pressures and concessions. Whether the color of our Party and our country would change depended upon this critical and decisive step.... This was the concession that we could not make. This was the concession that we absolutely would not make.[49]

Indeed, it was Deng's and his fellow party elders' determination not to allow Solidarity's story of success in Poland to be replayed in China that opened the door leading to the Tiananmen tragedy.

On April 26, *Renmin ribao* (People's Daily) published an editorial, branding the students' demonstration as a "turmoil," formed to fundamentally challenge the CCP's leadership role and socialism.[50] The editorial angered students and teachers throughout Beijing and China. On April 27, tens of thousands of students from thirty-eight Beijing universities and colleges poured into the city's streets, demanding that the CCP leadership take back the April 26 editorial. When the protest activities of the students continued, they coalesced with the seventieth anniversary of the May Fourth movement, which had long been regarded as a key moment in China's path toward democracy and modernity. Students from other cities also traveled to Beijing to join the demonstration. People from all walks of life in Beijing offered their unreserved support to the students.

Zhao returned to Beijing on April 30 and tried to persuade Deng and other top party leaders to take a different tone than the "April 26 editorial," but he was unsuccessful.[51] When the CCP leadership refused to respond to a formal request by Beijing students for dialogue, beginning on May 13, the students occupied the center of Tiananmen Square to hold a collective hunger strike. This occurred at the very moment when the world media were gathering in Beijing to report Gorbachev's visit.

During Gorbachev's visit, hundreds of thousands of students and Beijing residents continuously held demonstrations, forcing several of Gorbachev's scheduled activities, including the formal welcome ceremony in Tiananmen Square, to be canceled or relocated. Seeing one of his greatest diplomatic achievements turning into an embarrassment, Deng felt humiliated and offended. All of this further confirmed his judgment that the students' demonstrations were indeed a "big turmoil," which must be stopped by any means.[52]

On the afternoon of May 17, only hours after Gorbachev had left Beijing, the CCP Politburo Standing Committee held an enlarged meeting, which Deng attended. In spite of Zhao's strong opposition, the meeting responded to Deng's prodding and made the decision to impose martial law in Beijing.[53] Zhao still tried to avoid confrontation. On the morning of May 18, he visited the students in the hospital; and on the morning of May 19, he visited the students in the square. He tried to persuade them to stop the hunger strike and return to their campuses. But the students, without knowing Zhao's situation and intentions, refused to leave.[54] On May 20, martial law was formally imposed in Beijing.

To the great surprise of Deng and other top CCP leaders, hundreds of thousands of students and residents in Beijing, as well as many from other parts of China, took action spontaneously to prevent PLA soldiers from entering Beijing city, let alone reaching the square.[55] With the students continuously occupying Tiananmen Square, a two-week long stalemate emerged. In late May, Zhao was removed from the post of party general secretary; through discussions and compromises among party elders, Jiang Zemin, the party secretary in Shanghai, replaced him.[56]

By early June, it was increasingly clear that a showdown between the students and the government was inevitable. At 4:00 P.M. on June 3, the CCP leadership ordered the PLA units that had gathered in Beijing's surrounding areas to occupy Tiananmen Square by "any means necessary."[57] When the troops followed the order to move from the western suburb of Beijing, along the Changan Boulevard, the city's main east-west street, toward the Tiananmen Square, they encountered fierce resistance from the people. The troops opened fire. Finally, by early morning June 4, the troops had taken control of the square.

THE FALL OF THE BERLIN WALL

The Tiananmen tragedy shocked the whole world. Ironically, it was the rapprochement between Beijing and Moscow that made the crackdown much more widely exposed to the outside world, as hundreds of journalists and cameramen who reported on Gorbachev's visit stayed to cover the students' demonstrations. They showed the world, often on live television, how bloody violence was used during the crackdown. The scene of one young man who stood alone in front of the PLA's tanks, broadcast repeatedly throughout the world, moved the global audience to tears. This was a defining moment in twentieth-century history, the moment in which international Communism lost any moral strength that it once might have possessed.

During the days and weeks after the Tiananmen tragedy, the Chinese Communist state faced its gravest crisis in its forty-year history. Despite the party leadership's efforts to control the media and to impose upon the general public an official narrative that the crackdown was necessary for "pacifying a major turmoil" and "restoring social order," ordinary Chinese citizens, including many party cadres and members, refused to accept this explanation. Never before had the Chinese Communist state found itself in such a powerless position to influence the Chinese people's hearts and minds.

The international media almost unanimously denounced the crackdown. All governments in Western countries decided to impose economic sanctions against China. The image that Beijing had built during the years of reform and opening-up as a reasonable and responsible international actor was shattered almost overnight.[58]

The Tiananmen tragedy sent shockwaves throughout the Communist world, especially in the Soviet Union and the Soviet bloc countries of East Europe. In Moscow, Gorbachev, in spite of his disapproval of the CCP leadership's behavior, tried to avoid criticizing Beijing directly.[59] However, the impact of the Tiananmen crackdown indirectly restricted his ability to influence and control developments in the Soviet Union, and he was even less willing and likely to resort to force in dealing with activities related to the disintegration of the Soviet Union, often carried out in the name of democracy and self-determination.

In various East European countries, large-scale popular movements for democracy and self-determination were already on the rise. Although the Communist leaderships in these countries generally supported Beijing's use of "resolute measures" in dealing with the "counterrevolutionary forces" during the Tiananmen crackdown, the general public and even many members of the party and state apparatus opposed Beijing's actions.[60] The overwhelmingly negative international responses to the Beijing leadership's use of force made it very clear to the leaders in East European countries that any decision on their part to use force to suppress the pro-democracy movements would lead to denunciation by both their own people and the international community, as well as doom them in historical records. Indeed, the effects of the Tiananmen tragedy placed the entire Communist world on the defensive.

Against this background, the trend toward disintegration in the Soviet Union further developed, especially as the influences of Boris Yeltsin in Russia and the pro-democracy and pro-self-determination forces in such republics as the three Baltic countries—Estonia, Latvia, and Lithuania—increased continuously and significantly.[61] In almost every East European country, the pro-democracy movements grew rapidly in the summer and fall of 1989. The pro-democracy oppositions widely used the opportunity of international Communism's deepened legitimacy crisis to wage new offensives against the Communist authorities in their own countries. The Communist leaderships were all facing difficult dilemmas—they could neither afford to take a totally defensive attitude toward the pro-democracy movements nor dare to resort to violent means.[62]

As the primary decisionmaker in suppressing the students in Tiananmen, Deng knew very well that the crackdown had rendered a huge below to his own reputation and to the Chinese Communist state. Reportedly, like Josef Stalin in the first two weeks after the German invasion of the Soviet Union, Deng also experienced deep depression in the days after the Tiananmen crackdown. He lost much sleep and resumed smoking (which he had quit a few years earlier).[63] However, as a person who had been purged twice during the Cultural Revolution and reemerged both times, Deng was a man of iron will. He was determined to repair the serious damage that the crackdown had brought about, both to the Communist state and to his own perceived position in history.

Even before the crackdown, Deng already had stressed to other CCP leaders that the reform and opening policies should in no circumstances be abandoned. In selecting Jiang as the new top leader of the party and state, Deng contended that "the new central leading bodies should take on an entirely new look, so that people will feel that there is a promising new lineup of leaders who will carry out reform."[64] After the crackdown, Deng acknowledged in a series of internal speeches that the decision to use force had many side effects, but he contended that without it China would not have "a single day of stability and order." Yet Deng's emphasis was on the necessity to keep the momentum of the reform project. He believed that this was the time to "do several very practical things" for the Chinese people, so that their basic confidence in the party and the government would be restored.[65]

Thus, in the wake of the Tiananmen tragedy, the CCP leadership followed Deng's ideas to "do several practical things." In particular, it took a series of measures to fight against corruption, especially the profiteering behavior prevailing among party and government officials. The Chinese government exerted stricter control over the money supply, quickly placing the high inflation rate under control. The suppression of student leaders and the "black hands" behind the student movement was harsh, but it did not develop into a Cultural Revolution–style "mass purge." Several weeks after the crackdown, it seemed that the CCP had regained control of the situation.

Yet Deng, Jiang, and other CCP leaders knew that the challenges facing the party remained extremely serious. For the purpose of repairing the legitimacy of the party's rule, the CCP leadership intentionally highlighted "China versus the West" as a major theme that had dominated the agenda of the Tiananmen tragedy, stressing that, if the party had not adopted "resolute measures" to cope with the "turmoil," China would have been reduced to a "client state" of the Western imperialist countries. Deng particularly stated that if the CCP were allowed to fail, China would have to act "by taking the cue from the United States, or from the many developed countries, or from the Soviet Union." If so, asked Deng, "how can China remain a country with her own independent identity?"[66]

As *Heshang* was widely regarded as the cultural symbol and representation of the political discourse that both prepared and justified China's path toward 1989, the CCP leadership concentrated its efforts to delegitimate the pro-democracy movement on criticizing *Heshang*. In the many articles published in the party-controlled media and some academic journals, *Heshang* was labeled as a piece "totally negating China's own cultural and historical traditions," and "favoring wholesale Westernization of China's state, population and society." If the ideas of *Heshang* and, in a broader sense, of the "vicious forces" behind the students' demonstrations were enacted, China would lose its independent status, a main achievement of the Chinese revolution.[67] China has entered an age in which the Chinese *Communist* Party—albeit its persistence in taking communism as the official ideology—almost exclusively bases its legitimacy claim on nationalistic and patriotic representations.

By the end of June, the situation in Beijing and other parts of China had stabilized, and the CCP leadership increasingly turned its attention to the international challenges that China was facing. Most urgent for Beijing's leaders was to deal with the Western sanctions against China. Although Deng repeatedly told his colleagues that the CCP should not be scared by the protests and sanctions of the United States and other Western powers so long as it was able to "take good care of its own business,"[68] he knew clearly that it would be in China's best interests—and in the best interest of the reform project as well—to reduce external pressure. Therefore, on June 21, when Deng received a letter from the U.S. president George H. W. Bush, who proposed to send his national security advisor Brent Scowcroft to Beijing for a "frank discussion,"[69] he was immediately responsive. For Deng and the CCP leadership, this was an extremely important sign, indicating that the PRC's legitimacy remained valid in the eyes of the leaders of the strongest nation in the world. Scowcroft and Deng met in Beijing in early July. Deng pointed out that U.S. sanctions against China "violated China's interests and offended the Chinese people's feelings," but he obviously was happy to see that China's connections with the United States would not be cut off, as he fully understood that Beijing's relationship with Washington was crucial for the resumption of his reform and opening project.[70]

What most worried China's leaders in the summer of 1989 was the rapidly developing and spreading "unrest" in the Soviet Union and East European countries. In the Soviet Union, not only had pro-democracy activities been rising but the three Baltic countries were increasingly leaning toward independence. Beijing's leaders wondered how Gorbachev could continuously talk about glasnost without taking any substantial and effective actions when the structure and stability of the Soviet Union were being undermined.[71] In various East European countries—spearheaded by the rapid rise of Solidarity in Poland, which won a general election on June 4, the same day that the Tiananmen tragedy occurred—an anticommunism and pro-democracy tide was eroding the foundations of Communist parties in these countries.[72] Given their own recent experience, and given their need to inform the Chinese people that international Communism was still very much alive in the wake of the Tiananmen tragedy, Deng and other CCP leaders watched developments in the Soviet Union and East European countries with great anxiety.[73]

Yet top CCP leaders' understanding and assessments of the causes and meanings of the emerging crises in Eastern Europe were not identical. Deng firmly believed that the only way for China to go eventually beyond the negative impact of the Tiananmen tragedy was to continue the course of reform and opening. In a prolonged meeting with Jiang and other members of the Politburo Standing Committee on September 4, Deng elaborated that "an important dimension of the international situation today is that socialist countries have been experiencing turmoil." He pointed out that "the problem today is not whether the banner of the Soviet Union will fall...the problem is whether the banner of China will stand." Deng thus emphasized that the only way to hold firm China's banner was to "carry on genuine reform and to open wider to the outside." Following these ideas, Deng presented what would later be known as his "lying low" design for China's international strategy:

> First, we should observe the situation coolly. Second, we should hold our ground. Third, we should act calmly. Don't be impatient; it is no good to be impatient. We should be calm, calm, and again calm, and quietly immerse ourselves in practical work to accomplish something— something for China.[74]

Among top CCP leaders, however, there existed a very strong tendency to attribute the crisis situation facing China and other Communist countries to the conspiracies of Western imperialist countries. They therefore advocated a confrontational policy toward the West. Most conspicuous in this respect was Chen Yun. In a conversation on September 4, Chen contended that "Lenin's analysis of the five basic characteristics of imperialism, as well as his analysis of imperialist countries' essence of conducting aggression against other countries and competing for hegemony among themselves, is not out of date." He emphasized that the Western imperialist powers had been trying to "promote 'peaceful evolution' in socialist countries....It is the time now that we must give special attention to this important issue."[75] Chen's statement served as the core of the antireform counter-discourse to Deng's thesis, emphasizing "only continuous reforms can save China."

Deng understood the complicated domestic and international situation that he was facing; he also knew that many Chinese, and the younger generation in particular, compared him with Mao in his late years and attributed his decision to use force to his advanced age. So he decided to fully retire—at least in name—from all of his official posts. At the meeting with Jiang and others on September 4, Deng told them that "I have been determined to retire for several years, and now is the time for me to do so."[76] By doing so, Deng forced Chen Yun and several other party elders, most of whom were holding views against continuing the reform project, to retire with him.[77]

Despite Deng's and his fellow CCP leaders' serious assessment of the deteriorating situation in East Europe, they did not foresee that such a dramatic change as the fall of the Berlin Wall was imminent. Since both East Germany and Romania, among all Communist countries, had given the firmest support to Beijing's decision to use force, Beijing decided to send high-ranking delegations to these two countries to enhance China's ties with them.

In October, only a few weeks before the collapse of the Berlin Wall, Yao Yilin, representing the CCP leadership, visited East Germany, ostensibly to attend the celebration of the fortieth anniversary of the German Democratic Republic, but actually to thank Erich Honecker and the German party for their support during the Tiananmen crackdown. This was the first high-ranking Chinese delegation to visit East Germany since the CCP and the East German Communist Party resumed party-party relationships during Honecker's visit to Beijing in 1986.[78] In Beijing's eyes, among all Communist countries in East Europe, East Germany was the one that had done best in constructing a modern economy and improving people's standard of living. Several Chinese reports even pointed out that in some key statistics, East Germany even had surpassed West Germany.[79] Yao's visit had produced a more optimistic Beijing assessment of the situation in Germany. Therefore, the popular uprising in East Berlin and the subsequent collapse of the Berlin Wall came as a surprise to China's leaders.[80]

Yet, rather than the fall of the Berlin Wall, it was the dramatic change of situation in Romania—particularly the execution of Ceauşescu and his wife—that truly shocked leaders in Beijing. Ceauşescu had long been a friend of Beijing. Among all East European countries, Romania had been the only one that had maintained good relations with China throughout Mao's and Deng's times. Entering 1989, when pro-democracy tendencies were sweeping across East Europe, Romania seemed to be one of the few countries where the Communist Party still had firm control of the situation. During and after the Tiananmen tragedy, Ceauşescu firmly supported the CCP leadership's management of the crisis situation, including endorsing its use of force to suppress "activities of the reactionary elements."[81] In the fall of 1989, when more and more signs indicated that Romania was not immune to the pro-democracy tide, Beijing's leaders still tended to believe that Ceauşescu remained in a position to control the situation. In mid-November, Qiao Shi, a member of the Politburo Standing Committee, visited Bucharest for the purpose of "strengthening the solidarity between the Chinese and Romanian parties and states."[82] As late as mid-December, when Ceauşescu used force to suppress the gathering masses in Bucharest, Beijing still believed that "Romania is capable of managing its own affairs."[83] Thus the dramatic turn of events in Romania and, especially, the execution of Ceauşescu caught Beijing leaders totally off guard.

Beijing's responses, however, were quick and moderate. This was largely because Deng had already set the basic tone for the CCP's handling of possible dramatic changes of situation in the Soviet Union and Eastern Europe. He pointed out that the CCP should not try to take over the banner of international Communism in case Communism collapsed in the Soviet Union and East Europe—and certainly should not try to intervene in the internal development of other countries. "The most important thing is to take good care of our own business," Deng emphasized, "and this is the way for us to contribute to the international Communist movement and Marxism-Leninism."[84] Deng used his influence to make these ideas the CCP's consensus in coping with changes in East Europe. Only days after Ceauşescu's execution, Beijing recognized the new Romanian government and offered to establish "friendly relationship" with it.[85] When Communist governments collapsed one after another in East Europe, Beijing quickly and quietly accepted the changes.

Still the collapse of Communism in East Europe, as epitomized in the fall of the Berlin Wall, presented complex and urgent challenges to the CCP leadership, which was divided in its views on how China's development strategy should be defined in the future. Thus the Chinese Communist state was brought to its most critical juncture in forty years of existence.

THE SECOND LIFE OF THE CHINESE
REFORM PROJECT

The year 1989 ended for China with the government's lifting martial law in Beijing. Yet the society-wide "faith crisis" persisted, especially in the wake of the fall of the Berlin Wall. Watching the failure of international Communism in one country after another, CCP leaders and cadres could not help but worry about China's future. Despite Deng's repeated rallying cries, the reform project was continuously losing its momentum.

The CCP leadership's anxieties over the impact of the fall of the Berlin Wall were reflected in a series of internal party reports about the causes, processes, and consequences of the failure of Communism in Eastern Europe. These reports contended that these were the result of Western imperialist countries' persistent efforts to carry out "peaceful evolution" strategies vis-à-vis the Soviet Union and other socialist countries. The Communist leaderships in these countries, facing pressures from "pro-democracy" forces at home, especially under the impact of Gorbachev's glasnost and perestroika, were not alert to the serious threats to the Communist states from hostile forces at home and abroad and adopted the mistaken policy of yielding to these pressures. Consequently, the Communist leaderships had the illusion that "flexible policies" could help widen their support, and they encountered the harsh reality that the oppositions only took advantage of such policies to expand their own strengths for the purpose of overturning the Communist states. If the Communist regimes in Eastern Europe, according to these reports, had acted "more resolutely" toward "domestic and international enemies" they might not have been undermined.[86] A report by the CCP's External Liaison Department also detailed how Communist cadres had been ruthlessly purged and lived in miserable conditions in post-Communist Eastern European countries.[87]

In the meantime, the CCP leaders watched changes in the Soviet Union with deep worries. While labeling Gorbachev "a traitor of Communism" and attributing failures of Communist states in East Europe and difficulties facing the Communist leadership in the Soviet Union to Gorbachev's "surrenderist strategies and policies," they were worried that Communism in the Soviet Union would not be able to withstand the challenges of the "hostile forces" and would fail in the foreseeable future.[88]

In elaborating the lessons that the CCP should learn from the failure of European Communism, a report by the CCP's Central Party School emphasized the importance of "holding firm the banner of Marxism-Leninism," "rejecting resolutely a multi-party political system," and "casting away the illusion of benefiting from popular elections." The report, while acknowledging that "the origins of East Europe's fall lay in the economic field" and thus reforms should be continued, stressed that the reform and opening policies could be carried out only when the direction of socialism was guaranteed and the party was "unified on basic principles."[89]

Under these circumstances, even Deng himself seemed to have lost control over China's mainstream political discourse. In a series of talks in 1990–91, Deng remained persistent in emphasizing that the reform and opening process should continue. But he also repeatedly stressed that it was crucial to adhere to "the principles of Marxism-Leninism," as well as to the CCP's absolute leadership role, and to guard against the Western imperialists' "peaceful evolution strategies" against China.[90]

But Deng's heart was still with the reform and opening project. As a person who cared about his own position in history, Deng knew well—from being a student activist during his youth—that the decision to use force to crush the students had created a very bad image about him among the Chinese as well as in the world. The only way for him to regain his positive image was to regenerate the reform and opening project. He also understood that only by successfully carrying out the project would the Chinese Communist state be able to deal with the profound legitimacy challenges that it had been facing.[91]

Deng's first major action to regenerate the reform project occurred in early 1991, when he issued a series of pro-reform statements during a vacation tour in Shanghai. Taking as his target the discourse that treated market-oriented reform as capitalist by essence, Deng contended that "planning economy and market-oriented economy do not mark the difference between capitalism or socialism....Capitalism may include planning economy, and socialism can be compatible with market." Deng urged his CCP comrades to "think more courageously and creatively."[92]

But Deng's initiative encountered tough resistance. When he was in Shanghai, he proposed to meet with Chen Yun. But Chen refused to see him.[93] From early March to mid-April, *Jiefang Ribao* (Liberation Daily), a Shanghai-based newspaper, published three front-page commentaries, under the pen name Huangpu Ping, which contended that "the liberation of ideas must enter new realms, reform and opening up must explore new ways of thinking, and economic construction must make a breakthrough." In particular, the commentaries argued for the need to put aside the "market as either socialist or capitalist" debate and concentrate on "taking actions to promote the reform and opening-up."[94] Although it was quickly revealed that these essays were based upon Deng's remarks in Shanghai, they received no favorable treatment from the party's propaganda organs in Beijing. Reportedly, the editor of *Renmin Ribao,* the CCP's main organ, even conducted a secret investigation to pursue the "black hands" behind Huangpu Ping's essays.[95]

Jiang's initial response to the calls to regenerate reforms was dubious. Although he had been the CCP's general secretary for almost two years, his position remained vulnerable, and he had to maintain a subtle balance between the voices for and against reforms within the party leadership. As late as July 1991, Jiang had not made up his mind. In a speech dedicated to the seventieth anniversary of the CCP, Jiang emphasized the necessity of "continuously promoting reforms and opening up"; in the meantime, he contended that "class struggles remain serious" and that "the struggles against bourgeoisie liberalization is the reflection of serious class struggle in the realm of ideology."[96]

A critical turning point in the balance of power between forces for and against the reform project came during and after the failure of the August 19 coup in the Soviet Union. If Beijing's leaders had been rendered a heavy blow by the fall of the Berlin Wall and the ensuing collapse of Communist regimes throughout East Europe, they were truly shocked by the rapid disintegration of the Soviet Union.

When the Soviet coup occurred, the initial response by many leaders in Beijing—Jiang probably included—was sympathy and hope. At a Politburo meeting on the evening of August 19, the CCP leaders seemed pleased with the coup. They believed that "this is a good thing, and especially this is a good thing for China," as "when the West put more pressures on the Soviet Union, the pressures on us will be reduced."[97]

Deng, who had been predicting that "major unrest in the Soviet Union is inevitable," was concerned that Jiang and his colleagues would make a premature gesture to support the coup. Thus, late on the evening of August 19, he asked his secretary to convey to Jiang and others that "the event that occurred in the Soviet Union today is an urgent matter and an unusual development." He advised Jiang not to take action hurriedly, before "carefully observing and studying the situation."[98]

The next day, Deng summoned Jiang and several other top party leaders to discuss the situation in Moscow. Deng again emphasized that Beijing should not hurriedly take a stand on the coup before the situation was clear. In analyzing how the lessons of the coup should be learned, Deng pointed out that China now enjoyed a stable situation for two reasons: one was that the CCP leadership had adopted a firm attitude in managing the turmoil of 1989; the other was that the CCP had not abandoned the banner of continuing the reform project after 1989.[99] On August 22, at a banquet for Deng's eighty-seventh birthday, the senior Chinese leader, while advising other CCP leaders that the party should act cautiously toward the coup, stated that "China does not have the capacity to intervene in others' business, and China should not try to intervene even if it has the capacity." He emphasized that it should continuously pursue "the path of socialist development with Chinese characteristics," and he particularly clarified that "this is to take economic development as the central mission."[100] It was apparent that Deng was trying to turn the impact of the coup into new momentum for regenerating China's processes of reform and opening to the outside world.

The coup failed, but its impact upon the CCP leadership was significant. Deng's pro-reform opinions began to take the upper hand. The first public sign of the change appeared in early September 1991, when *Renmin Ribao* published a commentary. While favoring "going a step further in carrying out reform and opening to the outside world," it also stated that "we should never allow reforms to go along the bourgeois liberalization or capitalist line.... We should ask whether something is capitalist or socialist."[101] After the commentary was broadcast, the Xinhua News Agency later issued a different version deleting the "capitalist or socialist" reference. It was Jiang who ordered the deletion.[102] And this was an indication that momentum for reforms was gathering again.

In early 1992, Deng made another tour of southern China. This time, he made a series of statements to argue for the need to go all out to promote the reform and opening project. He emphasized that reforms should not only be continued but also be carried out on a broader scale and deeper levels. He again contended that "the market is only a means of economic development, and it is not necessarily in conflict with socialism." The essence of socialism, emphasized Deng, should be "the development of productivity." He particularly warned that while "rightist tendency" could be a threat to socialism, "leftist tendency"—namely, dogmatic attitudes toward socialism—could also "harm or even bury socialism."[103]

Chen Yun, the most important dissenter among influential party elders, decided to remain silent. Jiang was determined to fully endorse Deng's "accelerating and deepening reforms" initiative. On February 28, 1992, the CCP leadership formally issued the Central Committee's No. 2 Document of 1992, in which the main points of Deng's talks during his southern tour were relayed to all party members. In the introduction to the document, the CCP leadership emphasized that Deng's talks were "extremely important for directing the advance of the project of reform and opening up" and were "with important and profound significance for promotion of the great cause of socialist modernization."[104]

What followed was the regeneration of the reform and opening project. Like the reform process of the pre-1989 period, it remained an authoritarian one that concentrated on promoting economic development while continuously ignoring transforming China's one-party political structure. Yet, compared with the pre-1989 period, it was more bold in embracing "market" as the central agent in emancipating productivity and creativity, especially after the CCP's Fourteenth Congress, held in October 1992, which formally adopted the concept of "socialist market economy." China then registered rapid economic growth and experienced profound social and cultural transformations in the rest of the 1990s, a phenomenon that continued entering the twenty-first century.

REFLECTIONS

1989 has been recorded in Chinese and world history as a year of extraordinary importance. It witnessed the collapse of Communism as an alternative path to liberal capitalism toward modernity. It led to the disintegration of the Soviet Union and the "Soviet Bloc." It brought the global Cold War to an end.

By creating the Tiananmen tragedy, the Chinese Communist state pushed itself into a crisis most serious in essence and effectively undermined the last piece of legitimacy foundation of the international Communist movement. Yet the Chinese Communist state survived the tremendous shockwaves of 1989. In retrospect, this was because long before the coming of 1989 China had already withdrawn from the global Cold War, and had been profoundly involved in the "reform and opening to the outside world," which had made China anything but Communist. In terms of its connections with the coming of 1989, the reform and opening-up process served as a source as it was highly imbalanced in its design and development. By concentrating on economic development and "bypassing" political transformation, it greatly enhanced the legitimacy challenges—accompanied with an ever-deepening moral crisis—that the Chinese Communist state had been facing. In the meantime, the reform process—and the rapid economic growth that it had generated and the continuous improvement of China's international status in particular—had enhanced the image among the Chinese people that indeed "the Chinese people have stood up," thus creating the space for Deng and the CCP leadership to deal with the accumulated legitimacy challenge facing the Chinese Communist state. In coping with the crisis situation of 1989, Deng and the CCP attempted and, to a degree, succeeded in linking the challenges facing the Communist state to the "fate of China." In the name of stability and order as the necessary preconditions for China's continuous development, they controlled the banners of nationalism and patriotism, making themselves the representatives of China's vital national interests while, at the same time, branding dissident voices as agents of Western powers.

Indeed, if we compare China's experience of 1989 with those of the Soviet Union and the Soviet-bloc countries in East Europe, we may find that both the Soviet Union's disintegration and East European Communist countries' downfall and the Chinese Communist state's survival represented victories of nationalism. In the case of the Soviet Union and East European countries, nationalism justified tendencies toward self-determination, undermining the legitimacy of the Communist states. In the case of China, as the legitimacy representation of the Communist state was from beginning based upon the support of revolutionary nationalism, the CCP had possessed an ability far greater to "control" the banner of nationalism and to define the discourse of patriotism than the Soviet Union and East European countries. In other words, because the Chinese Communist state was more capable of justifying its legitimacy in nationalistic and patriotic terms, it thus achieved a larger capacity to survive (but not to resolve) the legitimacy challenges that it had been facing.

Deng played a central role in shaping China's path toward 1989, in making the Tiananmen tragedy, and in getting China out of the abyss of 1989 through re-embarking on the reform and opening process. In the final analysis, though, Deng played his role in regenerating China's reforms in the context of China's transformed economy and society. The rise of China's market-oriented economy, the changes in China's social conditions and structure (especially the emergence of new "middle classes"), and changes in everyday people's basic ways of thinking had combined together to make it next to impossible for China to return to the pre-reform era. The Chinese Communist state survived the shockwaves of 1989. Yet, as far as the contitituoal foundation and normative representation of the PRC are concerned, the legitimacy challenges facing it continued. In fact, the regeneration of China's reform and opening-up process in the post-1989 period, as well as the tremendous economic and social changes that it has brought about—Chinese economy has been further integrated into the world market and the Chinese society has become more diverse and plural, etc.—have resulted in deeper tension in China's one-Party-dominated political structure and institution, leading to a profound legitimacy crisis of the Chinese "Communist" state.

Twenty years have passed since 1989, and China and the world have experienced profound changes. Yet the impacts of 1989 remain and continuously play the role to define the trajectory of development of China and the world. The Chinese experience of 1989, and the Tiananmen tragedy in particular, remains a knot that must be untied and a barrier that must be removed in China's continuous advance toward modernity. Without doing so, the legitimacy narrative of the Chinese "Communist" state will always be burdened by its fundamental inability to justify itself.

NOTES

1. Deng, "Close the Past, Open the Future," May 16, 1989, *Deng Xiaoping xuanji* [Selected Works of Deng Xiaoping] (Beijing: Renmin, 1993), 3:291–95, Hereafter *Deng Xiaoping xuanji* will be abbreviated *DXJ*. All translations are mine, unless otherwise noted.

2. Mikhail Gorbachev, *Memoirs* (London: Bantam Books, 1996), 631.

3. The Chinese government announced that thirty-six people died on June 3–4. The unofficial number provided by survivors and international observers, however, is over several hundred.

4. There exists a large amount of literature on the Chinese story of 1989. Much of the early coverage of the Tiananmen tragedy was offered by journalists. In Jeffrey N. Wasserstrom and Elizabeth J. Perry eds., *Popular Protest and Political Culture in Modern China* (Boulder: Westview Press, 1992), a group of leading China scholars offer their observations and interpretations from non-high-politics-centered, cultural and social perspectives. Craig Calhoun, in *Neither Gods Nor Emperors: Students and the Struggle for Democracy in China* (Berkeley: University of California Press, 1994), presents nuanced analyses of the social, political and cultural contexts of the student protests in Tiananmen. With the support of personal experience, extensive interviews, and a wide range of social science theories, Zhao Dingxin, in *The Power of Tiananmen: State-Society Relations and the 1989 Student Movement* (Chicago: University of Chicago Press, 2001), offers insightful discussions of the social and political tension that brought about the 1989 student movement. Andrew Walder goes beyond the student-focus to discuss the roles played by Chinese workers in the 1989 uprising (Walder, "Workers, Managers, and the State: The Reform Era and the Political Crisis of 1989," *China Quarterly* 127, September 1991, 467–92). In Jonathan Unger, ed. *The Pro-Democracy Protests in China: Reports from the Provinces* (Armonk, N.Y.: M. E. Shape, 1991), contributors reconstruct the diversity and breadth of the Chinese story of 1989, revealing the interactive relations between the protests in Beijing and those in many other cities and provinces. Also highly revealing is the documentary, *Gate of Heavenly Peace*, directed by Richard Gordon and Carmar Hinton, which is associated with a continuously updated website: *http://tsquare.tv/*. Few studies, however, have reconstructed China's position in bringing about 1989 as a landmark year in twentieth-century world history.

5. An exception is Zhang Liang et al., *The Tiananmen Papers* (New York: Public Affairs, 2001). The book, by an anonymous Chinese source, includes valuable documents on

Beijing's decision making in 1989, although the authenticity of some documents needs further confirmation. Another highly revealing and valuable source is Zhao Ziyang, *Prisoner of the State: The Secret Journal of Premier Zhao Ziyang* (New York: Simon & Schuster, 2009), which is based on Zhao's recorded recollections during his prolonged house arrest.

6. Mao, "The Chinese People Have Stood Up," *Mao Zedong wenji* [A Collection of Mao's Papers] (Beijing: Renmin, 1995), 342–46.

7. For two excellent recent studies on the Sino-Soviet split, see Lorenz Luthi, *The Sino-Soviet Split: The Cold War in the Communist World* (Princeton, N.J.: Princeton University Press, 2008), and Sergey Radchenko, *Two Suns in the Heavens: The Sino-Soviet Struggle for Supremacy* (Washington, D.C.: Wilson Center Press, 2009).

8. In September 1971, Lin Biao, Mao's designated successor, fled China after the failure of an alleged plot to assassinate Mao. Lin died with his wife and son when his plane crashed in Mongolia.

9. Yang Kuisong, "The Sino-Soviet Border Clash of 1969," *Cold War History* 1.1 (August 2000): 25–31.

10. Chen Jian, *Mao's China and the Cold War* (Chapel Hill: University of North Carolina Press, 2001), chapter 9.

11. *Mao Zedong on Diplomacy* (Beijing: Foreign Languages Press, 1994), 454.

12. *Renmin ribao* [People's Daily], April 11, 1974, 1.

13. Li Ping et al., *Zhou Enlai nianpu, 1949–1976* [A Chronological Record of Zhou Enlai, 1949–1976] (Beijing: Zhongyang wenxian, 1997), 691.

14. Yu Guangyuan, *Deng Xiaoping Shakes the World: An Eyewitness Account of China's Party Work Conference and the Third Plenum* (Norwalk, Conn.: EastBridge, 2004), chapter 1.

15. Yu, *Deng Xiaoping Shakes the World,* especially chapters 9 and 13; Tang Tsou, "The Responsibility System in Agriculture," in his *The Cultural Revolution and Post-Mao Reforms* (Chicago: University of Chicago Press, 1986), 189–218.

16. Hu Yaobang, *Quanmian kaichuang shehui zhuyi jianshe de xin jumian* [Create a New Situation in All Fronts of Socialist Modernization] (Beijing: Renmin, 1982), part II.

17. Xue Mouhon et al., *Dangdai zhongguo waijiao* [Contemporary Chinese Diplomacy] (Beijing: Zhouguo shehui kexue, 1988), 229–30.

18. CCP Central Committee, "Instruction on Waging the War of Self-Defense against Vietnam and Safeguarding the Borders," February 14, 1979, CCP Central Institute of Historical Documents ed., *Sanzhong quanhui yilai zhongyao wenxian xuanbian* [Selected Important Documents since the Third Plenary Session] (Beijing: Renmin, 1982), doc. no. 8.

19. The editorial board of *Jiefangjun bao* [Liberation Army Daily], eds., *Xin shidai zui ke'ai de ren* [The Most Beloved People of the New Era] (Beijing: Jiefangjun wenyi, 1980).

20. For a good discussion of China's changing society and state-society relations in the 1980s, see Zhao, *The Power of Tiananmen,* 39–52.

21. Leng Rong et al., eds., *Deng Xiaoping nianpu, 1975–1997* [A Chronological Record of Deng Xiaoping, 1975–1997] (Beijing: Zhongyang wenxian, 2004), 498–500, 501–3. Hereafter, *Deng Xiaoping nianpu* will be abbreviated *DNP*.

22. Deng, "The Party's Urgent Tasks on the Personnel and Ideological Fronts," *DXJ*, 3:36–48; *DNP*, 939–40.

23. *DNP*, 492–93.

24. Xiao Donglian. *Lishi de zhuangui, 1979–1981* [Historical Transformation, 1979–1981] (Hong Kong: Chinese University Press, 2008), 267–83.

25. *DNP*, 721, 724–25.

26. Ibid., 1160–62, 1165–66; see also discussion in Zhao, *Prisoner of the State*, 169–176.

27. Chen Fongching and Jin Guantao, *From Youthful Manuscripts to River Elegy: The Chinese Popular Cultural Movement and Political Transformation* (Hong Kong: Chinese University Press, 1997).

28. *DNP*, 1174–75, 1201, 1215.

29. See, for example, Zhao Yuliang, *"Perestroika, Glasnost,* and Revolution in the Cultural Sphere: Preparations for Comprehensive Reforms in the Soviet Union," *Shijie jingji he zhengzhi* [World Politics and Economy] 10 (1988): 22–27; Lin Shichang, "Glasnost and Gorbachev's Reforms," *Eluosi yanjiu* [Russian Studies] 7 (1987): 1–6; Cui Shumei, "The Principle of Glasnost Is the Fundamental Feature of Socialist Democracy," *Kexue shehui zhuyi* [Scientific Socialism] 4 (1988): 41–46; see also Su Zhaozhi, "On Political Reforms," *Dushu* [Reading] 11 (1986): 3–9; Wang Huning, "On Political Transparency," *Shehui kexue* [Social Science] 3 (1988): 25–29.

30. Qian Qichen, *Ten Episodes in China's Diplomacy* (New York: HarperCollins, 2005), 17–18.

31. Wu Guogang, *Zhao Ziyuan he zhengzhi gaige* [Zhao Ziyang and Political Reform] (Hong Kong: Pacific Century Institute, 1997), 524–31; Zhao, *Prisoner of the State*, 226.

32. *Deng*, "Adjusting Prices, Accelerating Reforms," *DXJ*, 3:262–63; *DNP*, 1238, 1247–48; see also Yang Jisheng, *Zhongguo gaige niandai de zhengzhi douzheng* [Political Struggles in China in the Era of Reform] (Hong Kong: Zhuoyue wenhua, 2004), 368.

33. *Renmin ribao*, August 19, 1988, 1.

34. Tang Yingwu, *1976 nian yilai de zhongguo* [China Since 1976] (Beijing: Jingji ribao, 1997), 292.

35. A survey conducted by *Jingji yanjiu* [Economic Study, a Beijing-based journal] identified four main problems that had caused widespread popular discontent: corruption among party officials, unfair distribution of wealth and power, high inflation, and lack of clear direction of the reform. Yang, *Zhongguo gaige niandai de zhengzhi douzheng*, 374.

36. Zhao, *Prisoner of the State*, 233–36; Zong Fengming ed., *Zhao Ziyang ruanjin zhong de tanhua* [Zhao Ziyang: Conversations in Captivity] (Hong Kong: Kaifang, 2007), 226–27.

37. See, for example, Deng Xiaoping, "Take a Clear-Cut Stand Against Bourgeois Liberalization," "We Must Continue to Emancipate Our Minds and Accelerate the Reform," and "The Overriding Need Is for Stability," *DXJ*, 3:194–97, 264–65, 284–85.

38. Zhang Liang, ed., *Zhongguo liusi zhenxiang* [China's June Fourth: The True Story] (Hong Kong, Mingjing, 2001), 89.

39. See discussion in chapter 3, this volume, by William Taubman and Svetlana Savranskaya.

40. Among them were Bing Xin and Xiao Qian, Zhang Liang, *Zhongguo liusi zhenxiang,* 90.

41. Yang, *Zhongguo gaige niandia de zhengzhi douzheng,* 377.

42. *Renmin ribao,* March 15, 1989, 1; Yang, *Zhongguo gaige niandai de zhengzhi douzheng,* 377.

43. Yang, *Zhongguo gaige niandai de zhengzhi douzheng,* 378.

44. Qian, *Ten Episodes in China's Diplomacy,* 26–28.

45. Zhao, *Prisoner of the State,* 9–11, 13; Zong, *Zhao Ziyang ruanjin zhong de tanhua,* 9–10.

46. In his conversation with Li Peng, Zhao raised three points: That the students should be advised to return to the campuses after Hu's funeral, that multilevel dialogues should be held with the students to improve communication and mutual understanding; and that in any circumstance violent event should be avoided. See Zhao, *Prisoner of the State,* 5–6; Zong, *Zhao Ziyuan ruanjing zhong de tanhua,* 9.

47. Yang, *Zhongguo gaige niandai de zhengzhi douzheng,* 486.

48. *DNP,* 1273–74; see also Zhao, *Prisoner of the State,* 10–11.

49. When Yao made the speech, Li Peng, who was also present, commented: "If we were to legalize the Students' Autonomous Union as the students insisted, what about the workers? Do we also legalize a solidarity workers' union upon their insistence?" Yao Yilin, speech at a meeting of leading cadres of various departments of the CCP Central Committee and the State Council, June 13, 1989, *Xuechuan tongxun* [Propaganda Newsletter] 13 (1989): 16–18.

50. *Renmin ribao,* April 26, 1989, 1.

51. Zhao, *Prisoner of the State,* 16–18; Zong, *Zhao Ziyang ruanjin zhong de tanhua,* 51–54; Yang, *Zhongguo gaige niandai de zhengzhi douzheng,* 405.

52. Yang, *Zhongguo gaege niandai de zhengzhi douzheng,* 420–21.

53. *DNP,* 1276–77; Zhao, *Prisoner of the State,* 27–29.

54. Zhao, *Prisoner of the State,* 31; Zong, *Zhao Ziyang ruanjin zhong de tanhua,* 13–14.

55. Indeed, a main feature of the Tiananmen student movement of 1989 was that its participants came not only from universities in Beijing but also from other provinces and cities. One reason that the Square never emptied out, even under conditions of the martial law, was that students and, in occasions, workers from other parts of China continuously arrived in Beijing to join the protests. (The author would like to thank an anonymous reader of the manuscript for raising this important point.)

56. *DNP,* 1277.

57. Zhang, *The Tiananmen Papers,* 368–70.

58. Robert D. McFadden, "The West Condemns the Crackdown," *The New York Times,* June 5, 1989, A12; Zhang, *Tiananmen Papers,* 416–18.

59. Gorbachev, *Memoirs,* 636; "Turmoil in China, Kremlin Dismayed, Aide Says," *The New York Times,* June 10, A7, 1989.

60. Frank Columbus, ed., *Central and Eastern Europe in Transition* (Commack, N.Y.: Nova Science Publishers, 1998), 1: 22–24, 147–48.

61. See discussions in chapter 3, this volume, by Taubman and Savranskaya.

62. See chapters 1 and 2, this volume, by Jeffrey A. Engel and James J. Sheehan, respectively.

63. Yang, *Zhongguo gaige niandai de zhengzhi douzheng*, 476.

64. Deng, "We Must Form a Promising Collective Leadership That Will Carry out Reform," *DXJ*, 3:296–301.

65. Deng, "Urgent Tasks of China's Third Generation of Collective Leadership," *DXJ*, 3:309–14.

66. *DXJ*, 3:311.

67. See, for example, CCP Central Propaganda Department, ed., *Heshang de wuqu* (*River Elegy*'s Dark Visions) (Beijing: Renmin, 1990); *Heshang xuanyang le shenmo* [What Does *River Elegy* Advocate?] (Beijing: Zhongguo guanbo dianshi, 1990); and Li Fengxiang et al., *Heshang baimiu* [100 Mistakes of *River Elegy*] (Beijing: Zhongguo wenlian, 1990).

68. *DXJ*, 3:311–12.

69. For the text of the letter, see George H. W. Bush and Brent Scowcroft, *A World Transformed* (New York: Alfred A. Knopf, 1998), 100–102. That George H. W. Bush was the president of the United States at the time was an important factor for the post-1989 development of U.S.-China relations. Bush served as Chief of U.S. Liaison Office in Beijing (a position equivalent to U.S. ambassador) in the mid-1970s, and he believed that he had a good understanding of China and Chinese leaders (including Deng). Thus he was unwilling to take dramatic measures after the Tiananmen tragedy to undermine U.S.-China relations. See Engel, *The China Diary of George H. W. Bush*, for further discussion of Bush's time in Beijing and its long-term influence on his thinking.

70. *DNP*, 1284; for Scowcroft's account of the meeting, see Bush and Scowcroft, *World Transformed*, 106–107.

71. Yang, *Zhongguo gaige kaifang niandai de zhengzhi douzheng*, 486.

72. See chapters 1 and 2, this volume, by Engel and Sheehan, respectively.

73. *DNP*, 1287.

74. Deng, "With Stable Policies of Reform and Opening-Up, China Can Have Great Hopes for the Future," *DXJ*, 3:315–21.

75. Zhu Jiamu et al., *Chen Yun nianpu* [A Chronological Record of Chen Yen] (Beijing: Zhongyang wenxian, 2000), 3:428.

76. *DXJ*, 3:315.

77. As early as February 1989, Deng revealed his plan to "entirely retire," so that other party elders would also "stop intervening." Zhao, *Prisoner of the State*, 242.

78. *Renmin ribao*, October 10, 1989, 3.

79. Wei Si, "Four Decades of Glory of the Democratic Republic of Germany," *Renmin ribao*, October 7, 1989, 7.

80. The "big events" for the Chinese leaders on November 9–10 were Deng's decision to retire and the North Korean leader Kim Il-sung's visit to China. East Germany

certainly was not on the agenda on the CCP leadership's plenary held on November 6–10, and no evidence indicates that they discussed the fall of the Berlin Wall at the session.

81. *Renmin ribao*, June 28, 1989, 4.

82. *Renmin ribao*, November 23, 1989, 4.

83. *Renmin ribao*, December 22, 1989, 2.

84. *DNP*, 1286.

85. *Renmin ribao*, December 27, 1989, 1.

86. "Why Did Socialism Suffer from Major Setbacks?" *Neibu canyue* [Internal Reference] 29 (1991), and "The Soviet Union's Disintegration Is Inevitable," *Neibu canyue* 40 (1991).

87. The Bureau on Soviet-East European Affairs of External Liaison Department of the CCP Central Committee, "Communist Parties in East Europe Are in Miserable Conditions after Losing Political Power," *Neibu canyue* 57 (1991).

88. "The Soviet Union's Disintegration Is Inevitable," *Neibu canyue* 40 (1991).

89. Wu Zhenkun, "Five Models of 'Peaceful Evolution' in East Europe," *Neibu canyue* 11 (1991).

90. *DNP*, 1302–1303.

91. Deng, "Catch the Good Opportunity to Resolve the Question of Development," *DXJ*, 3:363–65.

92. *DNP*, 1307–1308; Yang, *Zhongguo gaige kaifang niandai de zhengzhi douzheng*, 477–78.

93. Yang, *Zhongguo gaige kaifang niandai de zhengzhi douzheng*, 477.

94. *Jiefang ribao* [Liberation Daily], March 2, March 12, and April 12, 1991.

95. Yang, *Zhongguo gaige kaifang niandai de zhengzhi douzheng*, 479.

96. *Renmin ribao*, July 2, 1991, 1.

97. Yang, *Zhongguo gaige niandai de zhengzhi douzheng*, 483.

98. *DNP*, 1330.

99. *DNP*, 1330–31.

100. Yang, *Zhongguo gaige niandai de zhengzhi douzheng*, 485–86.

101. Hu Jiwei, "On That the Main Attention Should Be Placed on Preventing Extreme 'Leftism,'" in *Lishi de chaoliu* [The Tide of History] (Beijing: Zhongguo renmin daxue chubanshe), 143.

102. Yang, *Zhongguo gaige niandai de zhengzhi douzheng*, 480–81.

103. Deng, "Excepts of Talks Given in Wuchang, Shenzhen, Zhuhai and Shanghai," January 18–February 21, 1992, *DXJ*, 3:358–70.

104. *DNP*, 1341.

Chapter 5

DREAMS OF FREEDOM,
TEMPTATIONS OF POWER

Melvyn P. Leffler

Many of us live with indelible images of the Cold War: mushroom
clouds over Hiroshima and Nagasaki, symbolizing the end of a hot war and the
beginning of another cold one; airplanes circling over Berlin in the summer of
1948, dropping supplies to the beleaguered people of that city; a barbed-wire
fence appearing along the fault lines of that city in August 1961; Soviet ships
dropping anchor and then turning around as they approached the blockade
line during the harrowing days of the Cuban missile crisis in October 1962;
helicopters taking off from the roof of a Saigon apartment in April 1975, packed
with fleeing Vietnamese; American flags ablaze in the street of Tehran during
the demonstrations that eventually overthrew the shah; Ronald Reagan standing before the Brandenburg Gate in Berlin in June 1987 calling upon Soviet leaders to "tear down this Wall"; a lone student standing before tanks in Tiananmen
Square, defying the power of the Chinese communist regime; and, remarkably,
throngs of East Germans traversing the Berlin Wall and dancing on its ramparts
during the thrilling days of November 9–10, 1989.

For Americans, these images invoke the trajectory of the Cold War: power,
determination, crisis, defeat, humiliation, resurgence, and, finally, triumph.
And Berlin, as evidenced by the frequency of its appearance in the landmark
events of the Cold War, remains at the center of the story. It symbolized, in
turn, resolve, tension, crisis, courage, resilience, and victory. For Americans,
it meant the conquest of freedom over tyranny, the liberation of a people, the

redemptive role of the United States of America. It confirmed the utility of power, the correctness of containment, the universal appeal of freedom, the triumph of good over evil. It foreshadowed the temptation to use power anew, when great threat appeared, in order to defeat a new devil and to fulfill God's intention for all men to be free.

People elsewhere interpreted the toppling of the Berlin Wall very differently. For many people in Western Europe, the meaning of the events of 1989–90 confirmed the rectitude of the trajectory they had taken since 1945: the embrace of integration, the salience of multilateral institutions, the political primacy of economic issues, and the rejection of force as the arbiter of differences among European states.[1] For leaders in Beijing, the crumbling of the Wall and the turmoil in Eastern Europe meant that they had to reactivate the economic reform agenda they had previously embarked upon and deflect the impulses for political change that had been the undoing of Communist oligarchs in Eastern Europe.[2] For many Russians, the demise of the Wall, the unification of Germany inside the North Atlantic Treaty Organization (NATO), and the dissolution of the Warsaw Pact demonstrated the consequences of what they regarded as naïve and pusillanimous leadership.[3]

But when the Wall came down, for many Americans, it did more than confirm their sense of righteous mission. Vindicating their Cold War policies, it intensified their determination to shape the evolving international system in ways that would comport with U.S. values and interests. Presidents George H. W. Bush and Bill Clinton began speaking of a "democratic peace"—a new world order dominated by democratic nations, whose norms and values encouraged the free flow of goods and capital and militated against the use of force to settle disputes among one another. But they also knew that nurturing democratic institutions and building peaceful norms would be a long and arduous process. In the interim, they tried to capitalize upon the opportunities afforded by the crumbling of the Berlin Wall. They wanted to solidify the preeminent position of the United States in the global arena, encourage orderly and liberal reform, and design a new military strategy to meet the challenges of the post–Cold War era. Yet they remained wary about employing force for humanitarian purposes or for regime change. Like Woodrow Wilson, they understood that there is a difference between making the world safe for democracy and making the entire world democratic.[4]

The self-imposed constraints disappeared after the sudden and cruel attack on the United States by al Qaeda terrorists on September 11, 2001. For President George W. Bush and his advisers, the end of the Cold War and the toppling of the Berlin Wall had conveyed dramatic lessons. Invoking memories of the recent past and inspired by recollections of Cold War triumphs, Bush proclaimed that hereafter November 9—the day the Wall was breached—would be "World Freedom Day." "Like the fall of the Berlin Wall and the defeat of totalitarianism in Central and Eastern Europe," Bush said, "freedom will triumph in this war against terrorism."[5] Seventeen months later, in April 2003, when American troops marched into Baghdad and when jubilant Iraqis pulled down the statue of Saddam Hussein and slammed their shoes against the deposed dictator's stone face, U.S. Secretary of Defense Donald Rumsfeld exclaimed, "Watching them...one cannot help but think of the fall of the Berlin Wall and the collapse of the Iron Curtain."[6]

This chapter will show how the discourse about the events of 1989 and the dismantling of the Berlin Wall assumed distinctive meanings and shaped distinctive policies in the United States. U.S. officials harnessed the past to mold the collective memory of Americans and used the rhetorical trope of freedom to mobilize support for their policies.[7] America's new foes, policy makers explained, were totalitarians akin to past adversaries. They, too, would be defeated, however protracted the conflict might be. Many people had once thought the Berlin Wall would last forever; but it was no more. Freedom would triumph over nihilism, much as it had vanquished fascism and communism because freedom—in George W. Bush's words—was "the design of our Maker, and the longing of every soul."[8] However, Americans would also learn, rather sorrowfully, that their peculiar mix of military power and ideological zealotry could have portentous consequences, facts well understood by George H. W. Bush and by Bill Clinton in the turbulent and unpredictable circumstances that initially followed the toppling of the Berlin Wall.

THE BERLIN WALL AND THE END
OF THE COLD WAR

No modern American president was more ideological than Ronald Reagan. He condemned communists for their beliefs in "treachery, deceit, destruction, & bloodshed."[9] They "are the focus of evil in the modern world," he declared in one of his most famous speeches as president.[10] The regime that these Communists had built in the Soviet Union was powerful militarily, but economically incapacitated and spiritually impoverished. It would founder, he said, because it ran "against the tide of history by denying freedom and human dignity to its citizens."[11] In contrast, America would be forever young, renewing itself and remaining a beacon for all humankind. America, he said, was not just a country;

it was an idea—"the love of freedom."[12] We Americans were "one people under God, dedicated to the dream of freedom that He has placed in the human heart, called upon now to pass that dream on to a waiting and hopeful world."[13]

In 1987, Reagan traveled to Berlin to commemorate the city's 750th anniversary. One of his speech writers, Peter Robinson, had gone to the city in advance, chatted with Berliners, and concluded that they longed to rid themselves of the Wall that divided them. He drafted a speech for the president in which he would challenge Mikhail Gorbachev, the chairman of the Communist Party of the Soviet Union, to tear down the Wall. Neither the State Department nor the National Security Council wanted Reagan to make such a pitch; he might antagonize or provoke the Soviet leader, who was seemingly embarked on promising reforms at home and calling for more openness and restructuring inside his country.[14] But Reagan wanted to speak of freedom. On June 12, 1987, with the chancellor of West Germany and the mayor of West Berlin at his side, he remarked, "Behind me stands a wall that encircles the free sectors of this city, part of a vast system of barriers that divides the entire continent of Europe." He went on, "As long as this scar of a wall is permitted to stand, it is not the German question alone that remains open, but the question of freedom for all mankind." And then, five paragraphs later, came the challenge: "General Secretary Gorbachev, if you seek peace, if you seek prosperity for the Soviet Union and Eastern Europe, if you seek liberalization: Come here to this gate! Mr. Gorbachev, open this gate! Mr. Gorbachev, tear down this wall!"[15]

Gorbachev was not impressed.[16] Nor was the Western media at the time. Despite the iconic place this speech has taken in our memory of the Cold War and despite the fact that it received attention on the nightly television news shows, press coverage in newspapers and magazines was rather muted and, to some extent, overshadowed by the president's lackluster performance at an economic summit meeting the week before in Venice. None of the major newsweeklies—*Time, Newsweek,* and *U.S. News and World Report*—focused much attention on the speech; to the extent that they covered it, they did not think that the American president was tarnishing the growing luster of the young Soviet leader in the East-West propaganda wars. *The Wall Street Journal* contained an opinion piece by Philip Revzin on June 17, arguing that Gorbachev was "outplaying the West." *The New York Times* put Reagan's speech on page 3 and made passing mention of it in an editorial calling for more reform inside the Soviet Union. *The Washington Post* did highlight it on page 1 but did not offer any editorial comment. Reagan's popularity did go up measurably in the week after the speech, perhaps because of the television coverage, but the speech itself lacked staying power, because German unification was simply not on anyone's policy agenda in June 1987.[17]

Yet two and a half years later, the Wall did come down. No one in the United States anticipated this development at the time, notwithstanding the signing of a treaty outlawing intermediate-range nuclear missiles in December 1987, notwithstanding Reagan's immensely successful trip to Moscow in late May 1988, notwithstanding the dramatic parliamentary changes taking place in Poland and Hungary during the summer of 1989, and notwithstanding the tumultuous demonstrations occurring on the streets of Leipzig and other East German cities in the early autumn. The ruling Communist Party (SED) in East Germany did not intend to open the gates; confusion was rampant; the regime's public spokesperson, Gunter Schabowski, did not grasp the import of his statements when he answered queries at a press conference and stated that people did not have to leave the GDR through other countries (as they had been doing, in record numbers). Yes, he said, they could "go through the border." Yes, they had freedom to travel. Television newscasters quickly reported that the borders had been opened. They created the reality as crowds gathered in front of several key crossings, and the guards, facing chaos and not having instructions, opened the gates. East German started flocking across the Wall, and then pulled parts of it down.[18]

Standing in front of the gate, the NBC anchorman Tom Brokaw conveyed the news to Americans: "This is a historic night....The East German Government has just declared that East German citizens will be able to cross the wall...without restrictions."[19] The news media in the United States reacted jubilantly. *Newsweek* declared that all "vestiges of the totalitarian past seemed gone." On November 12, *The New York Times* editorialized, "Crowds of young Germans danced on top of the hated Berlin wall Thursday night. They danced for joy, they danced for history. They danced because the tragic cycle of catastrophes that first convulsed Europe 75 years ago, embracing two world wars, a holocaust and cold war, seems at long last to be nearing an end."[20]

The president of the United States did not dance with joy. George H. W. Bush said he "welcomed" the decision of East German leaders to open the borders. When reporters noted that he did not seem elated, he said he was "not an emotional kind of guy." He was pleased, but wanted to remain prudent.[21] When German Chancellor Helmut Kohl called him to summarize the dramatic events taking place, Bush said that he wanted "to avoid hot rhetoric that by mistake might cause a problem."[22] Although Bush was chastised by his domestic foes for his restraint, he deemed such criticism to be ridiculous. "Some have wanted me to go jump up on top of the Berlin Wall," he told foreign journalists. "Well, I never heard such a stupid idea. I mean what good would it do for an American president to be posturing while Germans were flowing back and forth by the millions? It makes no sense at all. We are conducting ourselves in a prudent way."[23]

Prudence, of course, had been the watchword of Bush and his advisers since they had entered office in January 1989. Rather than quickly building upon the warm relations that Reagan and Gorbachev had cultivated with one another, the new president had decided to "pause" and reevaluate the significance of the changes taking place in the Soviet Union. In his inaugural address, Bush noted that the totalitarian era might be passing, but caution was imperative. Three weeks after taking office, he told Congress, "The fundamental facts remain that the Soviets retain a very powerful military machine in the service of objectives which are still too often in conflict with ours. So, let us take the new openness seriously, but let's also be realistic. And let's also be strong."[24]

The president and his key assistants—National Security Adviser General Brent Scowcroft, Secretary of State James A. Baker, Secretary of Defense Dick Cheney, Chairman of the Joint Chiefs of Staff General Colin Powell, and Deputy National Security Adviser Robert Gates—did not trust Gorbachev. "I was suspicious of Gorbachev's motives and skeptical of his prospects," recalled Scowcroft. He continued, "I believed that Gorbachev's goal was to restore dynamism to a socialist political and economic system and revitalize the Soviet Union domestically and internationally to compete with the West."[25] Cheney agreed: "We must guard against gambling our nation's security on what may be a temporary aberration in the behavior of our foremost adversary."[26] Thoroughgoing change in the Soviet Union was not likely to take place, thought Gates.[27] Consummate pragmatists, who believed in the art of realpolitik, the men who gathered around George H. W. Bush believed it was too soon to say the Cold War was over.

In May 1989, however, they announced that they wanted to go "beyond containment." They wanted to achieve a Europe "whole and free." They wanted to challenge Gorbachev with new initiatives in order to ascertain if he was sincere about being a reformer. If he was, they hoped to integrate the Soviet Union into an American-led world order, structured along liberal and capitalist lines. They hoped to push Soviet armies out of Eastern Europe or, at least, dilute the power of the Warsaw Pact in the middle of Europe. The initial goal, said Scowcroft, was "to lift the Kremlin's military boot from the necks of the East Europeans."[28]

Bush and his advisers were amazed when, during the late spring and summer of 1989, Gorbachev allowed the Communists to be ousted from power in Warsaw and to be challenged in Budapest. They were equally astonished by Gorbachev's willingness to make disproportionately large troop cuts in Europe.[29] When hundreds of thousands of East German citizens marched down the streets of their major cities calling for openness and political change, when the long-standing ruler of the nation—Erich Honecker—was removed from office, and when his successors allowed the Wall to be breached, however unintentionally, U.S. officials could hardly believe their good fortune. "With the fall of the Wall, suddenly anything was possible," thought Scowcroft.[30]

Nonetheless, Bush did not want to overreach. He was mightily affected by the turmoil in China and by the Chinese crackdown on dissidents in Tiananmen Square in June 1989. He vividly recalled the dashed hopes of reformers in Hungary in 1956 and Czechs in 1968. When Bush visited Poland and Hungary in July 1989, he heralded the democratic reforms taking place, but in measured words. He did not want to encourage violence. He did not want to "poke a stick in the eye of Mr. Gorbachev." The United States, he stressed, should "not overpromise, ought not to overexhort for others to be like us." He was extremely conscious, recalled Gates, that "if violence was avoided, reform would inexorably proceed."[31]

Four months later, as Berliners flocked across the border during the middle of November without signs of a Soviet crackdown, Bush was even more careful. He was delighted by the trajectory of events, but he did not want Gorbachev to think that he was fomenting disorder; he did not want the Kremlin to assume that the demonstrations in East Germany and throughout Eastern Europe were an "American project." He did not want to invite a "crackdown" that "could result in bloodshed." He knew he was being criticized for not doing enough. He believed, however, that "things were coming our way, so why do we have to jump up and down, risk those things turning around and going in the wrong direction." He could live with the fact that "he was not seen as a visionary, but I hope I'm seen as steady and prudent and able."[32]

On Thanksgiving Day 1989, President Bush addressed the nation and summarized his reactions to the remarkable events that were transpiring. For forty years, he said, Berlin had been "the test of Western resolve" and the symbol of the "contest between the free and the unfree." The West German foreign minister had given him a piece of the Berlin Wall, and he intended to keep it on his desk, "a reminder of the power of freedom to bring down the walls between people." Noting that he would be meeting with Gorbachev in about ten days, he again stressed that "a time of historic change is no time for recklessness." He hoped Gorbachev would permit the processes of reform in Eastern Europe to continue, and he was willing to offer support toward that objective. "Our goal is to see this historic tide of freedom broadened, deepened, and sustained."[33]

His advisers celebrated freedom's forward march, but they also remained wary. "The year 1989," Secretary of Defense Cheney told the Budget Committee of the House of Representatives, "may be one of those years, like few others in history—that is a watershed—that separates everything that went before from everything that comes after." But he and General Powell cautioned against substantial cuts in the defense budget. Gorbachev's future, they said, was uncertain; reforms were reversible. The Soviet Union, notwithstanding all the changes taking place, remained "a military superpower." Only when the "profound" changes in the Soviet system were "firmly rooted in democratic institutions— and that is certainly not the case at present," Powell said—could the United States make "deep, irrevocable changes to the foundations" of its own military strength.[34] "Simple common sense," Cheney admonished, "tells us that we should not abandon defense on the weight of one year's good news." Dangers would emerge quickly if the United States retrenched and permitted vacuums to develop in different parts of the globe.[35] It was essential, Undersecretary of Defense for Policy Paul Wolfowitz told the Senate Armed Service Committee, "to retain a prudent hedge against uncertainties." While some budget cutting made sense, dangers lurked in a world of "dizzying" change.[36]

On January 23, 1990, William Webster, the director of Central Intelligence, presented a comprehensive review of looming threats to the members of the Senate Armed Services Committee. He was especially worried about the Middle East and the Persian Gulf. "Western dependence on Persian Gulf oil will rise dramatically," he warned. At the same time, transnational terrorists were in the region, and they were developing capabilities "to operate in many parts of the world." For the moment, they were less active in Iraq, Libya, and Syria, but looming large in Iran. Some of these countries that supported terrorists were also developing ballistic missiles. "This is a particularly alarming prospect because many of them are also in the advanced stages of developing nuclear, chemical and biological warheads that could turn ballistic missiles into weapons of mass destruction. As a result, regional problems that have been of lesser policy importance to the United States could become significantly more urgent." Summing up, Webster noted that there was reason to rejoice over developments in Eastern Europe, where the conventional military threat had declined, but "the dangers inherent in rapid and unpredictable global change require that we remain firm and vigilant in our commitment to our national interests."[37]

In the wake of the collapse of the Berlin Wall, U.S. officials wanted to nurture the democratic revolutions taking place in Eastern Europe and design a new architecture for a Europe, whole and free, that would be appealing to the new noncommunist governments emerging in Poland, Hungary, and elsewhere.[38] But no matter of diplomacy and security was more important to the president and his advisers than German unification. Webster said it starkly, "The central question is the future of Germany."[39] And Bush, Scowcroft, and Baker knew precisely what they wanted: a united Germany inside NATO. For forty years NATO had been an institutional mechanism to absorb German power into a peaceful Western Europe. NATO had helped allay French anxieties and reconcile Franco-German differences. It had deterred the expansionist aspirations of Soviet Russia and projected American power and influence into the heart of Europe. From the perspective of Washington, NATO had been the key to postwar stability and order and to the Pax Americana that had made liberal democracy and consumer capitalism so attractive to the peoples of Eastern Europe. Once Germany was united, NATO would be even more vital for these purposes than ever before.[40]

But President Bush and his advisers also recognized the import of what they were doing: A united Germany inside NATO had ominous ramifications for the Soviet Union. "It would be fatal," acknowledged Scowcroft, "to post-war Soviet military strategy.... East Germany was the prize of World War II.... Losing it, and accepting that loss, would mean [the Kremlin] acknowledging the end of Soviet power in Eastern Europe and the complete erosion of Moscow's security buffer of satellite states, the very core of its security planning."[41]

Gorbachev and Foreign Minister Eduard Shevardnadze recognized that East Germans wanted unification. In elections in March 1990, the citizens of East Germany went to the polls and expressed their sentiments clearly. Candidates supporting retention of an East German state won less than 20 percent of the popular vote.[42] Soviet leaders understood they could not thwart the impulse toward unification without totally undercutting their professed commitment to democratic reform and self-determination. But they were not at all ready to accept the incorporation of a united Germany inside NATO.[43] No foreign policy matter had more resonance in the Soviet Union than this one. Germany was Soviet Russia's traditional enemy. Almost all Soviet citizens of Gorbachev's and Shevardnadze's generation remembered the anguish of the Great Patriotic War. "The past must never be repeated," Shevardnadze exclaimed. "The Soviet people have not forgotten and will never forget history's lessons."[44] These feelings, Secretary Baker recognized, were not feigned. He had the "overriding impression that Gorbachev was feeling squeezed.... Germany was over-loading his circuits. I had believed that Shevardnadze was more emotional and less logical on Germany than his boss, but...both of them were having trouble squaring the circle."[45]

Baker tried to allay the anxieties of Soviet leaders. He told them that if they would allow the German people to determine their own future and select whatever alliances they wanted, the United States and its allies would provide incentives and reassurances to the Soviet Union. Among other things, they would limit NATO forces in Europe; restate that Germany would never be allowed to possess or produce nuclear, biological, or chemical weapons; pledge that NATO forces would not be stationed on the territory of the former East Germany during a transition period; reorient the Western alliance toward a more political focus; reaffirm the integrity of the Polish-German border; and nurture increased economic ties between the new Germany and the Soviet Union. "Germany would not be untethered in the center of Europe, thus creating a dangerous instability," Baker promised Shevardnadze.[46]

When Gorbachev and Shevardnadze visited Washington at the end of May for another summit meeting, Bush pressed the issue of German unification. Did not Gorbachev agree that people could determine their own future? Did he not agree that the Helsinki accords permitted nations to choose whatever alliance they preferred? Should not a united Germany have the right to make its own choices? Grudgingly, and to the astonishment of his advisers, Gorbachev shrugged his shoulders and nodded agreement. "The dismay in the Soviet team was palpable," wrote Bush. "It was an unbelievable scene." Gorbachev quickly tried to retreat and started talking about a long transition period.[47]

Bush, Baker, and Scowcroft did not sew up the matter at the Washington summit. The president labored unsuccessfully to gain Gorbachev's unequivocal assent. "Germany can be trusted," he told Gorbachev. "For fifty years there has been democracy in Germany. This should not be ignored."[48] A democratic Germany, Bush was trying to reassure Gorbachev, would be a peaceful Germany. The reunited Germany, moreover, would be embedded in NATO and other supranational institutions like the European Community and the Conference on Security and Cooperation in Europe. These institutions would circumscribe the exercise of a united Germany's autonomous power.

But still more work needed to be done to allay Gorbachev's anxieties and win his support, and much of it was accomplished by the extraordinary efforts of the West German chancellor, Helmut Kohl. He was willing to offer huge amounts of money (about 12 billion deutsche marks) to assist Gorbachev's reform efforts, promise that Germany would never develop weapons of mass destruction, and recognize (yet again) the prevailing German-Polish border in exchange for the Kremlin's assent to the incorporation of a united Germany inside NATO. Kohl and Bush collaborated with other members of NATO to recast the alliance along more political and defensive lines. For three or four years, they agreed, NATO's activities would be restricted to the territory of the former West Germany, permitting Soviet troops to withdraw gradually from the eastern part of the country.[49] When Gorbachev finally agreed to a deal in talks that stretched through the summer of 1990, it marked a tremendous strategic victory for the West. "For me," commented Scowcroft, "the Cold War ended when the Soviets accepted a united Germany in NATO."[50]

Shaping the Post–Cold War World

Bush and his advisers were amazed and gratified by the march of events. On their watch—without the expenditure of any American blood or much money—Europe was being transformed and Germany reunited.[51] The United States was beginning to stand alone as the world's preeminent power, perhaps weakened economically relative to its allies in Western Europe and Japan, but still the linchpin of a burgeoning democratic capitalist world order. On October 2, 1990, President Bush heralded the unification of Germany and the advance of freedom: "Today the Wall lies in ruins, and our eyes open on a new world of hope."[52] But expectations could be dashed if complacency set in. The president and his advisers were worried that their successes would reignite the isolationist impulses of the American people.[53] They feared that Congress would decimate the defense budget. "We must understand," Cheney warned, "that there are threats outside those posed by the Soviet Union. . . . It is absolutely vital that we retain sufficient military force to sustain our worldwide commitments." Aside from defending American lives and territory, he emphasized, U.S. military capabilities had to be able to nurture "an environment in which freedom and democracy and market economics can flourish."[54]

As his advisers began to identify new challenges and threats, Bush outlined the contours of the nation's post–Cold War defense posture in a talk in Aspen, Colorado, on August 2, 1990. Although the arc of freedom was widening and forces could be reduced by as much as 25 percent over the next few years, peril remained. The United States, Bush said, had to guard its "enduring interests." Forces would be shaped and sized to meet regional contingencies. They would be configured "to respond to threats in whatever corner of the globe they may occur. . . . Terrorism, hostagetaking, renegade regimes and unpredictable rulers, new sources of instability—all require a strong and engaged America." The task was clear: "to shape our defense capabilities to these changing strategic circumstances."[55] With Soviet power in retreat, all regions of the world needed to be made secure for the onward rush of democratic capitalism.

As Bush spoke, Saddam Hussein's Iraqi armies marched into Kuwait. This unexpected aggression was precisely what administration officials worried about. "Unprovoked aggression," Secretary of State Baker told the Senate Committee on

Foreign Relations, "is a political test.... The Iraqi invasion of Kuwait is one of the defining moments of a new era. It is an era full of promise, but it is also one that is replete with new challenges...." The international community, Baker said, had to decide whether it had "the collective will" to thwart aggression. What most obviously was at stake, according to the secretary of state, was access to the energy resources of the Persian Gulf. The crisis emanated from "a dictator who, acting alone and unchallenged, could strangle the global economic order, determining by fiat, if you will, whether we all enter our recession [*sic*] or whether even we enter the darkness of a depression."[56] Secretary of Defense Cheney said much the same to the Senate Armed Services Committee: Saddam Hussein was seeking a "choke-hold on the world's economy." If he succeeded, he "would be in a position to blackmail any nation which chose not to do his bidding."[57]

Baker and Cheney clarified U.S. goals. "Our strategy," said Baker, "is to lead a global alliance . . . to isolate Iraq politically, economically, and militarily." This meant putting together an international coalition, including the Soviet Union and the Arab states of the Middle East as well as NATO allies. The coalition required Iraq to pull its troops out of Kuwait and restore its legitimate government. "Security and stability" had to return to the region.[58]

President Bush and his advisers were not seeking to spread freedom and democracy in the Persian Gulf through the use of force. They sought stability and access to petroleum. They also wanted to uphold a basic principle: territorial aggression (in a vital region) would not be tolerated. When French President François Mitterrand talked about repulsing Iraqi troops, not restoring the "legitimate" government of the al-Sabah family in Kuwait, Bush was upset. "I did not think we should impose democracy on the Kuwaitis," he recollected.[59] Nor for all their distaste for Saddam Hussein's brutality—in his diary Bush recounted how, in Kuwait, Saddam's troops were shooting citizens in their cars, ransacking their homes, and stealing their food—did the administration seek to remove the evil dictator from power.[60] Talking to reporters in mid-April 1991, Cheney bluntly stated, "We are not going to Baghdad. Our military objectives [do] not include changing the Iraqi government." The United States would not get into the business of governing Iraq; this, said Cheney, is

> a quagmire we don't want to involved in. I can't think of any way to make myself any clearer.... There isn't any way the President or those of us in the Administration would send American military forces into Iraq to take over the responsibility for governing that country.... It is not a military objective of the United States to go to Baghdad or to topple this government, or to get rid of Saddam Hussein.[61]

In the midst of the Persian Gulf crisis, President Bush began talking about "a new world order." Addressing a joint session of Congress on September 11, 1990, to explain American goals in Kuwait, he said:

> Out of these troubled times...a new world order can emerge: a new era—freer from the threat of terror, stronger in the pursuit of justice, and more secure in the quest for peace. An era in which the nations of the world, East and West, North and South, can prosper and live in harmony. A hundred generations have searched for this elusive path to peace, while a thousand wars raged across the span of human endeavor. Today that new world is struggling to be born, a world quite different than the one we've known. A world where the rule of law supplants the rule of the jungle. A world in which nations recognize the shared responsibility for freedom and justice. A world where the strong respect the rights of the weak.[62]

These were inspiring words, but it was not easy to discern exactly what would constitute this "new world order." In June 1991, Bush's aides summarized the contrasting ways in which the president had used the concept: sometimes emphasizing new forms of collaboration with the Soviet Union, sometimes focusing on stopping aggression and implementing collective security, sometimes highlighting the role of the United Nations and multilateral forms of collaboration.[63] While extolling the virtues of freedom, Bush reiterated in his state of the union message in January 1991 that military force was being used in the Persian Gulf War to achieve other purposes: to deter aggression, restore "legitimate" government in Kuwait, preserve access to the region's oil, and insure stability. "We seek a Persian Gulf," Bush declared, "where conflict is no longer the rule, where the strong are neither tempted nor able to intimidate the weak."[64]

During the run-up to the war in the Persian Gulf, Bush sought out Gorbachev's assistance, and he heralded the collaboration of the United States and the Soviet Union as a key element of the "new world order." But Gorbachev's position inside his country eroded as Boris Yeltsin gathered strength in the newly created Republic of Russia and as conservative elements in Gorbachev's Kremlin plotted an unsuccessful coup to remove him. Amidst the political turmoil in Moscow, U.S. officials had to determine whom they should support and to what extent they should champion the "center"—Gorbachev's base—as opposed to the newly emerging and rather autonomous republics led by Yeltsin's Russia. Although Bush still felt a strong bond with Gorbachev after the coup to topple the Soviet leader failed, geopolitical and strategic calculations in Washington trumped personal, political, and economic concerns. Cheney clearly wanted to use American influence to strengthen the republics at the expense of the center. Powell, too, favored the "dissolution of the old Soviet Union." Baker was not so inclined, but Scowcroft acknowledged that "our primary security interest would be best served by the breakup [of the Soviet Union], thus fractionating [*sic*] the military threat we faced." Bush eventually agreed: the "best arrangement would be diffusion, with many different states, none of which would have the awesome power of the Soviet Union."[65]

These policy preferences were of rather little consequence in the unfolding of events—Yeltsin outmaneuvered Gorbachev and the Soviet Union disintegrated. "It was a rare great moment in history," commented Scowcroft:

> The final collapse of Soviet power and the dissolution of its empire brought to a close the greatest transformation of the international environment since World War I and concluded nearly eight decades of upheaval and conflict.... We were suddenly in a unique position, without experience, without precedent, and standing alone at the height of power. It was, it is, an unparalleled situation in history, one which presents us with the rarest opportunity to shape the world....[66]

In this new environment, Bush and Cheney announced major changes in the nation's nuclear posture and significant cuts in the military budget. They grounded America's strategic bomber force for the first time since the 1950s and took 45 percent of its ICBM force off alert. They agreed to reduce the number of strategic and tactical nuclear warheads from about 21,000 to 8,000. Feeling enormous congressional and public pressure, Cheney cut over $250 billion out of the long-range five-year defense budget, abolished more than 85,000 civilian jobs in the Department of Defense, terminated over 100 different weapons systems, and planned to close about 300 bases worldwide. In real terms, he explained, the defense budget would be reduced 4 percent annually through fiscal year 1997.[67]

Notwithstanding these cuts, the aim of the Bush administration was to consolidate and perpetuate American geopolitical and strategic preponderance. Since the fall of the Berlin Wall, Secretary Cheney and General Powell told legislators, they had been thinking about reshaping strategy, reconfiguring forces, and making appropriate budget cuts. The strategy, said Cheney, "is designed to shape the future, to shape the course of events, and to change the course of history." Threats, he conceded, were now "remote," so remote "they are difficult to discern."[68] But in a more complicated world the United States had to prepare forces that could deal with uncertainty, anywhere. "I cannot tell," Powell said to members of the House Foreign Affairs Committee, "where the next...Saddam Hussein will appear to threaten stability in the world, but you can be certain that somewhere it will happen. It may be in the Middle East, in Europe, in East Asia, or in Latin America—wherever it occurs, we must be prepared to respond. The key to preparedness is building forces flexible enough to react to the unknown."[69]

Cheney and Powell warned Congress that it "would be a mistake of historic proportions" to cut too much or to retrench too far from Europe and Asia. The mistakes of the 1920s and 1930s must not be repeated. The United States had to lead the world, had to preserve its position of preeminence. "We are the world's sole remaining superpower," said Powell. There were no challengers, and none should be allowed. "This is a position we should not abandon," he declared. Facing a "turning point in world history," occasioned by the crumbling of the Berlin Wall, the demise of communism, the breakup of the Soviet Union, and the defeat of Saddam Hussein, Cheney emphasized that forces must be configured in new ways to preserve American leadership. We must work "to create a world in which free societies such as our own can thrive."[70]

The new strategy was designed to deal with regional contingencies, not a great war in the heart of Europe as had been the case during the Cold War. The "core goals of the regional defense strategy," Cheney told Congress, "are to protect American interests and to promote a more stable and democratic world." With little warning, threats could arise in Europe, East Asia, Southwest Asia, and Latin America. "We want to ensure that nondemocratic powers will not dominate regions of the world critical to us or come to pose a serious global challenge. To accomplish these goals, we must preserve U.S. leadership, maintain leading-edge military capabilities, and enhance collective security among democratic nations." The defense secretary outlined the four key elements of the strategy: strategic deterrence and defense; forward presence of U.S. military forces overseas; crisis response; and capacity to reconstitute additional capabilities quickly, should circumstances so dictate. The key ingredient, Cheney explained, was to have flexible forces, deployed in forward positions to "to help provide stability in critical regions of the world and to enable us to act quickly to meet crises that affect our security."[71]

In March 1992, *The New York Times* published excerpts from the Defense Policy Guidance (DPG) that Cheney's subordinates in the Pentagon had been drafting for more than six months. The news story ignited controversy. The *Times* reported that the United States was seeking to prevent the reemergence of any rival superpower in Western Europe, Asia, or the territories of the former Soviet Union. Why it stirred such emotions then (and since) is hard to fathom, because Cheney had been saying much of this publicly for many months. The new regional defense strategy was quite clear: its dominant rationale was "to prevent any hostile power from dominating a region whose resources would, under consolidated control, be sufficient to generate global power."[72] This type of thinking extrapolated previous Cold War strategy to the new era: from the late 1940s to the late 1980s, the overriding strategic goal was to prevent the Soviet Union from gaining control of the preponderant resources of Eurasia, either directly or indirectly.[73] Now, the objective was to prevent any aspiring regional hegemon from dominating any area deemed vital to U.S. security interests. According to Bush's defense strategists, mechanisms needed to be designed to deter "potential competitors from even aspiring to a larger regional or global role." Further, the new strategy required the United States to develop the capabilities to "address sources of regional conflict and instability." This meant promoting respect for international law, limiting international violence, and encouraging "the spread of democratic forms of government and open economic systems."[74]

In the February 18 draft of the DPG, defense officials acknowledged that the United States should not "become the world's policeman by assuming responsibility for righting every wrong." The objective was to design forces that could be employed selectively to address those wrongs which threatened its interests or those of its allies as well as those threats which "could seriously unsettle international relations." Cheney's subordinates clearly identified the "interests" they had in mind: "access to vital raw materials, primarily Persian Gulf oil; proliferation of weapons of mass destruction and ballistic missiles; threats to US citizens from terrorism or regional or local conflict; and threats to US society from narcotics trafficking."[75]

In short, the crumbling of the Berlin Wall and the dissolution of Soviet power meant that the United States had to consolidate and preserve its hegemonic position in the global arena, deter and dissuade challengers from arising, and "maintain a world environment where societies with shared values can flourish."[76] The aim was not to use force to promote democracy within particular nations or to deploy force for humanitarian ends or for the protection of human rights. Capabilities were designed for the purpose of nurturing an international environment conducive to American values and U.S. interests. "The concept that we have to work out every problem, everywhere in the world, is crazy," Bush cryptically wrote during the outbreak of civil war in Yugoslavia.[77]

The controversy aroused by the leaked DPG forced defense officials to revise and redraft, but the final product, signed by Secretary Cheney, put the administration's imprimatur on the new regional strategy. "Together with our democratic allies, we must preclude hostile nondemocratic powers from dominating regions critical to our interests and otherwise work to build an international environment conducive to our values." But if collective efforts were not likely to work, the United States had to have the capabilities and the will to act alone "to protect our critical interests." The challenge was "to preserve the extraordinary environment" that had emerged—"an environment within which the values of freedom that we and our principal allies hold dear can flourish. We can secure and extend the remarkable democratic 'zone of peace'…, preclude threats, and guard our national interests."[78]

While defense officials were configuring a strategy to preserve "a new world order," shaped by the United States and conducive to its interests and values, President Bush launched his campaign for reelection. The economy was contracting and he faced challengers within his own party as well as independent candidates seeking the support of traditional Republican voters. Bush now sought to claim credit for the new environment and to mold the nation's collective memory. "Think of it," he declared in his maiden speech as candidate Bush:

> The Berlin Wall came tumbling down. And last year, the Soviet Union collapsed. Imperial communism became a four-letter word D-E-A-D, dead. And today, because we stood firm, because we did the right things, America stands alone the undisputed leader of the world. We put an end to the decades of cold war and reaped a springtime harvest of peace. The American people should be proud of what together we have achieved. Now, together, we can transform the arsenal of democracy into the engine of growth.[79]

Candidate Bush now wanted Americans to take pride in their unique victory and to give him credit for it. Addressing the American Society of Newspaper Editors, he urged them to look around and take note of the extraordinary developments that had occurred. The Berlin Wall was down, communism had been vanquished, and Saddam's armies had been repulsed. Dispense with the gloom, he urged audiences, and bask in the glory that "we brought about the fall of the Iron Curtain" and "the death of imperial communism" without enduring the "cataclysm" of a third world war.[80]

The Republican Party tried to make the most of it. At its convention in August 1992, it adopted the following platform:

> "The Fall of the Berlin Wall symbolizes an epochal change in the way people live.…
>
> We Republicans saw clearly the dangers of collectivism: not only the military threat, but the deeper threat to the souls of people bound in dependence.…

Building on the legacy of Ronald Reagan, George Bush saw the chance to sweep away decadent Communism....He took the free world beyond containment, led the way to aiding democracy in Eastern Europe, and punched holes through the rusting Iron Curtain. We all remember the joy we felt when we saw the people of Berlin dancing on top of the crumbling Wall that had symbolized four decades of Communist oppression....

George Bush made it happen....

Yet now that we have won the Cold War, we must also win the peace. We must not repeat the mistake of the past by throwing away victory through complacency.[81]

At the Republican convention in August 1992, Ronald Reagan appeared for his last major political speech, putting his imprimatur on candidate Bush. It was vintage Reagan, celebrating America for being "forever young," with its "best days yet to come." Nor was he bashful about taking credit for recent events: "We stood tall and proclaimed that communism was destined for the ash heap of history." The sky would not fall, Reagan said, if an American president spoke the truth. "The only thing that would fall was the Berlin Wall." Americans should not forget that they were "the moral force that defeated communism"; they thwarted those who "would put the human soul itself into bondage."[82]

Notwithstanding Reagan's imprimatur, Bush could not overcome the economic woes and the deep divisions among conservatives. In a close election in which the independent candidate Ross Perot got almost 19 percent of the popular vote, Bush was defeated by Democratic nominee Bill Clinton. Many conservatives who ordinarily might have supported a Republican candidate wanted the United States to retrench after decades of onerous defense expenditures and dangerous commitments overseas. On December 15, 1992, at Texas A & M University, where he would build his library, Bush delivered a legacy address, seeking to shape how Americans would think about the past and plan for the future. "The Soviet Union did not simply lose the cold war," he stressed, "the western democracies won it," and U.S. leadership had been crucial. The American people now had to muster the will to win the democratic peace. "The advance of democratic ideals reflects a hard-nosed sense of our own, of American self-interest. For certain truths have, indeed, now become evident: Governments responsive to the will of the people are not likely to commit aggression. They are not likely to sponsor terrorism or to threaten humanity with weapons of mass destruction. Likewise, the spread of free markets...will sustain the expansion of American prosperity. In short, by helping others, we help ourselves."

Bush summarized the astounding achievements of the last four years: "The Berlin Wall demolished and Germany united; Russia democratic; whole classes of nuclear weapons eliminated, the rest vastly reduced...." He took great pride in forming the great coalition to thwart and reverse Saddam Hussein's aggression in Kuwait, and he trumpeted the progress that had been made in Arab-Israeli peace negotiations. But he warned: The "abandonment of the worldwide democratic revolution could be disastrous for American security....The new world could, in time, be as menacing as the old. And let me be blunt: A retreat from American leadership...would be a mistake for which future generations, indeed our own children, would pay dearly."[83]

Bush perhaps thought people might misconstrue his message. Before leaving office, he gave another thoughtful, reflective speech at West Point on January 5, 1993. The end of the Cold War was a great blessing; a new world order, a democratic peace, beckoned. To bring it about, he reiterated once again, the United States had to lead. But then he admonished that the United States should not become the world policeman; it should not "exhaust itself" in pursuit of a democratic peace. It should "not respond to each and every outrage of violence. The fact that America can act does not mean that it must." In other words, ideals should not undercut interests, he emphasized.

Force, Bush emphasized, must be used carefully and selectively. There were no rigid guidelines. There was no substitute for the exercise of judgment. "In the complex new world we are entering, there can be no single or simple set of fixed rules for using force. Inevitably, the question of military intervention requires judgment. Each and every case is unique." Even if an interest was vital, Bush explained, it did not mean that employing force was the best means of achieving it; and, paradoxically, he pointed out, sometimes using force might make sense to achieve a goal less than vital.

Whereas there were no fixed rules and judgment was the key, he did offer some guidelines: "Using military force makes sense as a policy where the stakes warrant, where and when force can be effective, where no other policies are likely to prove effective, where its application can be limited in scope and time, and where the potential benefits just the potential costs and sacrifice." He also explained that, whereas it was desirable to employ force as part of a coalition, "sometimes a great power has to act alone." Clearly, the outgoing president was agonizing over decisions he had just made to send limited troops for a humanitarian mission to Somalia while hesitating to deploy troops to the former Yugoslavia, where regional strife and civil conflict beleaguered the former Communist country. "But in every case involving the use of force," he concluded, "it will be essential to have a clear and achievable mission, a realistic plan for accomplishing the mission, and criteria to be realistic for withdrawing U.S. forces once the mission is complete."[84]

Prudence and the Democratic Peace

Three weeks later, a new man from the opposing party took the presidential oath. People expected vast changes. Bill Clinton had assailed Bush during the campaign for his restraint, for his realpolitik, and for his refusal to support freedom in China and to protect human rights and human lives in the Balkans and in Haiti. But after taking office, Clinton's rhetoric and actions resembled those of Bush: there was the same euphoria, the same determination to preserve America's preponderant power in the global arena, the same regional strategy, and the same ambivalence over the use of force.[85]

In his inaugural address, Clinton said the American people needed to embrace change and overcome drift. He then sounded much like his predecessor: "Today, a generation raised in the shadow of the Cold War assumes new responsibilities in a world warmed by the sunshine of freedom, but threatened still by ancient hatreds and new plagues." Suggesting that Bush had lacked vision and determination, Clinton stressed that he would tackle the new challenges that now appeared on the horizon. "The world," he emphasized, "was more free but less stable.... When our vital interested are challenged, or the will and conscience of the international community is defied, we will act—with peaceful diplomacy whenever possible, with force when necessary," as in the Persian Gulf and Somalia. But he then replicated the language of his former Republican foe and went on to say: "But our greatest strength is the power of our ideas, which are still new in many lands. Across the world, we see them embraced—and we rejoice. Our hopes, our hearts, our hands, are with those on every continent who are building democracy and freedom. Their cause is America's cause." The United States, he stressed, had to engage the world, avoid a return to isolationism, and enlarge the democratic peace.[86]

In Clinton's vision and memory, the collapse of the Berlin Wall also had a special place. "If the Soviet empire was a prison," he said, "then Berlin was the place where everyone could see the bars and look behind them. On one side of the wall lived a free people, shaping their destiny in the image of their dreams. On the other lived a people who desperately wanted to be free, that had found themselves trapped beyond a wall of deadly uniformity and daily indignities, in an empire that, indeed, could exist only behind a wall." What brought the Wall down, Clinton opined, was courage, vision, determination, persistence, power, conviction, and, most of all, U.S. leadership. "America's resolve and

American ideals so clearly articulated by Ronald Reagan helped to bring the wall down."[87]

According to Clinton, the crumbling of the Wall and the embrace of freedom in Berlin ignited a wave of democratic revolutions. "More people live in freedom today, he exclaimed at the end of his administration, "than at any other time in history." The march of events, moreover, began in the divided city of Berlin in November 1989. "The fall of the Berlin Wall a decade ago," Clinton declared in July 1999, "finally enabled us to pursue democratic reform in Central and Eastern Europe and to lay the firm foundations of freedom, peace, and prosperity."[88]

These beliefs did not simply inform President Clinton's rhetoric, they shaped the central contours of his foreign policy. The crumbling of the Wall, in other words, not only demonstrated the rectitude of past American policies but also served as a reminder of how things would turn out in the future if policy was conceived wisely. Clinton and his advisers defined their strategy as one of "engagement and enlargement." They sought to enlarge the democratic peace by incorporating Eastern European nations into NATO, establishing a "partnership" with democratic Russia, and expanding open trade through the adoption of the North American Free Trade Act and the embrace of the World Trade Organization. They wanted to repulse isolationist impulses, harness the forces of globalization, and embrace new technologies to advance American interests. "Underpinning our international leadership," Clinton's national security advisers explained, was "the power of our democratic ideals":

> In designing our strategy, we recognize that the spread of democracy supports American values and enhances both our security and prosperity. Democratic governments are more likely to cooperate with each other against common threats, encourage free trade, and promote sustainable economic development. They are less likely to wage war or abuse the rights of their people. Hence, the trend toward democracy and free markets throughout the world advances American interests. The United States will support this trend by remaining actively engaged in the world. This is the strategy to take us into the next century.[89]

The fall of the Berlin Wall shaped Clinton's military strategy, much like it had molded the planning of Bush and Secretary of Defense Cheney. In the first "bottom-up" strategic review conducted by Clinton's Pentagon, the thinking was remarkably similar to the final version of the Bush administration's Defense Policy Guidance. It began: "The Cold War is behind us. The Soviet Union is no longer the threat that drove our defense decision-making for four and a half decades....In 1989, the fall of the Berlin Wall and the collapse of communism throughout Eastern Europe precipitated a strategic shift away from containment of the Soviet empire." The new strategy was focused on engaging the international community, enlarging democratic alliances, and expanding world trade. There was no longer any great immediate danger; but there were looming threats—the same ones identified by the earlier Bush administration: proliferating weapons of mass destruction, regional strife, backsliding in the former Soviet Union, and a faltering American economy. To meet these threats, "our primary task, then, as a nation is to strengthen our society and economy for the demanding competitive environment of the 21st century, while at the same time avoiding the risks of precipitous reductions in defense capabilities and the overseas capabilities they support." Specifically, to meet these dangers the United States needed to engage in counter-proliferation and cooperative threat reduction activities, but the heart of the military strategy was based on a strategy designed to promote regional stability.[90]

Clinton's military strategists, like Bush's, believed that the United States had to have the capabilities to fight two regional wars simultaneously. Such capabilities provided "a hedge against the possibility that a future adversary might one day confront us with a larger-than-expected threat...."[91] During the 1990s, the concept was refined, but its core principles did not alter from Cheney and Powell's articulation in 1991–92. "As a global power with worldwide interests," stated Clinton's strategists in the 1997 Quadrennial Defense Review:

it is imperative that the United States now and for the foreseeable future be able to deter and defeat large-scale, cross-border aggression in two distant theaters in overlapping time frames, preferably in concert with regional allies. Maintaining this core capability is central to credibly deterring opportunism—that is, to avoiding a situation in which an aggressor in one region might be tempted to take advantage when U.S. forces are heavily committed elsewhere—and to ensuring that the United States has sufficient military capabilities to deter or defeat aggression by an adversary that is larger, or under circumstances that are more difficult, than expected. We can never know with certainty when or where the next major theater will occur, who our next adversary will be....A force sized and equipped for deterring and defeating aggression in more than one theater ensures the United States will maintain the flexibility to cope with the unpredictable and the unexpected. Such a capability is the sine qua non of a superpower and is essential to the credibility of our overall national security strategy.[92]

The overriding motif was that the United States had to preserve its position of preponderance against all potential competitors and challengers. "As we move into the next century," Clinton's strategists emphasized, "it is imperative that the United States maintain its military superiority in the face of evolving, as well as discontinuous, threats and challenges. Without such superiority, our ability to exert global leadership and to create international conditions conducive to the achievement of our national goals would be in doubt." And in order to preserve this leadership, the military had to embrace new technologies, modernize its business practices and intelligence capabilities, and enhance the forward positioning of U.S. troops and capabilities overseas. Prudent steps needed to be taken "today" to "respond more effectively to unlikely, but significant, future threats, such as the emergence of a regional great power or a 'wild card' scenario. Such steps provide a hedge against the possibility that unanticipated threats will emerge."[93]

The goal, as President Clinton stated in his second inaugural address, was for the United States to stand alone "as the world's indispensable nation."[94] He supported the goal of "full spectrum dominance," as his military chiefs called it, because it afforded the United States the ability to act in concert with others if it could, but to act alone if it must.[95] Clinton, like Bush, never tired of emphasizing that the United States had to lead the world. And to lead required courage, vision, determination, and, when necessary, the will to act alone. "We must always be prepared to act alone," said his national security team in 1998.[96]

Furthermore, as the perception of threat multiplied and as the reality and frequency of terrorist actions grew, Clinton's doctrine embraced the concept of possible preemption (or prevention) as well as unilateralism. In Presidential Decision Directive 39, Clinton endorsed preventative action as well as deterrence in the fight against terrorism.[97] "As long as terrorists continue to target American citizens," his strategists wrote, "we reserve the right to act in self-defense by striking their bases and those who sponsor, assist, or actively support them...."[98]

For Clinton, as for Bush, the military capabilities of the United States had to be used selectively. The reconfiguration of world power in America's favor after the demise of the Berlin Wall and the break-up of the Soviet Union meant that the United States had unprecedented strength. But Clinton's national security advisers acknowledged that force had to be used carefully. "Our strategy is tempered by recognition that there are limits to America's involvement in the world. We must be selective in the use of our capabilities...."[99] Accordingly, Clinton did not challenge China's repressive political policies or use force to avert genocide in Rwanda or to sustain a humanitarian mission in Somalia.

Late in his second administration, he did employ force against Serbia, retaliated against an alleged terrorist factory in Sudan, and readied to take action against Osama bin Laden in Afghanistan.[100] In these instances, Clinton's advisers felt that "our interests and values were affected to a sufficient degree to warrant U.S. military intervention."[101]

But, in general, Clinton and his advisers believed they could be patient, much as U.S. Cold Warriors had demonstrated patience and resolve—leading eventually to the crumbling of the Wall. Freedom would come to oppressed peoples everywhere, much as it had cracked the Wall and lured East Germans into the West. "I believe," said Clinton, "that the impulses of society and the nature of the economic change will work together, along with the availability of information from the outside world, to increase the sphere of liberty over time. I don't think there is any way that anyone who disagrees with that in China can hold back that [sic], just as eventually the Berlin Wall fell. I just think it's inevitable."[102]

Existential Threats and the Use of Force

Clinton's hesitation to act in Iraq to overthrow Saddam Hussein, however, evoked increasing ridicule from neoconservative foes and other opponents. In January 1998, Donald Rumsfeld, Paul Wolfowitz, Richard Armitage, and Robert Zoellick (among others) signed a letter calling upon Clinton "to act decisively" to remove "Saddam's regime from power," employing a "full complement of diplomatic, political, and military efforts." Their rationale said nothing of Saddam's brutality and repression, but focused on his alleged development of weapons of mass destruction and their "destabilizing effect on the entire Middle East."[103] Their sponsor, The Project for the New American Century, followed this up with a more comprehensive strategic study, completed in September 2000. Written by Donald Kagan, Gary Schmitt, and Thomas Donnelly, it harkened back to Cheney's Defense Policy Guidance in 1992, but its findings also strikingly resembled those that had shaped the Clinton national security strategy. "At present the United States faces no global rival. America's grand strategy," they wrote, "should aim to preserve and extend this advantageous position as far into the future as possible." Their gripe with Clinton was that he had not been doing enough (even though the United States was spending more on defense than all the rest of the countries in the world combined). The "core missions" they delineated were almost precisely the ones enumerated in Clinton's defense documents: defend the American homeland; fight and decisively win multiple, simultaneous major theater wars; perform the "constabulary" duties associated with shaping the security environment in critical regions; and transform U.S. forces to exploit the "revolution in military affairs."[104]

What they really sought to do was not to reconfigure strategy, but to highlight the greater scale of forces required to implement it. They pontificated briefly about expanding the "zones of democratic peace," but their focus was on deterring the rise of great-power competitors, defending key regions around the globe, developing ballistic missile defenses, and preserving "American preeminence...." The key to preeminence was in not allowing aspiring regional hegemons to acquire weapons of mass destruction lest they use such capabilities "to deter U.S. military action" and thereby gain the potential to blackmail the United States.[105]

In their campaign to win the presidency in 2000, the Republicans accused Democrats of weakness. The Republican platform stated: "The administration has run America's defenses down over the decade through inadequate resources, promiscuous commitments, and the absence of a forward looking military strategy."[106] George W. Bush, the Republican nominee for president, chose foreign policy advisers, like Condoleezza Rice, renowned for their commitment to realpolitik. Rice condemned the Clinton administration for eroding the nation's military strength and employing U.S. military forces for humanitarian purposes and nation-building.[107] When asked during a presidential debate whether he "had formed any guiding principles for exercising [America's] enormous power," Bush responded, "I have. I have. First question is what's in the best interests of the United States? What's in the best interests of our people? When it comes to foreign policy that will be my guiding question. Is it in our nation's interests?"[108]

But the trope of freedom was too tempting for the Republican candidate. He was deeply conflicted about the respective roles of interests and of values in the formation of policy. The United States, he insisted, had to have more power, but it had to use it humbly. It had to have greater capabilities, but they must not be used, Bush said, "for what's called nation-building."[109] In his inaugural address, he said that the United States must "build our defenses beyond challenge, lest weakness invite challenge." But despite these references to power and interests, the theme of freedom was the defining feature of his inaugural address: "Through much of the last century, America's faith in freedom and democracy was a rock in a raging sea. Now it is a seed in the wind, taking root in many nations. Our democratic faith is more than the creed of our country, it is the inborn hope of our humanity, an ideal we carry but do not own, a trust we bear and pass along. And even after near 225 years, we have a long way yet to travel."[110]

To reconcile his concern for power and his embrace of freedom, Bush concocted the notion, rarely defined or explained, "of a balance of power in favor of freedom." America, Bush emphasized, "remains engaged in the world by history and by choice, shaping a balance of power that favors freedom. We will defend our allies and our interests. We will show purpose without arrogance. We will meet aggression and bad faith with resolve and strength. And to all nations, we will speak for the values that gave our nation birth."[111]

Freedom dominated the new president's discourse—although it did not shape his foreign policy—during his first nine months in office. In speech after foreign policy speech, George W. Bush talked about freedom. Addressing Congress about the administration's goals, he said that he would promote "a distinctly American internationalism. We will work with our allies and friends to be a force for good and a champion of freedom. We will work for free markets, free trade, and freedom from oppression." On March 4, 2001, while championing missile defense, he exclaimed, "America, by nature, stands for freedom." On May 1, at the National Defense University, he noted the vastly different world that had evolved in recent years. "The Wall is gone," and the sun rises on a transformed international landscape. On May 3, to the American Jewish Committee, he voiced alarm about freedom of religion in the world: We must protect that freedom—"the first freedom of the human soul." On May 25, at the Naval Academy, he stressed "that no one can be neutral between right and wrong, tyranny and freedom." And, in Poland, on June 15, he heralded the spread of freedom: "Today, a new generation makes a new commitment....The Iron Curtain is no more. Now we plan and build a house of freedom, whose doors are open to all of Europe's peoples and whose windows look out to global challenges beyond." And, on July 17, at the World Bank, he offered his own interpretation of globalization: "What some call globalization is, in fact, the triumph of human liberty stretching across national borders."[112]

Freedom, however, was beleaguered by rogue states and terrorist organizations. Bush warned that they might acquire weapons of mass destruction and blackmail the United States. "Unlike the cold war," he noted,

> today's most urgent threat stems not from thousands of ballistic missiles in Soviet hands but from a small number of missiles in the hands of these states, states for whom terror and blackmail are a way of life....Like Saddam Hussein, some of today's tyrants are gripped by an implacable hatred of the United States of America. They hate our friends. They hate our values. They hate democracy and freedom and individual liberty....In such a world cold war deterrence is not enough.[113]

The United States, according to President Bush, needed to use its power "for a broad strategy" of counter-proliferation. "We need new concepts of deterrence," he explained, "that rely on both offensive and defensive forces." He wanted the United States to move beyond the constraints of the 1972 Anti-Ballistic-Missile Treaty, harness technology for new forms of defense, and reconfigure (and downsize) the composition of nuclear forces to meet the new threats of a post–Cold War world. The overriding task was to thwart the spread of weapons of mass destruction. Should adversaries acquire these weapons, Bush reiterated, they would blackmail the United States and deter it from "forward thinking about fighting terrorism." The president asked Congress for an increase of $39 billion over the original 2001 military request submitted by the previous administration—the largest expansion in military spending since the Reagan buildup in the early 1980s.[114] The discourse about freedom and its universal appeal—reinforced by recollections of the Wall's coming down—buttressed the administration's case to augment U.S. military capabilities to meet the challenges of a new era.

But alongside the plans to augment U.S. power, Bush's focus during these first nine months in office was also on the role of trade in the promotion of liberty. "Open trade," he emphasized, was one of his top priorities. "Open trade fuels the engines of economic growth.... It applies the power of the market to the needs of the poor. It spurs the processes of economic and legal reform.... And open trade reinforces the habits of liberty that sustain democracy over the long term." And, again, on May 29, he reiterated that open trade "is a force for freedom in China, a force for stability in Asia, and a force for prosperity in the United States."[115]

This eclectic and ill-defined amalgam of freedom, power, interests, and openness came to an end on September 11, 2001. On that day, the looming threat materialized with dramatic suddenness: not long before, it had seemed distant and inchoate; now it was ferocious and omnipresent. Administration officials felt that war had been declared on the United States. Danger lurked everywhere, reinforced by the anonymous delivery of letters containing anthrax in the immediate aftermath of the attack on the Twin Towers and the Pentagon. The events of 9/11, said Condoleezza Rice, "crystallized our vulnerability." "After 9/11," she went on, "there is no longer any doubt that today America faces an existential threat to our security—a threat as great as any we faced during the Civil War, World War II, or the Cold War."[116]

Facing peril, the Bush administration unleashed America's awesome military power, first against the Taliban in Afghanistan and then against Saddam Hussein in Iraq. Its rationale was straightforward: "the greater the threat, the greater is the risk of inaction." Peril justified the preemptive and unilateral use of America's military force. Peril meant that the United States had to shock and overwhelm the adversary. But the president and his advisers emphasized that the mission was larger than defense of country: "We fight, as we always fight," they stressed, "for a just peace—a peace that favors liberty."[117]

The tropes of the Cold War and the memories of Berlin were vivid. When Iraqi forces were crushed, and American troops entered Baghdad, the president rejoiced. America's mission had been accomplished; its commitment to liberty vindicated. Iraqis—like Germans, and like all human beings—yearned to be free.[118] "The toppling of Saddam Hussein's statue in Baghdad," he later explained, "will be recorded alongside the fall of the Berlin Wall as one of the great moments in the history of liberty."[119] Most Americans shared this viewpoint. They believed that the crumbling of the Wall had been an important, perhaps even one of the most decisive, moments in the twentieth century.[120]

Tragedy and peril transformed the quest for a democratic peace into a national security imperative that justified the use of force and the exercise of America's unparalleled power. Advancing America's ideals, Bush proclaimed in his second inaugural address, had "become the urgent requirement of our nation's security and the calling of our time." It was now the policy of the United States, he declared, "to seek and support the growth of democratic movements and institutions in every nation and culture, with the ultimate goal of ending tyranny in our world."[121] Tolerating tyranny, he explained, had been a strategic as well as moral failure. "Pursuing stability at the expense of liberty does not lead to peace—it leads to September the 11th, 2001."[122] Although the quest for freedom was fraught with difficulty, and the liberation of Iraq had become a nightmare, the challenge could not be avoided. During the long Cold War, he recollected, people also had despaired, but courage and persistence had paid off. "When Harry Truman promised American support for free peoples resisting Soviet aggression," Bush told the American people on the fifth anniversary of the September 11 attacks, Truman "could not have foreseen the rise of the Berlin Wall, but he would not have been surprised to see it brought down. Throughout our history," Bush continued, "America has seen liberty challenged, and every time, we have seen liberty triumph with sacrifice and determination." In other words, the battle of ideas could not be forsaken. Freedom now prevailed across the European continent, and one day it would "ring out across the world." Like President Clinton before him, Bush loved to remind audiences that "more people now live in freedom than ever before."[123]

Except that they didn't. The Freedom House, an organization with no wish to embarrass George W. Bush, reported in 2007 and 2008 that worrisome trends had set in: "The year 2007 was marked by a notable setback for global freedom," it reported. It was the first time in fifteen years that freedom had registered setbacks in two consecutive years. In 2007, thirty-eight countries showed evidence of declines in freedom, while only ten displayed a positive trajectory. In the Middle East, in particular, the region that George W. Bush so desperately wanted to transform, the signs were especially portentous: declines were evident in Egypt, Syria, Lebanon, and the Palestinian Authority. Many of these countries had been moving in a positive direction, but that no longer was the case.[124]

Freedom was faltering for many reasons, but one of the most conspicuous was the fallout of 9/11. America's use of force had tarnished America's reputation and undercut its capacity to be a force for democratic change.[125]

Power, Mission, and Threat Perception

Power and a sense of mission can be intoxicating as well as uplifting. George H. W. Bush and Bill Clinton rejoiced in the crumbling of the Berlin Wall. They believed it confirmed America as the world's one indispensable nation. They sought to rebuff isolationist impulses, solidify U.S. preponderance, and enhance the nation's capabilities to intervene in regions far from America's shores. Yet they also recognized that force had to be used soberly, prudently, and judiciously. Freedom did not come easily—certainly not through the barrel of a gun or even by simply depositing a ballot in an election box. Freedom required tolerance, openness, and the rule of law.[126] Their actions and inactions—for good and for bad—illuminated how complicated such matters were.

George W. Bush embraced many of the same ideas of his predecessors and wanted to employ and augment the capabilities they had nurtured to effectuate a more open world conducive to U.S. interests and values and amenable to U.S. power. He wanted to build missile defenses and deter potential foes. He wanted to promote U.S. interests and spread its ideals, ideals that in his view had universal appeal and a divine imprimatur. He hoped to do all these things without acting arrogantly and counterproductively. But once the United States was attacked and its vulnerabilities exposed, the temptation to use its unmatched capabilities was irresistible.[127]

Threat and peril transformed rhetorical tropes into an action agenda. After all, policymakers in Washington had been planning for regional wars for almost a decade and now had justification and incentive to put planning to practice. Declaring a righteous mission, President George W. Bush set out to defeat evil and end tyranny, confident that the story of the Cold War and the crumbling of the Berlin Wall vindicated America's past efforts and portended ever more glory, more freedom, and more power in the future.

No matter how desperate the situation appeared in Baghdad during the awful days of 2004–7, the president and his advisers could recall the bleakest days of the Cold War—the blockade of Berlin in 1948 and the face-off of Soviet and American tanks at checkpoint Charlie in 1961—and then recall the unanticipated joys of victory on November 9, 1989. For them, the mystic chords of memory ran deep and long. Freedom would prevail—even in the Middle East—if the United States demonstrated its resolve and applied its power. Were not those the best-informed lessons of the long twilight struggle with communism? Or were they illusory dreams emanating from rhetorical tropes and manufactured memories that associated the end of the Cold War with Berliners traversing the Wall—dancing for joy, dancing for history?[128]

NOTES

I am indebted to Seth Center, Andrew Ferguson, and James Wilson for their research assistance, most especially to Seth for his thoughtful advice and illuminating suggestions. This chapter also benefited greatly from dialogue with Jim Sheehan, Chen Jian, William Taubman, Svetlana Savranskaya, Frank Gavin, Jeffrey Engel, and Susan Ferber as well as from a colloquium with my colleagues and graduate students at the Miller Center of The University of Virginia.

1. See chapter 2, this volume, by James J. Sheehan; also see, for example, Frederic Bozo, "France, German Unification and European Integration," in *Europe and the End of the Cold War: A Reappraisal,* edited by Frederic Bozo et al. (London: Routledge, 2008), 148–61.

2. See chapter 4, this volume, by Chen Jian.

3. See, for example, the account of Gorbachev in Vladislav M. Zubok, *A Failed Empire: The Soviet Union in the Cold War from Stalin to Gorbachev* (Chapel Hill: University of North Carolina Press, 2007), 303–35.

4. For this distinction, see the incisive analysis by David Kennedy, "Two Concepts of Sovereignty," in *To Lead the World: American Strategy After the Bush Doctrine,* edited by Melvyn P. Leffler and Jeffrey W. Legro (New York: Oxford University Press, 2008), 165–74.

5. George W. Bush, "Proclamation 7499—World Freedom Day, 2001," November 9, 2001, http://www.presidency.ucsb.edu/ws/index.php?pid=61796 (accessed May 16, 2009).

6. "Dod News Briefing–Secretary Rumsfeld and Gen Myers," April 9, 2003, http://www.defenselink.mil/transcripts/transcript.aspx?transcriptid=2339 (accessed May 17, 2009).

7. For the use of "keywords" in American history, see Daniel T. Rodgers, *Contested Truths: Keywords in American History* (New York: Basic Books, 1987), esp. 3–16, 212–17.

8. Bush, "Remarks to the Democracy and Security Conference in Prague," June 5, 2007, http://www.presidency.ucsb.edu/ws/index.php?pid=75306&st=&st1= (accessed May 17, 2009); Bush, "Speech to the OECD," June 13, 2008, http://www.oecd.org/document/50/0,3343,en_2649_201185_40835506_1_1_1_1,00.html (accessed May 16, 2009).

9. Kiron K. Skinner, Annelise Anderson, and Martin Anderson, eds., *Reagan in His Own Hand* (New York: Simon and Schuster, 2001), 15.

10. Ronald Reagan, "Remarks at the Annual Convention of the National Association of Evangelicals [March 8, 1983]," in *Public Papers of the Presidents: Ronald Reagan* (Washington, D.C.: Government Printing Office, 1984), 743. Hereafter, citations of the Reagan volumes of *Public Papers of the Presidents* are abbreviated "*RR* (year), page."

11. Reagan, "Address to Members of British Parliament [June 8, 1982]," *RR* (1982), 745.

12. Quoted in Paul Kengor, *God and Ronald Reagan* (New York: HarperCollins, 2004), 94–96.

13. Reagan, "Second Inaugural Address [January 21, 1985]," *RR* (1985), 58; also see Hugh Heclo, "Ronald Reagan and American Public Philosophy," in *The Reagan Presidency: Pragmatic Conservatism and Its Legacies,* edited by W. Elliot Brownlee and Hugh Davis Graham (Lawrence: University Press of Kansas, 2003), 17–39.

14. Peter Robinson, "Tear Down This Wall," *Reader's Digest,* http://www.rd.com/content/printContent.do?contentId=28515&KeepThis=true&TB_iframe=true&height=500&width=790&modal=true (accessed May 16, 2009).

15. Reagan, ""Remarks on East-West Relations at the Brandenburg Gate [June 12, 1987]," *RR* (1987), 635.

16. Anatoly S. Chernyaev Diary, June 15, 1987, translated by Anna Melyakova and Svetlana Savranskaya. Manuscript on file at the National Security Archive, George Washington University, Washington, D.C., http://www.gwu.edu/~nsarchiv/NSAEBB/NSAEBB220/index.htm.

17. George J. Church, "Back to the Wall: Reagan Rallies with a Strong Speech," *Time,* June 22, 1987, 18; Russell Watson et al., "Waiting for Gorbachev," *Newsweek,* June 22, 1987, 18; William L. Chaze, "Once Again, the President's Age Is at Issue," *U.S. News & World Report,* June 22, 1987, 20; Gerald M. Boyd, "Raze Berlin Wall, Reagan Urges Soviet," *The New York Times,* June 13, 1987, 3; Helen Thomas, "Reagan to Call for Berlin Wall's End," *The Washington Post,* June 12, 1987, A1; Lou Cannon, "Reagan Challenges Soviets to Dismantle Berlin Wall, *The Washington Post,* June 12, 1987, A1; and Philip Revzin, "Gorbachev Plays All the Right Cards against Allies," June 17, 1987, The Wall Street Journal, 22. I am indebted to two research assistants, Andrew Ferguson and James G. Wilson, for their research in newspapers and newsweeklies. Also see Philip Zelikow and Condoleezza Rice, *Germany Unified and Europe Transformed: A Study in Statecraft* (Cambridge, Mass.: Harvard University Press, 1997), 20.

18. Hans-Hermann Hertle, "The Fall of the Wall: The Unintended Self-Dissolution of East Germany's Ruling Regime," [Cold War International History Project] *Bulletin* 12/13 (Fall/Winter 2001): 134–37.

19. Ibid., 137.

20. Michael Meyer et al., "The Wall Comes Down: Is It Possible?" *Newsweek*, November 20, 1989, 24; "The End of the War to End Wars," *The New York Times*, November 11, 1989, 26; also see, for example, George J. Church, "Freedom! The Wall Crumbles Overnight, Berliners Embrace in Disbelieving Joy, and a Stunned World Ponders the Consequences," *Time*, November 20, 1989, 24ff.

21. "Remarks and a Question-and-Answer Session with Reporters [November 9, 1989]," *Public Papers of the Presidents: George Herbert Walker Bush* (Washington, D.C.: Government Printing Office, 1989), 1488–90. Hereafter, citations of the Bush volumes of *Public Papers of the Presidents* are abbreviated "*GHWB* (year), page."

22. Memorandum of Telephone Conversation, November 10, 1989, box 3, End of Cold War Collection, National Security Archive, Washington D.C. Manuscript on file at the National Security Archive, George Washington University, Washington, D.C., http://www.gwu.edu/~nsarchiv/NSAEBB/NSAEBB220/index.htm.

23. Bush, "Interview with Foreign Journalists [November 21, 1989]," *GHWB* (1989), 1588.

24. "Inaugural Address [January 20, 1989]," *GHWB* (1989), 1; "Address Before a Joint Session of Congress [February 9, 1989]," *GHWB* (1989), 79.

25. George Bush and Brent Scowcroft, *A World Transformed* (New York: Vintage Books, 1998), 13.

26. "Remarks at the Swearing-in Ceremony [March 21, 1989]," *GHWB* (1989), 277.

27. Robert M. Gates, *From the Shadows: The Ultimate Insider's Story of Five Presidents and How They Won the Cold War* (New York: Touchstone, 1997), 474.

28. Bush and Scowcroft, *World Transformed*, 44; James A. Baker, III, with Thomas M. DeFrank, *The Politics of Diplomacy: Revolution, War and Peace, 1989–1992* (New York: G. P. Putnam's Sons, 1995), 93–94.

29. For background, see Melvyn P. Leffler, *For the Soul of Mankind: The United States, the Soviet Union, and the Cold War* (New York: Hill and Wang, 2007), 423–27; and Tim Naftali, *George H. W. Bush* (New York: Times Books, 2007), 1–100. For an example of the astonishment, see Cheney, "Interview with Reporters," October 30, 1989, Public Statements of Richard B. Cheney, Secretary of Defense, George Herbert Walker Bush Presidential Library (Texas A & M University). Hereafter, the Richard B. Cheney public statements collection in the Bush Presidential Library will be abbreviated RBC-BPL.

30. Bush and Scowcroft, *World Transformed*, 151.

31. "Interview with Members of the White House Press Corps [July 13, 1989]," *GHWB* (1989), 951–53; "Interview with Hungarian Journalists [July 6, 1989]," *GHWB* (1989), 914; "President's News Conference [July 6, 1989]," *GHWB* (1989), 899, 900; "The President's News Conference in Paris [July 16, 1989]," *GHWB* (1989), 973; and Gates, *From the Shadows*, 466.

32. George Bush, *All the Best, George Bush: My Life in Letters and Other Writings* (New York: Scribner, 1999), 446, 451; Bush and Scowcroft, *World Transformed*, 148–49.

33. Bush, "Thanksgiving Address to the Nation [November 22, 1989]," *GHWB* (1989), 1581–84.

34. Cheney and Powell, testimony and statements, February 7, 1990, House Committee on the Budget, *Administration's Defense Budget,* 101st Cong., 2nd sess. (Washington, D.C.: Government Printing Office, 1990), quotations on 5, 12, 114.

35. Cheney, "Remarks prepared for Delivery at the National Newspaper Association," March 16, 1990, RBC-BPL; Cheney, "Remarks Prepared for Delivery at the United Jewish Appeal National Young Leadership Conference," March 13, 1990, RBC-BPL.

36. Paul D. Wolfowitz, statement, December 12, 1989, Senate Committee on Armed Services, *Threat Assessment; Military Strategy; and Operational Requirements,* 101st Cong., 2nd sess. (Washington D.C.: Government Printing Office, 1989), 5–10, 32.

37. William H. Webster, statement, January 23, 1990, Senate Committee on Armed Services, *Threat Assessment; Military Strategy; and Operational Requirements,* 101st Cong., 2nd sess. (Washington D.C.: Government Printing Office, 1989), 57–61 (quotations on 60 and 61).

38. See, for example, James Baker, "A New Europe, A New Atlanticism: Architecture for a New Era," Vital Speeches of the Day, 56(January 15, 1990), 195–99.

39. Webster, Statement, January 23, 1990, Senate, Armed Services, *Threat Assessment,* 58.

40. Baker, "A New Europe, A New Atlanticism."

41. Bush and Scowcroft, *World Transformed,* 186; Leffler, *For the Soul of Mankind,* 439–48.

42. Konrad Jarausch, *The Rush to German Unity* (New York: Oxford University Press, 1994), 115–17.

43. Leffler, *For the Soul of Mankind,* 439–46; Zelikow and Rice, *Germany Unified and Europe Transformed;* Mary Elise Sarotte, *1989 and the Architecture of Order: The Competition to Lead the Post–Cold War World* (Princeton, N.J.: Princeton University Press, 2009).

44. Shevardnadze, speech, November 17, 1989, Foreign Broadcasting Information Service (FBIS), November 20, 1989, 46.

45. Baker, *Politics of Diplomacy,* 252.

46. For a cogent summary, see Hannes Adomeit, "Gorbachev's Consent to United Germany's Membership of NATO," in *Europe and the End of the Cold War: A Reappraisal,* edited by Frederic Bozo et al. (London: Routledge, 2008), 112; Baker, *Politics of Diplomacy,* 244–54 (quotation on 245).

47. Bush and Scowcroft, *World Transformed,* 281–83.

48. Mikhail Gorbachev, *Memoirs,* 533; Bush and Scowcroft, *World Transformed,* 281–82.

49. Sarotte, *1989 and the Architecture of Order,* especially chapters 3–5; Adomeit, "Gorbachev's Consent to United Germany's Membership of NATO," 113–15.

50. Bush and Scowcroft, *World Transformed,* 299.

51. For the standard account by two officials, see Zelikow and Rice, *Germany Unified and Europe Transformed.*

52. Bush, "Address to the German People on the Reunification of Germany [October 2, 1990]," *GHWB* (1990), 1348.

53. For a traditional account of isolationism in American history, see Selig Adler, *The Isolationist Impulse: Its Twentieth Century Reaction* (New York: Abelard-Schuman, 1957).

54. Cheney, "Commencement Address at Graduation Ceremonies of the National War College," June 13, 1990, RBC-BPL; Cheney, "Address to the Tenth Anniversary Celebration of the World Affairs Council," June 8, 1990, RBC-BPL.

55. "Remarks at the Aspen Institute Symposium [August 2, 1990]," *GHWB* (1990), 1089–93.

56. Statement by Baker, September 5, 1990, Senate Committee on Foreign Relations, *U.S. Policy in the Persian Gulf,* 101st Cong., 2nd sess. (Washington, D.C.: Government Printing Office, 1990), 8–11; for background, also see Hal Brands, *From Berlin to Baghdad: America's Search for Purpose in the Post-Cold War World* (Lexington: University Press of Kentucky, 2008), 1–73.

57. Cheney, statement, September 11, 1990, Senate Committee on Armed Services, *Crisis in the Persian Gulf: U.S. Policy Options and Implications,* 101st Cong., 2nd sess. (Washington, D.C.: Government Printing Office, 1990), 643–44.

58. Baker, statement, *U.S. Policy in the Persian Gulf,* 10, 11; Cheney, statement, *Crisis in the Persian Gulf,* 644.

59. Bush and Scowcroft, *World Transformed,* 376.

60. Ibid., 374.

61. Cheney, "Interview with Editors and Reporters," April 16, 1991, RBC-BPL.

62. Bush, "Address Before a Joint Session of the Congress [September 11, 1990]," *GHWB,* 1990, 1219.

63. Dan Jahn to John Snow, June 26, 1991, Speech File, George Herbert Walker Bush Presidential Library (Texas A & M University); for assessments of the "New World Order," also see Brands, *Berlin to Baghdad,* 74–100; Derek Chollet and James Goldgeier, *America Between the Wars From 11/9 to 9/11* (New York: Public Affairs, 2008), 6–41; Zbigniew Brzezinski, *Second Chance: Three Presidents and the Crisis of American Superpower* (New York: Basic Books, 2007), 45–82.

64. Bush, "Address on the State of the Union [January 29, 1991]," *GHWB* (1991), 78.

65. Bush and Scowcroft, *World Transformed,* 541–43; Cheney, "Interview with Jim Lehrer," January 17, 1992, RBC-BPL. Although Bush agreed, his affection and admiration for Gorbachev were clear. See Bush, *All the Best,* 532–33, 542–43.

66. Bush and Scowcroft, *World Transformed,* 564.

67. Powell and Cheney, testimony, March 24, 1992, House Committee on Foreign Affairs, *The Future of U.S. Foreign Policy in the Post-Cold War Era,* 102nd Cong., 2nd sess. (Washington, D.C.: Government Printing Office, 1992), 354–61, 297–98, 331; Cheney, "Interview with *San Diego Union,*" November 12, 1991, RBC-BPL; Cheney, "Interview with Judy Woodruff," October 1, 1991, RBC-BPL.

68. Cheney, testimony, *Future of U.S. Foreign Policy,* 291, 304; also see Cheney, "Remarks to the U.S. Naval Academy," October 8, 1991, RBC-BPL.

69. Powell, testimony, *Future of U.S. Foreign Policy,* 369–70.

70. Ibid., 425, 367; Cheney, "Remarks to the World Affairs Council of Northern California," February 12, 1992, RBC-BPL.

71. Cheney, testimony, *Future of U.S. Foreign Policy,* 320–21; Cheney, "Remarks to the World Affairs Council of Northern California," February 12, 1992, RBC-BPL.

72. Dick Cheney, Defense Strategy for the 1990s: The Regional Defense Strategy, 1–3, in "The Nuclear Vault—The Making of the Cheney Regional Defense Strategy, 1991–1992," National Security Archive, Washington, D.C., http://www.gwu.edu/~nsarchiv/nukevault/ebb245/doc15.pdf (accessed May 17, 2009).

73. Melvyn P. Leffler, *A Preponderance of Power: National Security, the Truman Administration, and the Cold War* (Stanford, Calif.: Stanford University Press, 1992).

74. Chollet and Goldgeier, *America Between the Wars,* 44–45; successive drafts of the Defense Policy Guidance, from which I am quoting, may be found in "The Nuclear Vault—The Making of the Cheney Regional Defense Strategy, 1991–1992," http://www.gwu.edu/~nsarchiv/nukevault/ebb245/index.htm.

75. "Defense Policy Guidance, FY 1994–1992," February 18, 1992, 2, http://www.gwu.edu/~nsarchiv/nukevault/ebb245/index.htm.

76. Ibid., 8.

77. Bush, *All the Best,* 527.

78. Cheney, *Defense Strategy for the 1990s: The Regional Defense Strategy,* January 1993, 1, 27, http://www.gwu.edu/~nsarchiv/nukevault/ebb245/index.htm (accessed May 17, 2009).

79. Bush, "Remarks Announcing the Bush-Quayle Candidacies for Reelection [February 12, 1992]," *GHWB* (1992), 233–34.

80. Bush, "Remarks at the Ohio Freedom Day Celebration [May 21, 1992]," *GHWB* (1992), 812–14.

81. "Republican party Platform of 1992," August 17, 1992, The American Presidency Project, http://www.presidency.ucsb.edu/ws/index.php?pid=78545.

82. Reagan, "Address to the Republican National Convention," August 17, 1992, http://en.wikisource.org/wiki/Ronald_Reagan's_Speech_to_the_1992_GOP_Convention.

83. Bush, "Remarks at Texas A & M University [December 15, 1992]," *GHWB* (1992), 2189–94.

84. Bush, "Remarks at the United States Military Academy [January 5, 1993]," *GHWB* (1992–93), 2228–33.

85. For background, see David Halberstam, *War in a Time of Peace: Bush, Clinton, and the Generals* (New York: Simon and Schuster, 2001), 1–194.

86. Bill Clinton, "First Inaugural Address [January 21, 1993]," *Public Papers of the Presidents: William Jefferson Clinton* (Washington, D.C.: Government Printing Office, 1993), 1–3. Hereafter, citations of the Clinton volumes of *Public Papers of the Presidents* are abbreviated *"WJC* (year), page." Also see The White House, "A National Security Strategy of Engagement and Enlargement," (Washington, D.C.: The White House, 1996).

87. Clinton, "Remarks at Georgetown University [November 8, 1999]," *WJC* (1999), 2009; Clinton, "Remarks at the Dedication of the Ronald Reagan Building and International Trade Center [May 5, 1998]," *WJC* (1998), 690–92.

88. Clinton, "Proclamation 7386—Human Rights Day, Bill of Rights Day, and Human Rights Week, 2000," December 9, 2000, http://www.presidency.ucsb.edu/ws/

index.php?pid=62339; Clinton, "Proclamation 7209—Captive Nations Week, 1999," July 16, 1999, http://www.presidency.ucsb.edu/ws/index.php?pid=57894&st=proclamation+7209&st1=.

89. White House, *A National Security Strategy for a New Century*, October 1998 (Washington, D.C.: The White House, 1998), 2 (for quotation), 5, 6, 33, 41, 47, 50, 54; for Clinton's own summary of his policies, see Clinton, "Remarks on Receiving the International Charlemagne Prize in Aachen, Germany [June 2, 2000]," *WJC* (2000–2001), 1064–68.

90. Secretary of Defense, *National Security in the Post–Cold War Era*, October 1993, quotations on 1, 3, http://www.fas.org/man/docs/bur/part01.htm (accessed May 17, 2009).

91. Ibid., 3–4.

92. Secretary of Defense, *Quadrennial Defense Review*, May 1997, 6, http://www.fas.org/man/docs/qdr/ (accessed May 17, 2009).

93. Ibid., 7–11 (quotations on 7, 9).

94. Clinton, "Inaugural Address [January 20, 1997]," *WJC* (1997), 43–46.

95. "To act alone," see White House, *National Security Strategy of Engagement and Enlargement*, ii; for "full spectrum" dominance, see Secretary of Defense, *Quadrennial Defense Review*, 8.

96. White House, *National Security Strategy for a New Century*, 2.

97. Presidential Decision Directive 39, "U.S. Policy on Counterterrorism," June 21, 1995, http://www.fas.org/irp/offdocs/pdd39.htm (accessed May 17, 2009).

98. White House, *A National Security Strategy for a Global Age* (Washington, D.C.: The White House, 2000), 11–15 (quotation on 14).

99. White House, *National Security Strategy of Engagement and Enlargement*, ii; White House, *National Security Strategy for a New Century*, 2.

100. White House, *National Security Strategy for a Global Age*, 3–4; for background, also see Warren I. Cohen, *America's Failing Empire: U.S. Foreign Relations since the Cold War* (Malden, Mass. Blackwell Publishing, 2005), 56–122; Chollet and Goldgeier, *America Between the Wars;* Halberstam, *War in a Time of Peace;* Brands, *Berlin to Baghdad.*

101. White House, *National Security Strategy for a Global Age*, 3.

102. "The President's Press Conference [January 28, 1997]," *WJC* (1997), 84.

103. The Project for the New American Century (PNAC) Clinton Letter, January 26, 1998, http://www.newamericancentury.org/iraqclintonletter.htm.

104. A Report of The Project for the New American Century, *Rebuilding America's Defenses: Strategy, Forces and Resources For a New Century*, September 2000 [http://www.newamericancentury.org/RebuildingAmericasDefenses.pdf], i, iv (accessed May 17, 2009); for relative military expenditures, see William E. Odom and Robert Dujarric, *America's Inadvertent Empire* (New Haven, Conn.: Yale University Press, 2004), 64–96; Andrew Bacevitch, *American Empire: The Realities and Consequences of U.S. Diplomacy* (Cambridge, Mass: Harvard University Press, 2004).

105. Project for the New American Century, *Rebuilding America's Defenses*, 2, 6, 13.

106. Republican Party Platform of 2000, July 31, 2000, http://www.presidency.ucsb.edu/ws/index.php?pid=25849 (accessed May 17, 2009).

107. Condoleezza Rice, "Campaign 2000—Promoting the National Interest," *Foreign Affairs* 79 (January-February 2000): 1–8.

108. "Presidential Debate in Winston-Salem, North Carolina," October 11, 2000, http://www.debates.org/pages/trans2000b.html (accessed May 17, 2009).

109. Ibid.

110. Bush, "Inaugural Address [January 20, 2001]," *Public Papers of the Presidents: George Walker Bush* (Washington, D.C.: Government Printing Office, 2001), 1–3. Hereafter, citations of the George W. Bush volumes of *Public Papers of the Presidents* are abbreviated "*GWB* (year), page."

111. Ibid.

112. Bush, "Address Before a Joint Session of Congress [February 27, 2001]," *GWB* (2001), 145; Bush, "Remarks at the Christening Ceremony for the U.S.S. Ronald Reagan at Newport News, Virginia [March 4, 2001]," *GWB* (2001), 190; Bush, "Remarks at the National Defense University [May 1, 2001]," *GWB* (2001), 471; Bush, "Remarks to the American Jewish Committee [May 3, 2001]," *GWB* (2001), 487–88; Bush, "Commencement Address at the United States Naval Academy [May 25, 2001]," *GWB* (2001), 579; Bush, "Address at Warsaw University [June 15, 2001]," *GWB* (2001), 681; and Bush, "Remarks at the World Bank," July 17, 2001, http://www.presidency.ucsb.edu/ws/index.php?pid=73621 (accessed May 17, 2009).

113. Bush, "Remarks at the National Defense University [May 1, 2001]," *GWB* (2001), 471–72.

114. Ibid.; Bush, "The President's News Conference [June 12, 2001]," *GWB* (2001), 640–41; Bush, "The President's News Conference [June 15, 2001]," *GWB* (2001), 672; Bush, "Remarks at the Veterans of Foreign Wars Convention, August 20, 2001, http://www.presidency.ucsb.edu/ws/index.php?pid=63225&st=remarks+at+the+veterans+of+foreign+wars+convention&st1 (accessed May 17, 2009).

115. Bush, "Remarks to the Organization of American States [April 17, 2001]," *GWB* (2001), 408–409; Bush, "Remarks to the Los Angeles World Affairs Council [May 29, 2001]," *GWB* (2001), 593–98.

116. Condoleezza Rice, "A Balance of Power that Favors Freedom," October 1, 2002, http://www.manhattan-institute.org/html/wl2002.htm (accessed May 17, 2009).

117. The administration's clearest statement of strategy was "The National Security Strategy of the United States of America," September 17, 2002 (Washington, D.C.: The White House, 2002)].

118. Bush, "Remarks from the USS Abraham Lincoln," May 1, 2003, http://www.presidency.ucsb.edu/ws/index.php?pid=68675&st=&st1= (accessed May 17, 2009).

119. Bush, "Remarks at Fort Hood," April 12, 2005, http://www.presidency.ucsb.edu/ws/index.php?pid=62995&st=&st1= (accessed May 17, 2009).

120. Gallup Poll, November 1999, Roper Center for Public Opinion Research, University of Connecticut.

121. Bush, "Second Inaugural Address," January 20, 2005, http://www.presidency.ucsb.edu/ws/index.php?pid=58745&st=&st1= (accessed May 17, 2009).

122. Bush, "Remarks to the Democracy and Security Conference in Prague," June 5, 2007, http://www.presidency.ucsb.edu/ws/index.php?pid=75306&st=&st1= (accessed May 17, 2009).

123. Bush, "Address to the Nation on the War on Terror," September 11, 2006, http://www.presidency.ucsb.edu/ws/index.php?pid=73962&st=&st1= (accessed May 18, 2009); Bush, "Speech to the OECD," June 13, 2008, http://www.presidency.ucsb.edu/ws/index.php?pid=77488&st=&st1= (accessed May 17, 2009); Bush, "Remarks to the Democracy and Security Conference in Prague," June 5, 2007, http://www.presidency.ucsb.edu/ws/index.php?pid=75306&st=&st1= (accessed May 17, 2009).

124. Arch Puddington, "Findings of Freedom in the World 2008—Freedom in Retreat: Is the Tide Turning?" http://www.freedomhouse.org/template.cfm?page=130&year=2008 (accessed May 17, 2009); also see Arch Puddington, "Freedom in the World 2007: Freedom Stagnation Amid Pushback Against Democracy," http://www.freedomhouse.org/template.cfm?page=363&year=2007 (accessed May 17, 2009).

125. See, for example, Peter W. Galbraith, *Unintended Consequences: How War in Iraq Strengthened America's Enemies* (New York: Simon and Schuster, 2008).

126. See, for example, George H. W. Bush's highly criticized but quite thoughtful "chicken Kiev" speech in the Ukraine, August 1, 1991, *GHWB* (1991), 1005–8.

127. For an elaboration of my views on this matter, see Melvyn P. Leffler, "9/11 and American Foreign Policy," *Diplomatic History* 29 (June 2005): 395–413.

128. This evokes the language of the editorial, "The End of the War to End Wars," *The New York Times*, November 11, 1989, 26.

FOR FURTHER READING

Adams, A. James. *Germany Divided: From the Wall to Reunification.* Princeton, N.J.: Princeton University Press, 1993.

Adler, Selig. *The Isolationist Impulse: Its Twentieth Century Reaction.* New York: Abelard-Schuman, 1957.

Adomeit, Hannes. "Gorbachev's Consent to United Germany's Membership in NATO." In *Europe and the End of the Cold War: A Reappraisal,* edited by Frederic Bozo et al., 107–18. London: Frank Cass, 2008.

Alter, Peter. *The German Question and Europe.* New York: Hodder Arnold, 2000.

Antohi, Sorin, and Vladimir Tismaneanu. *Between Past and Future: The Revolution of 1989 and Their Aftermath.* New York: Central European University Press, 2000.

Ash, Timothy Garton. *In Europe's Name: Germany and the Divided Continent.* New York: Vintage Books, 1994.

———. *The Magic Lantern: The Revolution of '89 Witnessed in Warsaw, Budapest, Berlin, and Prague.* New York: Vintage Books, 1993.

Bacevitch, Andrew. *American Empire: The Realities and Consequences of U.S. Diplomacy.* Cambridge, Mass: Harvard University Press, 2004.

Bahr, Egon. *Zu meiner Zeit.* Munich: K. Blessing, 1996.

———. *Zum Europäischen Frieden. Eine Antwort auf Gorbatschow.* Berlin: Siedler, 1988.

Baker, James A., with Thomas DeFrank. *The Politics of Diplomacy: Revolution, War and Peace, 1989–1992.* New York: G. P. Putnam's Sons, 1995.

Bange, O., and G. Niedhart, eds. *Helsinki 1975 and the Transformation of Europe.* New York: Berghan Books, 2008.

Beschloss, Michael. *The Crisis Years: Kennedy and Khrushchev, 1960–1963*. New York: HarperCollins, 1991.

Beschloss, Michael, and Strobe Talbott. *At the Highest Levels*. Boston: Back Bay Publishing, 1993.

Blasius, R., et al., eds. *Akten zur Auswärtigen Politik der Bundesrepublik Deutschland 1949/50: September 1949 bis Dezember 1950*. Munich, 1997.

Brands, Hal. *From Berlin to Baghdad: America's Search for Purpose in the Post-Cold War World*. Lexington: University Press of Kentucky, 2008.

Bozo, Frederic. "Before the Wall: French Diplomacy and the Last Decade of the Cold War." In *The Last Decade of the Cold War: From Conflict Escalation to Conflict Transformation*, edited by Olav Njølstad. 240–264. London: Frank Cass, 2004.

———. *Mitterrand, la Fin de la Guerre Froide et l'unification allemande de Yalta à Maastricht*. Paris: Jacob, 2005.

———. "Mitterrand's France, the End of the Cold War, and German Unification: A Reappraisal." *Cold War History* 7.4 (2007): 455–78.

Bozo, Frederic, et al., eds., *Europe and the End of the Cold War: A Reappraisal*. London: Frank Cass, 2008.

Brown, Archie. *The Gorbachev Factor*. New York: Oxford University Press, 1997.

Brown, Michael, et al. *Debating the Democratic Peace*. Cambridge, Mass: MIT Press, 1996.

Brzezinski, Zbigniew. *Second Chance: Three Presidents and the Crisis of American Superpower*. New York: Basic Books, 2007.

Buckley, William. *The Fall of the Berlin Wall*. New York: Wiley, 2004.

Bunce, Valerie. *Subversive Institutions: The Design and Destruction of Socialism and the State*. New York: Cambridge University Press, 1999.

Bush, George. *All the Best: My Life in Letters and Other Writings*. New York: Scribner, 1999.

Bush, George, and Brent Scowcroft. *A World Transformed*. New York: Alfred A. Knopf, 1998.

Campbell, Edwina. "Comment on Cox, 'Another Transatlantic Split." *Cold War History* 8.1 (February 2008): 103–13.

Chen, Fongching and Jin, Guantao. *From Youthful Manuscripts to River Elegy: The Chinese Popular Cultural Movement and Political Transformation*. Hong Kong: Chinese University Press, 1997.

Chen Jian. *Mao's China and the Cold War*. Chapel Hill: University of North Carolina Press, 2001.

Chernyaev, Anatoly. *My Six Years with Gorbachev*. University Park: Penn State University Press, 2000.

———. *Shest' Let s Gorbachevym*. Moscow: Progress Kultura, 1993.

Chirot, Daniel, ed. *The Crisis of Leninism and the Decline of the Left*. Seattle: University of Washington Press, 1992.

Chollet, Derek, and James Goldgeier. *America Between the Wars: From 11/9 to 9/11*. New York: Public Affairs, 2008.

Clark, Michael, and Simon Sefarty, eds. *New Thinking and Old Realities: America, Europe, and Russia.* Washington, D.C.: Seven Locks Press, 1991.

Cohen, Warren. *America's Failing Empire: U.S. Foreign Relations since the Cold War.* Malden, Mass.: Blackwell Publishing, 2005.

Columbus, Frank, ed. *Central and Eastern Europe in Transition.* Commack, N.Y.: Nova Science Publishers, 1998.

Cox, Michael. "Another Transatlantic Split? American and European Narratives and the End of the Cold War." *Cold War History* 7.1 (February 2007): 121–46.

Cui, Shumei. "The Principle of Glasnost Is the Fundamental Feature of Socialist Democracy." *Kexue shehui zhuyi* 4 (1988): 41–46.

Cushing, Lincoln, and Ann Tompkins. *Chinese Posters: Art from the Great Proletarian Cultural Revolution.* New York: Chronicle Books, 2007.

Davy, Richard, ed. *European Détente: A Reappraisal.* London: Sage Publications, 1992.

Dawisha, Karen. *Eastern Europe, Gorbachev and Reform: The Great Challenge.* Cambridge: Cambridge University Press, 1990.

Deng Xiaoping. *Deng Xiaoping Xuanji.* Beijing: Renmin, 1993.

Desch, Michael. *Power and Military Effectiveness: The Fallacy of Democratic Triumphalism.* Baltimore, Md.: Johns Hopkins University Press, 2008.

Editorial Board of *Jiefangjun bao* [Liberation Army Daily], eds. *Xin shidai zui ke'ai de ren.* Beijing: Jiefangjun wenyi, 1980.

Engel, Jeffrey A. *The China Diary of George H. W. Bush.* Princeton, N.J.: Princeton University Press, 2008.

English, Robert. *Russia and the Idea of the West: Gorbachev, Intellectuals and the End of the Cold War.* New York: Columbia University Press, 2000.

Fairbank, John, and Merle Goldman. *China: A New History.* Cambridge, Mass: Belknap Press, 2006.

Fontaine, Pascale. *A New Idea for Europe: The Schuman Declaration, 1950–2000.* 2nd edition. Luxembourg: Office for Official Publications of the European Communities, 2000.

Fukuyama, Francis. *The End of History and the Last Man.* New York: Free Press, 2006.

Fulbrook, Mary. *The People's State: East Germany Society from Hitler to Honecker.* New Haven, Conn.: Yale University Press, 2005.

Gaddis, John Lewis. *The Cold War: A New History.* New York: Penguin, 2006.

———. *We Now Know: Rethinking Cold War History.* New York: Oxford University Press, 1997.

Gaidar, Yegor. *Gibel Imperii: Uroki dlya sovremennoi Rossii.* Moscow: Rosspen, 2006.

Galbraith, Peter. *Unintended Consequences: How War in Iraq Strengthened America's Enemies.* New York: Simon and Schuster, 2008.

Gates, Robert. *From the Shadows: The Ultimate Insider's Story of Five Presidents and How They Won the Cold War.* New York: Touchstone, 1997.

Gelb, Norman. *The Berlin Wall: Kennedy, Khrushchev and a Showdown in the Heart of Europe.* New York: Dorset Press, 1986.

Gillingham, John. *European Integration, 1950–2003: European Superstate or Market Economy?* Cambridge: Cambridge University Press, 2003.

Gorbachev, Mikhail. *Memoirs.* New York: Doubleday, 1995.

———. *Ponyat' Perestroiku....Pochemu eto vazhno seychas.* Moscow: Al'pina Biznes Buks, 2006.

———. *A Road to the Future: Address by Mikhail Sergeyevich Gorbachev, General Secretary of the Central Committee of the Communist Party of the Soviet Union...At the Plenary Meeting of the 43rd Session of the United Nations General Assembly in New York.* Santa Fe, N.M.: Ocean Tree Books, 1990.

———. *Zhizn i reformy.* Moscow: Novosti Press, 1995.

Görtemaker, Manfried. *Unifying Germany.* New York: St. Martin's Press, 1994.

Grachev, Andrei. *Gorbachev's Gamble.* London: Polity, 2008.

Greenwood, Sean. "Helping to Open the Door? Britain in the Last Decade of the Cold War." In *The Last Decade of the Cold War: From Conflict Escalation to Conflict Transformation,* edited by Olav Njølstad, 265–276. London: Frank Cass, 2004.

Haftendorn, Helga, et al., *The Strategic Triangle: France, Germany, and the United States in the Shaping of the new Europe.* Washington, D.C.: Woodrow Wilson Center Press, 2005.

Halberstam, David. *War in a Time of Peace: Bush, Clinton, and the Generals.* New York: Simon and Schuster, 2001.

Han Minzu [pseud.]. *Cries for Democracy: Writings and Speeches from the 1989 Chinese Democracy Movement.* Princeton, N.J.: Princeton University Press, 1990.

Heclo, Hugh. "Ronald Reagan and American Public Philosophy." In *The Reagan Presidency: Pragmatic Conservatism and Its Legacies,* edited by W. Elliot Brownlee and Hugh Davis Graham, 17–39. Lawrence: University Press of Kansas, 2003.

Hertle, Hans-Hermann, "The Fall of the Wall: The Unintended Self-Dissolution of East Germany's Ruling Regime." *Cold War International History Project Bulletin* 12/13 (Fall/Winter 2001): 134–37.

———. "Germany in the Last Decade of the Cold War." In *The Last Decade of the Cold War: From Conflict Escalation to Conflict Transformation,* edited by Olav Njølstad, 365–87. London: Frank Cass, 2004.

Hitchcock, William. *The Struggle for Europe: The Turbulent History of a Divided Continent.* New York: Doubleday, 2002.

Hu Yaobang. *Quanmian kaichuang shehui zhuyi jianshe de xin jumian.* Beijing: Renmin, 1982.

Hurd, Douglas. *Memoirs.* London: Little, Brown, 2003.

James, Harold and Marla Stone, eds. *When the Wall Came Down: Reactions to German Unification.* New York: Routledge, 1992.

Jarausch, Konrad. *The Rush to German Unity.* New York, Oxford University Press, 1994.

Joffe, J. "The 'Revisionists': Germany and Russia in a Post-Bipolar World." In *New Thinking and Old Realities: America, Europe, and Russia,* edited by M. Clark and S. Serfaty, 95–125. Washington, D.C.: Seven Locks Press, 1991.

Jowitt, Ken. *New World Disorder: The Leninist Extinction*. Berkeley: University of California Press, 1992.

Judt, Tony. *Postwar: A History of Europe since 1945*. New York: Penguin Books, 2005.

Kaiser, Robert. *Why Gorbachev Happened: His Triumphs and His Failure*. New York: Simon and Schuster, 1991.

Kashlev, Yuri. *Helsinskii Protsess 1975–2005: Svet i Teni Glazami Uchastnika*. Moscow: Izvestia, 2005.

Kengor, Paul. *God and Ronald Reagan*. New York: HarperCollins, 2004.

Kennedy, David. "Two Concepts of Sovereignty." In *To Lead the World: American Strategy After the Bush Doctrine*, edited by Melvyn P. Leffler and Jeffrey W. Legro, 165–74. New York: Oxford University Press, 2008.

Kenney, Padraic. *A Carnival of Revolutions*. Princeton, N.J.: Princeton University Press, 2002.

Keohane, Robert, Joseph Nye, Jr., and Stanley Hoffmann, eds. *After the Cold War: International Institutions and State Strategies in Europe, 1989–1991*. Cambridge, Mass: Harvard University Press, 1993.

Kissinger, Henry. *Diplomacy*. New York: Simon and Schuster, 1995.

Kohl, Helmut. *Erinnerungen 1982–1990*. Munich: Droemer Knaur, 2005.

Kovrig, Kenneth. *Of Walls and Bridges: The United States and Eastern Europe*. New York: New York University Press, 1991.

Kramer, Mark. "The Czechoslovak Crisis and the Brezhnev Doctrine." In *1968: The World Transformed*, edited by Carol Fink et al. New York: Cambridge University Press, 1998.

———. "The Myth of a No-NATO-Enlargement." *The Washington Quarterly* 32.2 (April 2009): 39–61.

———. "The Soviet Union and the 1956 Crises in Hungary and Poland: Reassessments and New Findings." *Journal of Contemporary History* 33.2 (1998): 163–214.

Kuesters, Hans Jürgen, and Daniel Hoffmann, eds. *Dokumente zur Deutschlandspolitik. Deutsche Einheit Sonderedition aus den Akten des Bundeskanzleramtes 1989/90*. Munich: Oldenbourg Verlag, 1998.

Kvitsinsky, Yuli. *Vremya i sluchai: Zametki professionala*. Moscow: Olma-Press, 1999.

LaFeber, Walter. *America, Russia, and the Cold War, 1946–2006*. New York: McGraw-Hill, 2006.

Leffler, Melvyn. "9/11 and American Foreign Policy." *Diplomatic History* 29 (June 2005): 395–413.

———. *For the Soul of Mankind: The United States, the Soviet Union, and the Cold War*. New York: Hill and Wang, 2007.

Leffler, Melvyn, and Jeffrey Legro, eds. *To Lead the World: American Strategy After the Bush Doctrine*. New York: Oxford University Press, 2008.

Leng Rong et al., eds. *Deng Xiaoping nianpu, 1975–1997*. Beijing: Zhongyang wenxian, 2004.

Lévesque, Jacques. *The Enigma of 1989: The USSR and the Liberation of Eastern Europe*. Berkeley: University of California Press, 1997.

————. *Italian Communists versus the Soviet Union: The PCI Charts a New Foreign Policy*. Berkeley: University of California Press, 1987.

————. "The Messianic Character of 'New Thinking': Why and What For?" In *The Last Decade of the Cold War: From Conflict Escalation to Conflict Transformation*, edited by Olav Njølstad, 159–76. London: Frank Cass, 2004.

Li Fengxiang, et al. *Heshang baimiu*. Beijing: Zhongguo wenlian, 1990.

Lieberthal, Kenneth. *Governing China: From Revolution to Reform*. New York: W. W. Norton, 2006.

Lilley, James. *China Hands: Nine Decades of Adventure, Espionage, and Diplomacy in Asia*. New York: Public Affairs, 2004.

Lin, Shichang. "Glasnost and Gorbachev's Reforms." *Eluosi yanjiu* 7 (1987): 1–6.

LiPing et al., eds. *Zhou Enlai Nianpu, 1949–1976*. Beijing: Zhongyang wenxian, 1997.

Liu, Binyan. *Tell the World: What Happened in China and Why*. New York: Pantheon Books, 1989.

Loth, Wilfried. "Germany in the Cold War: Strategies and Decisions." In *Reviewing the Cold War: Approaches, Interpretations, Theory*, edited by Odd Arne Westad, 242–257. London: Frank Cass, 2000.

Ludlow, N. Piers, ed. *European Integration and the Cold War: Ostpolitik-Westpolitik, 1965–1973*. London: Routledge, 2007.

Luthi, Lorenz. *The Sino-Soviet Split: The Cold War in the Communist World*. Princeton, N.J.: Princeton University Press, 2008.

MacFarquhar, Roderick. *The Politics of China: The Eras of Mao and Deng*. New York: Cambridge University Press, 1997.

MacFarquhar, Roderick, and Michael Schoenhals. *Mao's Last Revolution*. Cambridge, Mass: Belknap Press, 2006.

Maier, Charles. *The Cold War in Europe: Era of a Divided Continent*. Princeton, N.J.: Princeton University Press, 1996.

————. *Dissolution: The Crisis of Communism and the End of East Germany*. Princeton, N.J.: Princeton University Press, 1997.

Mann, James. *About Face: A History of America's Curious Relationship with China, from Nixon to Clinton*. New York: Vintage Books, 2000.

————. *The China Fantasy: How Our Leaders Explain Away Chinese Repression*. New York: Viking, 2007.

————. *The Rebellion of Ronald Reagan*. New York: Viking, 2009.

Mao Zedong. *Mao Zedong on Diplomacy*. Beijing: Foreign Languages Press, 1994.

————. *Mao Zedong Wenji*. Beijing: Renmin, 1995.

Matlock, Jack. *Autopsy on an Empire*. New York: Random House, 1995.

Maynard, Christopher. *Out of the Shadow: George H. W. Bush and the End of the Cold War*. College Station: Texas A&M University Press, 2008.

Mearsheimer, John. "Back to the Future: Instability in Europe after the Cold War." *International Security* 15.1 (Summer 1990): 5–56.

Medvedev, Vadim. *V Komande Gorbacheva*. Moscow, 1994.

Meisner, Maurice. *The Deng Xiaoping Era*. New York: Hill and Wang, 1996.

Merkl, P. *German Unification in the European Context*. University Park: Penn State University Press, 1993.

Mitterand, François. *De l'Allemagne. De la France*. Paris: Odile Jacob, 1996.

Naftali, Tim. *George H. W. Bush*. New York: Times Books, 2007.

Njølstad, Olav, ed. *The Last Decade of the Cold War: From Conflict Escalation to Conflict Transformation*. London: Frank Cass, 2004.

Odom, William E., and Robert Dujarric. *America's Inadvertent Empire*. New Haven, Conn.: Yale University Press, 2004.

Ostermann, Christian. "This is Not a Politburo, But a Madhouse." *The Cold War International History Project Bulletin* 10 (March 1998): 61–110.

Qian, Qichen. *Ten Episodes in China's Diplomacy*. New York: HarperCollins, 2005.

Radchenko, Sergey. *Two Suns in the Heavens: The Sino-Soviet Struggle for Supremacy*. Washington, D.C.: Wilson Center Press, 2009.

Ratti, Luca. "Britain, the German Question and the Transformation of Europe: From Ostpolitik to the Helsinki Conference, 1963–1975." In *Helsinki 1975 and the Transformation of Europe,* edited by O. Bange and G. Niedhart, 83–97. New York: Berghan Books, 2008.

Remnick, David. *Lenin's Tomb: The Last Days of the Soviet Empire*. New York: Vintage Books, 1994.

Rey, Marie-Pierre. "'Europe is our Common Home': A Study of Gorbachev's Diplomatic Concept." *Cold War History* 4.2 (2004): 33–65.

Richardson, Louise. "British State Strategies after the Cold War." In Nye, and Hoffmann, *After the Cold War,* edited by Robert Keohane et al., 148–169. Cambridge, Mass: Harvard University Press, 1993.

Robinson, Peter. *How Ronald Reagan Changed My Life*. New York: Regan Books, 2003.

Rodgers, Daniel. *Contested Truths: Keywords in American History*. New York: Basic Books, 1987.

Rubbi, Antonio. *Incontri con Gorbaciov. I Colloqui di Natta e Occhetto con il leader sovietico 1984–1989*. Rome: Editori Riuniti, 1990.

Sarotte, Mary Elise. *1989 and the Architecture of Order: The Competition to Lead the Post–Cold War World*. Princeton, N.J.: Princeton University Press, 2009.

Savranskaya, Svetlana. "In the Name of Europe: Soviet Withdrawal from Eastern Europe." In *Europe and the End of the Cold War: A Reappraisal,* edited by Frederic Bozo et al., 36–48. London: Frank Cass, 2008.

Schell, Orville. *Mandate of Heaven: The Legacy of Tiananmen Square and the Next Generation of China's Leaders*. New York: Simon and Schuster, 1995.

Schmeman, Serge. *When the Wall Came Down*. New York: Kingfisher, 2006.

Schwabe, Klaus. "The Cold War and European Integration, 1947–1963." *Diplomacy and Statecraft* 12.4 (2001): 18–34.

Sheehan, James. *Where Have All the Soldiers Gone? The Transformation of Modern Europe*. Boston: Houghton Mifflin, 2008.

Skilling, H. Gordon. *Czechoslovakia's Interrupted Revolution*. Princeton, N.J.: Princeton University Press, 1976.

Skinner, Kiron, Annelise Anderson, and Martin Anderson, eds. *Reagan in His Own Hand*. New York: Simon and Schuster, 2001.

Soutou, Georges-Henri. *L'Alliance incertaine: Les Rapports Politico-stratégiques Franco-allemande, 1954–1996*. Paris: Fayard, 1996.

———. "France and the Cold War, 1944–1963." *Diplomacy and Statecraft* 12.4 (2001): 35–52.

———. "The Linkage between European Integration and Détente: The Contrasting Approaches of DeGaulle and Pompidou, 1965–1974." In *European Integration and the Cold Wa: Ostpolitik-Westpolitik, 1965–73*, edited by N. Piers Ludlow, 11–35. London: Routledge, 2007.

Spence, Jonathan. *The Search for Modern China*. New York: W. W. Norton, 1999.

Stokes, Gale. *From Stalinism to Pluralism: A Documentary History of Eastern Europe since 1945*. New York: Oxford University Press, 1996.

———. *Three Eras of Political Change in Eastern Europe*. New York: Oxford University Press, 1997.

———. *The Walls Came Tumbling Down: The Collapse of Communism in Eastern Europe*. New York: Oxford University Press, 1993.

Su, Zhaozhi. "On Political Reforms." 11 *Dushu* (1986): 3–9.

Suri, Jeremi. *Power and Protest: Global Revolution and the Rise of Détente*. Cambridge, Mass: Harvard University Press, 2005.

Tang Tsou. *The Cultural Revolution and Post-Mao Reforms*. Chicago: University of Chicago Press, 1986.

Tang, Yingwu. *1976 nian yilai de zhongguo*. Beijing: Jingji ribao, 1997.

Taylor, Frederick. *The Berlin Wall*. London: Bloomsbury, 2006.

Teltschik, Horst. *329 Tage: Innenausichten der Einigung*. Berlin: Siedler, 1993.

Thatcher, Margaret. *Downing Street Years*. New York: HarperCollins, 1993.

Urban, George. *Diplomacy and Disillusion at the Court of Margaret Thatcher*. New York: St. Martin's Press, 1996.

Van Oudenaren, J. "Gorbachev and His Predecessors: Two Faces of the New Thinking." In *New Thinking and Old Realities: America, Europe, and Russia,* edited by M. Clark and S. Serfaty, 2–28. Washington, D.C.: Seven Locks Press, 1991.

Wang, Huning. "On Political Transparency." *Shehui kexue* 3 (1988): 25–29.

Westad, Odd Arne. *The Global Cold War: Third World Interventions and the Making of Our Time*. New York: Cambridge University Press, 2007.

———, ed. *Reviewing the Cold War: Approaches, Interpretations, Theory*. London: Frank Cass, 2000.

White, Stephen. *After Gorbachev*. Cambridge: Cambridge University Press, 1993.

Williams, Kieran, *The Prague Spring and Its Aftermath*. New York: Cambridge University Press, 1997.

Wohlforth, William, ed. *Cold War Endgame: Oral History, Analysis, Debate*. University Park: Pennsylvania State University Press, 2003.

————. "Reality Check: Revising Theories of International Relations in Response to the End of the Cold War." *World Politics* 50.4 (July 1998): 650–80.

Wu Guogang. *Zhao Ziyuan he zhengzhi gaige.* Hong Kong: Pacific Century Institute, 1997.

Xiao,Donglian. *Lishi de zhuangui, 1979–1981.* Hong Kong: Chinese University Press, 2008.

XueMouhon, et al., eds. *Dangdai zhongguo waijiao.* Beijing: Zhouguo shehui kexue, 1988.

Yang, Kuisong. "The Sino-Soviet Border Clash of 1969." *Cold War History* 1.1 (August 2000): 25–31.

Yu, Guangyuan. *Deng Xiaoping Shakes the World: An Eyewitness Account of China's Party Work Conference and the Third Plenum.* Norwalk: EastBridge, 2004.

Zelikow, Philip, and Condoleezza Rice. *Germany Unified and Europe Transformed.* Cambridge, Mass: Harvard University Press, 1995.

Zhang, Liang. *The Tiananmen Papers.* New York: Public Affairs, 2001.

————, ed. *Zhongguo liusi zhenxiang.* Hong Kong, Mingjing, 2001.

Zhao, Dingxin. *The Power of Tiananmen: State-Society Relations and the 1989 Student Movement.* Chicago: University of Chicago Press, 2001.

Zhao, Yuliang. "*Perestroika, Glasnost,* and Revolution in the Cultural Sphere: Preparations for Comprehensive Reforms in the Soviet Union." *Shijie jingji he zhengzhi* 10 (1988): 22–27.

Zhu, Jiamu, et al. *Chen Yun nianpu.* Beijing: Zhongyang wenxian, 2000.

Zong, Fengming, ed. *Zhao Ziyang ruanjin zhong de tanhua.* Hong Kong: Kaifang, 2007.

Zubok, Vladislav. *A Failed Empire: The Soviet Union in the Cold War from Stalin to Gorbachev.* Chapel Hill: University of North Carolina Press, 2007.

————. "Gorbachev and the End of the Cold War: Perspectives on History and Personality." *Cold War History* 2.2 (January 2002): 61–100.

————, ed. *Understanding the End of the Cold War: Reagan/Gorbachev Years.* Providence, R.I., 1998.

INDEX